The Union As It Is

The Union As It Is

CONSTITUTIONAL UNIONISM

AND SECTIONAL COMPROMISE,

1787–1861

PETER B. KNUPFER

THE UNIVERSITY OF NORTH CAROLINA PRESS

CHAPEL HILL & LONDON

Manufactured in the United States of America

The paper in this book meets the guidelines for permanence and durability of the Committee on Production Guidelines for Book Longevity of the Council on Library Resources.

95 94 93 92 91
5 4 3 2 1

Library of Congress Cataloging-in-Publication Data

Knupfer, Peter B.

The Union as it is : constitutional unionism and sectional compromise, 1787–1861 / by Peter B. Knupfer.

p. cm.

ISBN 0-8078-1996-4 (cloth : alk. paper)

1. United States—Politics and government—1783–1865. 2. United States—Constitutional history. 3. Sectionalism (United States) I. Title.

E302.1.K58 1991

973—dc20 91-50254

CIP

Portions of this work appeared earlier, in somewhat different form, in "Henry Clay's Constitutional Unionism," *Register of the Kentucky Historical Society* 89 (Winter 1990–91), and "The Rhetoric of Conciliation: American Civic Culture and the Federalist Defense of Compromise," *Journal of the Early Republic* 11, no. 3 (Fall 1991), and are reproduced here with permission of the journals.

The Middle Course

I gave the people as much privilege as they have a right to:

I neither degrade them from rank nor give them free hand;

and for those who already held the power and were envied for money,

I worked it out that they also should have no cause for complaint.

I stood there holding my sturdy shield over both the parties;

I would not let either side win a victory that was wrong.

—SOLON

Contents

Preface

Madisonian principles mean . . . peace, harmony, union, amiableness, justice, and conciliation and the *conservative* principle; it means dignity, honor, order—it means the Constitution.
—*Daily Madisonian*, January 11, 1838

Predictably, the bicentennial of the Constitution and the Bill of Rights has produced a flood of new works about the origins and development of American constitutionalism. Perhaps the most innovative and penetrating work has been directed toward uncovering and analyzing the connection between political culture and the Constitution. Michael Kammen's path-breaking book, *A Machine That Would Go of Itself* (Knopf, 1986), comes immediately to mind as representative of this genre, for it makes an ambitious attempt to escape the traditional legalistic and juridical method of understanding the Constitution in order to discern how the Constitution was taught to and interpreted by the common citizen. Kammen's conclusions are pretty depressing. For in the end, the Constitution's chaotic career, troubled by civil war, intellectual ferment, staid conservatism, and general public indifference, leaves Kammen lamenting the low civic IQ of both ordinary citizens and national leaders.[1]

Of course, complaints about the poverty of constitutional education in the United States have been a staple of public discourse since the instrument was framed in 1787. Yet if Kammen's conclusion is valid, then the Republic long ago should have collapsed from a terminal case of civic ignorance. I began this book with this apparent contradiction in mind, hoping at once to answer Merle Curti's call back in 1963 for a study of the role played by moderates in ideological conflicts and also to find any connection between civic attitudes and constitutional development.[2]

I cannot say that I have entirely succeeded, but what I have found does offer some interesting avenues for further research. I chose to examine the changing meanings of compromise in American constitutionalism, mainly by using the gathering sectional quarrel as my subtext and the essential themes of "constitutional unionism" as my yardstick. I think that ordinary citizens—certainly those citizens with more than a casual interest in their political future—did have a stronger grasp of the Constitution's meaning, significance, and content than Kammen allows. The instrument permeated public discourse; its very language—legalistic, sterile, dry—came alive in the vigorous, chaotic debates over the nature of the Union, over taxation and the distribution of public resources, and of course over slavery's moral and political status in a republic. Textbooks reprinted the Constitution, editors quoted it endlessly, bleary-eyed pupils practiced their handwriting with it. And any confrontation with the Constitution automatically confronted Americans with its compromises.

Political moderates played a vital role in these controversies, but remarkably they have not as a group received the attention that reformers, reactionaries, ideologues, and idealists have received. One reason is that it's too hard to categorize and classify them—one might argue that the very definition of a moderate implies a defiance of rigid categories. But I have attempted to make the definition by placing moderates within a unique constitutional unionist tradition that rested on basic, if superficial, tenets of the Madisonian constitutional heritage. Moderates generally acted on a set of assumptions about the nature of civic life; they believed that there must be limits to political controversy and that civility, rational discourse, and attachment to procedure were among the most important determinants of those limits. Readers will detect here vestiges of classical political ideas going back to Aristotle.

Of course compromise, especially the sectional variety, was very important to political moderates. They operated within a compromise tradition that contained special ethical and historical meanings for the three generations living in the period between the Constitutional Convention and the Civil War. To them, compromise was not a doctrine, a philosophy, or even a first principle in republican politics. Properly conceived and honorably executed, compromise was the expected outcome of republican political action: the reconciliation of principles and interests.

As a part of the language of public discourse and of the "popular constitutionalism" of the early Republic, compromise reflected the belief that the Constitution was a compact that imposed mutual sacrifices on the parties to it. This conception of the relationship between compromise and the Constitution was especially clear during the dangerous sectional conflicts that punctuated the young nation's early political history. Within this context, it was apparent that the concept of compromise rested on a cluster of assumptions, rather than formal theories, about the duties of citizens and the process of governing. Apparently, the Constitution could be viewed not only as a legal framework but also as a symbol of political moderation. Compromise could reconcile Americans to this imperfect Constitution and shield the constitutional union from rupture.

Two other purposes lie behind this book. Currently there is no study of the intellectual or cultural continuities in the rhetoric of sectional compromise, despite the prominence of important antebellum compromises and of the critical political and constitutional issues they raised. The advocates of sectional compromise, like the sectional militants they faced, offered a battery of distinctive historical, ethical, and practical arguments for finding a middle way through divisive confrontations. I have tried to resurrect and dissect those arguments and the conservative constitutionalism they expressed.

It should be clear from the start, then, that what follows is not an examination of the opposition to compromise or of the antislavery or proslavery ideologies that challenged the compromise tradition. Certainly it is arguable that the views of anticompromisers must be addressed in a work about popular perceptions of compromise. Although I give these positions some treatment, I think they have been thoroughly examined in a number of excellent works. The underpinnings of the compromise argument have also been studied, but not with the objective of connecting constitutional political culture to the idea of compromise. Nor is this study designed to turn compromise into an explanatory principle of political action: to argue that the existence of a distinctive meaning for compromise somehow required all who discussed its assumptions about politics to compromise in any and all conflicts would do violence to the record and deny that moderates could choose among alternative methods of resolving conflict.

Although historians have fully examined the contract theory and classical republican thought that undergird the Constitution, only recently have they begun to map the Constitution's place in the civic culture of the past.

In particular, historians of political thought and political scientists in search of their own historical roots have been treating the informal political commentary of stump speeches, editorial opinion, and private correspondence as texts that reveal the contours of popular political ideas. And others are noting the importance of simple as well as complex political customs and rituals, embedded in the civic culture and eventually challenged by the economic and social changes that swept the early Republic before the Civil War.

Historical discussions of compromise tell us much about contemporary political "science"—especially about what Americans expected would be the course and consequences of certain special categories of political conflict. We can learn much about conventional attitudes toward important institutions designed to mediate conflict, especially political parties and deliberative assemblies. My examination of the constitutional lineage of compromise has uncovered conceptions—about majority rule, the strengths and limitations of party action, statesmanship, and the evolution of constitutional customs—that hint at a variant of common constitutional thought somewhat different from the now dominant modes of analyzing political ideology in the early Republic.

In particular, constitutionalism can be seen as a more specific, operative form of republicanism, a form more readily comprehensible to the public and to historians of political ideas. It gave real shape to the diffuse, ambiguous assumptions that have come to make up the modern conception of republicanism. I hope this study will reinforce our growing interest in constitutionalism as a way of life. And I hope that it will in some ways be a brief respite from the rarefied abstractions of "republicanism" and "liberalism" that historians are fond of applying to antebellum political discourse. Useful as these categories may be, nonetheless I think that most statesmen (and especially those advocating sectional compromise) would be reticent to use them in the ideological mode so fashionable among modern historians.

My second purpose has been to place the idea of compromise within the post-1815 debate over the nature of the Union. The postwar generation, having secured the Republic against foreign dangers to the republican system, engaged in a rich and fascinating debate about the distinctive union created in this Republic. It is easy to deprecate the narrow legalism of this important public conversation about the Union and to ignore its relevance to the second generation of statesmen who were genuinely concerned about the nation's survival. Compromise was essential to the maintenance of the "Union as it is" and was a useful and critical component of the Madisonian constitutionalism on which advocates of sectional compromise often relied.

IN THE LONG PROCESS of research and writing, I incurred many debts that I am very happy to acknowledge. This book began as a dissertation at the University of Wisconsin-Madison; the Departments of History and Political Science provided a stimulating and productive atmosphere in which to work on it. Dr. John P. Kaminski of the Center for the Study of the Constitution carefully critiqued the first chapter and saved me from several fatal errors; he has been a strong friend and amiable critic. Professor Robert Booth Fowler presided over the germ of this study, a paper on compromise, which he urged me to expand. Harold T. Mahan, currently at work on a biography of the popular historian Benson J. Lossing, generously shared his extensive bibliography of nineteenth-century civics and history books.

Professor John Milton Cooper, Jr., enriched every stage of this project with his cheerful advice, steady friendship, and willingness to share his observations about the nature of American statesmanship. Professor Allan G. Bogue spared time from a crowded schedule to give the manuscript a thorough reading; I have greatly profited from his wisdom and support. Professor Richard H. Sewell guided my work with a patient, firm hand. His unrelenting criticism refused to let a single foolish thought escape unnoticed. Any surviving mistakes are mine, not his.

Robert Seager II, the former editor of *The Papers of Henry Clay*, and his assistants Anna Perry and Mackelene Smith kindly opened their offices and files to me during my visit to the Clay project at the University of Kentucky in 1985. Professor Seager was particularly helpful and generous with his time. His many comments and criticisms forced me to clarify my ideas and hone my intuitions about Clay and compromise.

At Arizona State University, Professor Philip R. Vandermeer gave me much support, criticism, and friendly counsel, for which I am very grateful. Professors Robert Trennert, Peter Iverson, and Paul Hubbard and the

ASU History Department provided comfortable working space and a friendly, encouraging atmosphere in which to complete the first draft of this book while I was juggling a heavy teaching load.

Portions of this book have been presented or published elsewhere. Parts of chapters 4, 5, and 6 were discussed in "Henry Clay's Constitutional Unionism," *Register of the Kentucky Historical Society* 89 (Winter 1990–91). Parts of chapter 1 were discussed in "The Rhetoric of Conciliation: American Civic Culture and the Federalist Defense of Compromise," *Journal of the Early Republic* 11, no. 3 (Fall 1991). I am grateful for the permission to reprint what I wrote in these articles. Some of the ideas in chapters 2 and 4 were presented in "Clay and the Constitution in 1850: The Compromise Ethic at Work," a paper given at the 81st Annual Meeting of the Organization of American Historians in Reno, Nevada, March 25, 1988. I thank Jean H. Baker and Daniel W. Howe for their perceptive and incisive comments on that paper. Professor Howe in particular has been a source of inspiration and support. I also expanded on the materials and ideas in chapter 2 for "Civic Education and the Problem of Parties, 1820–1860," a paper I presented at the annual meeting of the Society of Historians of the Early American Republic in Toronto, August 3, 1990. I am grateful to Professor Bernard Friedman for his helpful criticisms.

Several very special people deserve mention too. Peter J. Lysy has guided me in countless ways, especially by sharing his contagious thrill in the hunt for clues through darkened stacks and dusty tomes. Hans Van Dyk read and criticized two chapters and would not permit a lunch to end without words of encouragement and enlightenment. My wife, Nancy, has made compromises too numerous to mention. I look forward to making good on my debt to her. Rebecca Lee Knupfer and Kelly Marie Knupfer arrived in this world mercifully late enough to be spared the agony of living with a harried graduate student. Their joyful indifference to my work has refreshed me through the struggle with revisions. Sis and Paul Knupfer raised me to respect the past; both were delighted when I launched my own voyage of discovery into history. Paul did not live to see his son make this first of many landfalls along the way, but his spirit guided the journey and with knowing, silent smiles has shared my delight at the treasures I have found.

The Union As It Is

Introduction

A compromise is not a question of law or abstract justice, but something adapted to the prejudices and feelings of men.
—"X," Baltimore *Sun*, May 21, 1850

"I call the work of compromise emphatically American," James Shields declared to the United States Senate in April 1850, for unlike people in other countries that settle conflicts by force, "the people of this country are trained and educated to settle all their difficulties, public and private, by just and honorable compromise." The intensity of sectional conflict by 1850 invited many doubts about the thoroughness of that training and education in the "great Republican and American work of compromise," but apparently Shields saw no difficulty in tying compromise to the special history and character of the American people, a connection that his audience well understood.[1]

Surely Senator Shields's comment suggests that the term *compromise* engaged his intellect on a number of levels, evoking deeper intuitions about the rhythms of American political life. For him, compromise had an American and republican context that shaped its contemporary meaning, if not its abstract definition. And it is important to uncover this connection between compromise and political culture—to determine how Americans used compromise to construe experience, especially political experience—because compromise is at the heart of the American polity.[2]

Whether one defines that polity as an aggregate of conflicting socioeconomic interests that the varying majorities and minorities recombine into a common interest or as a political order seeking to cultivate individual self-restraint and consensus on behalf of a disembodied common good above the polity, compromise is vital to its survival. Both definitions of the polity assume human fallibility and government by consent, the essential prerequisites of conflict and political compromise. And because compromise is not only a dynamic process of mutual concession but also a form of association that stamps its outcome with distinctive qualities, historical formulations of its use, abuse, and context can tell us something about how Americans analyzed and understood the sources of conflict within the polity and how they went about sifting alternatives when facing a major crisis.

The long, deep, and ultimately violent controversy about Americanism and republicanism in the period between the Constitutional Convention and the Civil War offers plenty of evidence with which to explore contemporary meanings of the relationship between compromise and political culture. During this time, the nation's "public moralists"—its statesmen, editors, politicians, ministers, educators, literati, and other shapers and philosophers of national civic attitudes—earnestly discussed the most basic assumptions of politics and culture in a search for what they called the "American character."[3]

The period's explosive economic growth and extreme social dislocations fostered intense apprehensions about the future of the new experiment in liberty and about how to preserve republican institutions and to reconcile the tensions between minority rights and majority rule. As this dialogue about Americanism and republicanism raised the ageless tension between continuity and change, it revealed that compromise had indeed become one of what John Stuart Mill called "the obvious and universal facts which every one sees and no one is astonished at, [and which] it seldom occurs to any one to place upon record."[4]

The search for an American character capable of encompassing the nation's cultural and social extremes also revealed how cultural and institutional circumstances influenced the contemporary meaning of compromise. Political systems that combine a basic consensus on what values are closed to compromise with established structures for mediating conflict will not only encourage the practice of compromise but also make the justification of such political activity both a personal and a political imperative. These conditions can elevate compromise above its function as a strategy to a higher plane of abstraction, where it becomes a symbol of political legitimacy endowed with an emotional and intellectual significance, a symbol whose meaning vibrates with the changing tenor of political life.

The United States between 1787 and 1860 fit these conditions. The novelty of its political system, the structure of its constitutional order, and the tensions generated by the development of new political styles, institutions, and issues naturally magnified the importance of compromise's peculiar emphasis on reconciling extremes. When political compromisers had to justify their actions, they articulated its republican and American qualities by binding the abstract ethical and procedural features of compromise in general to popular perceptions of American political ethics that still glowed from the heat of constitutional arguments raging since 1787.[5]

By trying to explain important compromises, public moralists frequently ended up trying to explain America. This study, then, focuses less on how Americans made major compromises—especially of the sectional variety—and more on how they justified and explained their compromises. Specifically, it traces the relationship between the concept of compromise—as a strategy and as a symbol—and what may be termed *constitutional unionism:* a belief system encompassing the theory, ethics, operation, and structure of a constitutional system as it was perceived by those who framed and implemented it. Constitutional unionism assumed that the Union was neither automatically self-perpetuating nor completely supreme over the states. The Union was limited by the Constitution; its legitimacy and therefore its perpetuity rested on consensus—the "mutual affections" of its citizens who, short of outright revolution, could gather constitutional majorities (presumably a number equivalent to three-fourths of the states) to end the Union at any time. Therefore, constitutional unionists did not accept the legitimacy of secession or nullification; they could accept the idea of federal supremacy within the sphere marked out by the Constitution and established by congressional, administrative, and judicial precedent over long stretches of time. The ambivalent and apparently contradictory character of constitutional unionist thought was an understandable outgrowth of the pragmatic outlook common to denizens of the political center. And it could have predictable consequences, for when faced with sectional crises that exposed the inherent conflicts between states and nation, freeman and slaveholder—conflicts that were incorporated into the compromises of the Constitution—constitutional unionists preferred old formulas to new institutions or ideas for advising a troubled country.

But neither were constitutional unionists entirely paralyzed or static in their understanding of the operative side of American politics. Their assumptions were dynamic—that the Union at some future date would surely become self-perpetuating and therefore capable of managing severe sectional and ideological crises. This was not mere wishful thinking; it rested on simple propositions about how constitutionalism and pluralism slowly strengthen the process of resolving conflict and thereby enhance the legitimacy of the regime.

It should be clear that constitutional unionists did not compose a single party (until, significantly, the old Madisonians adopted the label in the presidential election of 1860). They could be active partisans, strongly antiparty, or a bit of both. As moderates along the political spectrum, they believed that America's unique circumstances had shaped a special kind of republic, unlike any other. In sum, constitutional unionism was the heir of James Madison's conception of the Constitution as partly federal, partly national. It marked the center of American politics through the 1850s.

What, then, was "republican" and "American" about compromise, and how could Americans be trained and educated in it? How did Americans fit compromise into the context of their constitutional order? And did the term *compromise* help them to explain how that system worked and the extent to which it fulfilled its purposes? Did compromise's particular combination of mutuality and concessions signify more than the everyday settlement of conflicts? Did Americans link grand political compromise to prevailing notions of American uniqueness? Addressing these questions naturally requires a foray into the civic culture, because in antebellum America that was where Americanism and republicanism converged.

Before we can tackle these issues, we must define the concept of compromise. The moral ambiguities of any historic compromise too often tempt the historian to issue weighty judgments about its "genuineness" without exploring the contemporary understanding of the concept, the modern prejudices about compromise's moral dilemmas, or the simple generic definition of the term itself.

COMPROMISE HAS A LONG PEDIGREE marked by its own occasional and significant concessions to human fallibility. Moralists have debated its virtues, historians have contemplated its role in the rise or fall of civilizations, and politicians have praised its blessings and damned its unholy alliances. In general, however, there has been less disagreement about the definition of compromise than about its interpretation and application.

A compromise is the settlement of a conflict through mutual concessions. Other definitions offer variations on this one, modifying certain terms—using diplomatic *adjustment* in place of sterile *settlement,* for instance. Some definitions stray from description to prescription, conflating compromise with consensus or amputating the quality of mutuality by sermonizing about making compromises "with reality." Compromise is not consensus, and reality never makes compromises but only demands concessions. To avoid the common confusion of compromise with other forms of conflict resolution, we need to delineate its component elements—conflict, concession, mutuality, and settlement—and explain their unique relationship to one another.[6]

With apologies to James Madison, one might say that if men were angels, no compromise would be necessary. Our imperfections generate conflicts that our settled nature and social conditions urge us to resolve. And resolution requires an understanding of what a dispute is all about—the substance of the opposing claims, the relative intensity of the disputants' physical and mental commitments to their claims, and the arena in which the conflict appears. All of these determine in some degree the strategy for resolving the conflict, especially, in the case of compromise, as they reveal the presence of any grounds for concessions.

Our common tendency is to classify a conflict according to the degree of its abstractness, by denoting whether it is a conflict of inalienable principles or of tangible interests. A conflict of interests is generally over the allocation of resources, public or private, whereas a conflict of principles supposedly pits rival conceptions of the public good against each other. But this distinction needs to be refined simply because all conflicts theoretically can be reduced to their purest essences and thereby abstracted beyond the reach of mortal negotiators. All rule making, for instance, encounters the basic conflict between liberty and obedience.[7]

It is better to recognize that public conflicts routinely involve rival, tangible claims backed by appeals from a cluster of prescriptive principles. They are disputes about the relationship of principles to interests, not conflicts simply between principles or between interests. If rival claims rest on different principles, then the resulting confusion of voices clouds the discussion; the disputants must create a common context for debate in order to make any progress. If rival claims rest on different interpretations of similar principles, then the disputants face the daunting task of redefining those principles to accommodate their different viewpoints.

In any case, the disposition to advance beyond the initial clash will depend on the parties' relative commitments to their respective arguments, because the chain of an advocate's reasoning from the claim back to supporting principles is an alloy of emotions and logic. The parties' attitudes about conflict in general—its sources, what magnifies it, whether it is intrinsically acceptable at any level—and about an issue in particular are very important considerations when the decision about strategies must be made.

In particular, when severe conflicts arise, a common language of concession and conciliation is necessary, both to soothe tempers and to prepare disputants for upcoming negotiations. Rhetoricians have long noted and studied the rhetoric of conciliation, seeing it as vital to conflict resolution not only because it reaffirms a common commitment to a process of resolving disputes but also because it reveals the bedrock of cultural assumptions that support the process of adjustment.[8]

The unique constraints of democratic politics further complicate the relationship between conflict and compromise. Politics is a collective enterprise that requires action and commands obedience. In theory, all members of the polity are potential disputants; from the standpoint of the politician, they are potential enemies or potential allies. The relative strength of opposing sides adds the problem of majorities and minorities to the emotional engagement of the two sides. Close divisions in the polity will heighten tension and make compromise more imperative because the large number of potential losers on a simple majority vote raises the possibility of continued agitation and of the erosion of the legitimacy of the political process. These conflicts between closely matched forces can broaden enough to endanger the social order by paralyzing the normal processes for resolving conflict. At such a point, the urge to retreat to the familiar, to retain some institutional and procedural continuity and integrity, makes compromise more attractive than other forms of resolution. In this sense, a compromise becomes a bulwark of majority rule because it reconciles losers and winners.[9]

In sum, the nature, the intensity, and the arena of a conflict are inseparably connected to the convictions of the disputants. Naturally the would-be compromiser views most conflict not so much as a clash between interests and principles as a confrontation between fallible people advocating or holding modifiable opinions that integrate principles and interests.

It is possible that concession was a latecomer to the concept of compromise. The early forms of the term *compromise* at most implied but probably did not comprehend the notion of actual sacrifice. *Compromise* derives from the past participle, *compromissus,* of the Latin verb *compromittere,* meaning "to agree to refer a cause to arbitration" or, more simply, to "promise together." There seems to have been no suggestion that such a promise would entail any sacrifice of principle, honor, or interest, but apparently experience warranted some expression for the frequent risks accompanying a decision to "promise together" because the French and the Germans began to employ variations on the root's forms in order to distinguish positive intentions from the ensuing costs of compromise. Thus, the French verb *compromettre,* its noun relative *compromission,* and the German verb *kompromittieren* connote an unfortunate, fatal sacrifice of virtue resulting from exposure to the risk of censure for one's misconduct. But the French noun *compromis* and the German noun *Kompromiss* refer only to a mutual agreement or a settlement of a dispute.[10]

English maintained the distinction, but experience blurred it. Although the now obsolete term *compromit* admitted both positive and negative meanings, the latter seems to have been prevalent in the United States during the early nineteenth century. In fact, the term suggested the risk of permanent, not just temporary, sacrifice through a "compromise commitment."[11]

The eventual demise of *compromit* abandoned the different English meanings of *compromise* to the discretion of the speaker. In the clouded atmosphere of political debate, the discerning individual must sniff the air to distinguish the fragrance of magnanimous concession from the odor of spoiled virtue. The passive and reflexive forms ("one has been compromised," and "one compromises oneself") convey a more certain, pejorative meaning than do the noun and the active verb ("to compromise"), whose meaning depends on detecting a telltale raised eyebrow or altered pitch in voice.[12]

Concession—and the double-edged sword associated with sacrificing principles, interests, or morals—reveal the powerful tug of public and private ethics in compromise. Concession has consequences for principles and interests; the prospect of giving up one in the service of the other injects ethical questions into the problem of compromise. Advocates of compromise portray themselves as practical people fighting moral absolutists, but successful compromisers understand that ethics both limits and reinforces compromise. Ethics helps to determine what claims are not subject to concession, and it is one measure of the justice of means and ends.[13]

Some observers proclaim wide boundaries for concessions and claim that prescriptive principles ought not to impede concessions. They argue that the primary objective of compromise is peace, usually achieved through the fundamental ambiguity of compromise that permits the coexistence of different but compatible interpretations of any concessions made. Ethics should not restrain concessions; compromise should instead restrain the force of rigid ethical commitments. On the other hand, others proclaim the value of principle, arguing, as Lord Morley does in an essay on compromise, that "it is better to bear the burden of impracticableness, than to pare away principle until it becomes hollowness and triviality."[14]

Max Weber attempted to reconcile these two positions by outlining what he called the "ethics of responsibility," which became the ethical basis for the pluralist scholars' celebration of compromise during and after World War II. According to the ethics of responsibility, the failure to concede on one principle could easily result in the sacrifice of another, more urgent and superior one. According to Robert Dahl's interpretation of Weber, "if sheer opportunism is ignoble, then rigid morality in politics is dangerous and inapplicable." The answer to the ethical problem of compromise settled on the idea of moderation—of recognizing that the outcome of political conflict is usually a plurality of moral ends limited by the process of resolution itself.[15]

At the very least, compromise must occur within a framework of values that the negotiators agree on—a consensus must be present, and it must comprise a hierarchy of enduring values compatible with the moral autonomy of individuals within the polity. This foundation of principle both excludes certain claims from negotiation and recognizes others crucial to the process. The renegotiation of that consensus cannot terminate in an ethically defensible compromise if it concedes the moral autonomy of its participants.

But the mere fact of concessions is insufficient evidence that a compromise has occurred. (A majority can impose concessions on a minority, for instance.) A compromise requires mutuality, reciprocity, between the parties to it. Mutuality confirms that compromise is a unique form of association.

Mutuality can be understood on two levels, contractual and affective. The contractual type of mutuality proceeds from the parties' self-interest to the negotiation of exact, balanced equivalents. The compromise is essentially a contractual exchange of sacrifices, with any rival principles remaining in distant contention. The symmetry of this mutuality balances the purities of extremes against each other while blending agreeable qualities in the middle, a kind of Aristotelian golden mean. Self-interest is the fulcrum in this balance, for it draws the emotionally or ideologically divided parties together. Thus, a moderate in politics is usually viewed as a centrist whose self-interested pragmatism makes him an artful, levelheaded negotiator.

The central feature of contractual mutuality is equipoise—uncompromisable opposites remain in contention. This notion of contractual mutuality suits well the idea that societies comprise aggregations of self-interested individuals whose conflicts require adjustment instead of melioration. The parties to the agreement are acting as independent, rational beings whose creative energy compromise releases instead of restrains.

The other level of mutuality is affective: the relationship between the parties reflects a degree of intimacy, of dependence. Compromise in this sense is a communal act, almost a ritual, that confirms mutual dependence. The process of compromise, then, has an intrinsic value apart from the material gains it produces. The parties seek conciliation, so their arguments for concessions appeal to common symbols of fraternity, honor, affection, and duty.

These two forms of mutuality suggest different conceptions of the social bond—indeed, they reflect the cultural differences between the rival syndromes of thought that historians have uncovered in the political culture of the early Republic. Contractual mutuality recalls to mind the understanding of compromise and pluralism that runs throughout the scholarship of the postwar generation of social scientists and historians. Clinton Rossiter, David Truman, Richard Hofstadter, Daniel Boorstin, John P. Roche, and especially Robert Dahl devoted much of their work on American politics to explaining the common beliefs in ordered liberty, individualism, private property, and constitutional self-government, beliefs that enabled Americans to compromise their differences without subjecting their political system to suicidal stresses.[16]

These scholars generally celebrated compromise as the primary strategy for reconciling the many conflicting interests that they detected at the heart of the liberal American polity. Viewing politicians as brokers among interests, they tended to approach compromise as a way to advance one's self-interest through pragmatic accommodation of interests vital to the bargainers' own political ambitions. Contractual mutuality can also be seen as an offshoot of the commercial culture of American liberal capitalism and as the cement of political parties and interest-group politics into the nineteenth century and beyond.[17]

Over the past twenty years, this pluralist vision of the polity has been supplemented by research that confirms a communal, classical republican strain in early political culture. Its roots in the civic humanism of the Renaissance stressed the incompatibility of commerce and virtue and defined republican citizenship in terms of the citizen's ability to sacrifice self-interest for the public good. Compromise in this context signifies mutual sacrifice and a reaffirmation of mutual affections through the common restraint of passions in politics.[18] This idea recalls to mind the classical emphasis on moderation and balance that permeated Greek political thought.

The debate about the appearance and disappearance of these parallel worlds of social and political thought continues to rage, but it is important to note that both languages of politics accommodate a conception of compromise, for in both cases compromise is a form of association, a social act, that requires civility and moderation in order to go forward. And both visions of the polity admit the moral and practical need for government by consent.[19]

To return to the problem of definitions: if we understand mutuality and concessions, then it is possible to understand *settlement,* the last and perhaps most misunderstood component of compromise. A compromise eventuates in a settlement, but not all settlements require mutual concessions. There are alternative types of settlements, such as integrative solutions (in which the parties reformulate the dispute in terms that permit a settlement in which neither side sacrifices anything), third-party arbitration (which occurs when the parties are so polarized that a solution must be imposed), and simple weight of numbers (majority rule).[20]

Indeed, the very nature of democratic decision making greatly confuses the definition and the meaning of compromise settlements in politics. Much of this difficulty is rooted in the complex relationship of compromise, consent, and obligation. Consider the following scenario. Two bills embodying sharply different policies are introduced into a legislature. Their respective sponsors, groups A and B, could risk an immediate, simple majority vote, but the prospect of a slim victory, of a thin mandate, and of being a convenient target for a large contingent of losers is not very reassuring to them. They could take their rival positions to the country, drum up support at the polls, and reinforce their ranks for a later session, but the time, the expense, and the likelihood of being sidetracked by peripheral issues make this option undesirable for the present. The other option, of course, is to compromise the two bills, so that each side can proclaim its magnanimity and sagacity to the voters, with little evident risk. The bills go to committee, but during the process of arranging mutual concessions, a cluster of standpatters, group C, defects from A and B, protesting the arrangement. Nonetheless, the compromise emerges from committee over C's objections and wins on a close vote after a sharp debate.

Several questions arise from this rather common scenario. Does C's dissent from the compromise bill mean that the condition of mutuality was not met and that A and B's claim of a compromise settlement is therefore spurious? Does it matter which group's claim is accurate, given that the status of a law created through compromise should be no different from that of a law not resulting from compromise? Surely a compromise occurred. A majority of equals arranged mutual concessions that did not sacrifice the minority's moral autonomy (that is, its right to dissent and seek redress). The bill is a compromise, but the decision to make it law is not. And the law's status as a compromise is irrelevant to the issue of obedience: all persons subject to the law must obey it at least as a law, if not as a compromise.

But the problem does not end there. The compromise did not have the consent of more than a slim majority, and group C can take its case to the country if it desires. If A and B wish to avoid the problem of a thin mandate and the possibility of repeal, then they must try to use their compromise strategy to build a stronger, *concurrent majority* reconciled to at least some of C's objections. Unlike a simple majority vote on the pure question of A's or B's original bill, a compromise encourages further compromises because it leaves a residue of dissatisfaction among the parties to it and because, in this case, an unreconciled minority could spell future trouble. And if C stubbornly resists further negotiation with A and B, then the latter have the additional advantage of appealing to the voters' sense of fair play and patriotism by making an issue of C's inflexibility. William E. Nelson labels this mode of decision making "instrumental reasoning," which aims at the incorporation of minority sentiments into concurring majorities instead of the mere reconciliation of clashing interests.[21]

On the other hand, if A and B claim that their compromise is final and that the majority's victory effectively ends further discussion with C, then they are more wishful than accurate. They would endanger their already precarious position by precluding further concessions between themselves and the minority. By confusing obligation with consent and settlement with finality, they succeed only in isolating a tenuous compromise from reinforcement by future recruits. The absence of finality does not mean the absence of compromise, whereas an insistence on finality endangers further compromise.

But when would the compromising end? Is it hypothetically possible to use compromises to achieve consensus, or at least a complete solution to the original conflict? Not if consensus means unanimity, the elimination of conflict. At the most, compromise can be used to build coalitions of consenting individuals willing to settle a conflict even if they cannot unanimously solve it. Over time, a series of compromises might help to build concurring majorities—that is, sequentially larger majorities that absorb former dissenters and thereby enhance the legitimacy of the settlement and of the process of resolving conflict. Despite the implication of permanence in the term *settlement,* compromise settlements are only as final as the parties' willingness to live with the agreement's imperfections. In politics this should be particularly obvious because politics never solves conflicts the way, say, a student solves a problem in geometry. As Bertrand de Jouvenel observes, politics can only settle conflicts, leaving an aftertaste of controversy that may or may not goad politicians into arranging yet another settlement. "A solution makes no enemies and requires no defenders," he says. "It is otherwise in the case of a settlement. Its permanence cannot be taken for granted; its chances of enduring depend upon its fostering forces which will work to uphold it."[22]

THE GENERIC DEFINITION of compromise as a settlement of a conflict through mutual concessions permits us to examine how historical context gives meaning to that definition. Because compromise comprises potentially conflicting elements—especially of mutuality and sacrifice—its meaning can change as the emphasis on one or another element is changed. The contractual implications of compromise might at some times seem more important than its affective connotations; arguments for the former could be more appealing than for the latter. In the present case, the changing meaning of compromise through time did not necessarily alter the practice itself but actually moved it to different contexts and applied the concept in new venues. Meanings can outrun definitions, even after critical points in history when the reconstitution of political vocabulary accompanies new ways of practicing politics.[23] Compromises that at one time were celebrated as honorable compacts might become corrupt bargains under the pressure of new issues and styles of politics. The pressures generated by the ambiguities inherent in compromise could become irreconcilable conflicts of principle and conscience. And in response, compromisers themselves might begin to apotheosize compromise in an attempt to head off its natural consequences. The meaning of compromise might change as the practice's context changes.

The evolution of American politics through the colonial and early national periods set the context for public perceptions about political compromise, especially by forging a relationship between compromise and a constitutional union, statesmanship, sectionalism, and political parties. The generation that wrote and ratified the Constitution would inherit a set of assumptions about the context of compromise that they would connect to the larger problem of creating a constitutional union. The distinctive history of compromise, then, would not be found in the colonial period or even after the Civil War but in the period between the two—when the special nature of a union partly federal, partly national, and perplexed by the unique conflicts arising from slavery and sectional tensions gave compromise its real significance in American politics.

Compromise had been an important means of reconciling differences in the colonial tradition—it was not invented with the creation of a national republican polity in 1787. Before the crisis of independence and union in the 1770s and 1780s, Americans learned the importance of compromise through the actions of their local assemblies, governors, and emissaries to Great Britain. The development of a legislative tradition in the colonial assemblies created fertile grounds for compromise, especially given the cultural diversity and geographical dispersion of the colonial population. Compromise did not arise as a doctrine but as a custom that slowly obtained a special significance with the growing popularity of contract theory and the increasing awareness by the colonists that the customary "concessions" by people and sovereign implied a contract that could not be rashly broken.[24] In a sense, compromise became important in related legal, social, commercial, and legislative spheres, where the exchange of concessions contributed both to the peaceful workings of government, the economy, and the law and to the rising acceptance of a colonial elite practiced in the arts of negotiation. In sum, the creation of consociational polities in the colonies contributed to the political stability necessary for intercolonial union by creating a common set of political procedures and a political language that elites could understand.[25]

Americans would not become aware of this development until the custom was challenged and they were forced through a series of crises concerning independence and perpetual union. The constitutional and political conflict over the nature of the imperial constitution in the 1760s and 1770s raised the difficult issue of compromising with a sovereign who would brook no opposition at all, a problem that colonists would eventually resolve by rejecting halfway solutions and seeking their own temporary union in the Continental Congress. By creating a common interest in national defense, the Revolution built upon the growing recognition of a common interest in a more uniform set of laws, commercial regulations, and interstate relations. A basis for mutual concessions by fractious states very slowly developed in the forge of revolution and confederation.

The practical problem of reacting to Parliament's refusal to concede any authority to the colonies also pushed the colonists into a search through their constitutional past to justify their actions and construct a blueprint for the future. The ideological dimension of this problem revealed the extent to which provincial political culture had come to explain and justify compromise by associating it with temperaments valued deep in the colonial past and recently connected to Enlightenment political science. The tie between personal temperament and the fate of a constitutional republic was an article of faith for Americans. George Mason thought the point important enough to incorporate in Virginia's Declaration of Rights in 1776, equating "moderation" and "temperance" with "frequent recurrence to first principles" as essential to the preservation of any free government. John Adams agreed, writing essentially the same language into the Massachusetts Bill of Rights four years later.[26] Moderation, the parent of compromise, was basic to constitutional liberty because it was the nucleus of personal and public constitutions. And its importance was heightened by the wave of Revolutionary constitution making in the states, which recalled the Aristotelian preference for moderate, balanced constitutions as the proper form of government.

Indeed, the embedding of compromise into local civic cultures enabled the nationalist elite of the 1780s to offer a strong alternative to disunion. They could appeal not only to the imperative of making sacrifices for liberty during the Revolution but also to the imperative of making sacrifices for the restoration of order in 1787. In both cases, the overarching objective was national unity of some kind, either to defeat the British or to create and ratify a constitution. In sum, union and compromise were inextricably linked by the Revolution, the failure of confederation, and the creation of a more perfect union in 1788.[27]

What matters here is the growing connection between national union and compromise, which after the ratification of the Constitution became the context for more comprehensive discussions of the technique. For most Americans, the framework for political compromise had become constitutional, and its reification in the Constitution lay not so much in the Constitution's structure and the laws flowing out of it as in the ability of statesmen to bridge the Constitution's built-in divisions and devise workable agreements on legal, social, political, and economic issues. The ability to mediate among interests, to impose acceptable and equitable sacrifices on them, and to maintain the people's attachment to the Union, then, was the great challenge of early republican statesmanship.

The relationship of union, compromise, statesmanship, and the Constitution evolved through the colonial period, paralleling the rise of intercolonial elites practiced in the legislative arts with which a people already inured to local self-legislating were quite familiar. But the shift of focus in politics from local problems to the constitutional conflict with Great Britain introduced sectional questions to the now normative practice of compromise. Here the problem of reconciling firmly entrenched majorities and minorities—or, more ominously, the problem of large, rival minorities with no majority to control them—made compromise a matter of the greatest necessity.

In the period between the Constitutional Convention and the Civil War, no other single issue so persistently and powerfully peeled away the layered sediments of accumulating political detritus to reveal the underlying bedrock of assumptions as did the sectional quarrel over black slavery. As David Brion Davis has observed, the fundamental contradiction of slavery—its treatment of humans as objects—is deeply interwoven with fears and with rationalizations for authority and subordination that inevitably involve compromise.[28]

Slavery's entanglement of principle and interest required high statesmanship to maintain the continuity and tenuous balance of a political system founded on compromise yet professing attachment to eternal principles. The paradox of human slavery in a free republic recalled timeless issues of freedom and order, bringing into battle array a host of historical and ethical arguments that had puzzled and plagued the ancients. The conflict over slavery is the context and the underlying theme of my discussion because like no other issue, it forced the convergence of the ethical and practical dilemmas that make compromise so unique and imperfect. Furthermore, slavery and compromise have a common history in this country; many issues required compromise, but no other so persistently focused the nation's attention on compromise and the legitimacy of the political process, especially after 1787.

Although American political culture and institutions enhanced the importance of compromise, the issues that forced compromise to the forefront of public discourse infused the concept with an urgent relevance unknown in any other period in American history. As the conflict over slavery in the United States produced more frequent and alarming crises that paralyzed the nation's public business, the very process of adjustment became an issue, even to the point of being identified with specific proposals for resolving the dispute. Flexible method became rigid policy; simple compromise was inflated to *the* Compromise, the elusive final settlement that would end the controversy.

Historical consciousness combined with contemporary fears of the dissolution of the Union to imbue compromise with a special constitutional significance as well. When Americans thought of compromise, frequently they remembered the framers of the Constitution, the "bundle of compromises" negotiated at Philadelphia in 1787, and the statesmanship of the first generation of national leaders. Responsible constitutional systems foster the reconciliation of principles and interests. The ongoing public debate about the Constitution and the Union therefore provided a further subtext for subsequent compromise discussions that occurred during flash points in the sectional debate, when the constant conflict over the status of slavery rekindled the ethical and strategic questions that had troubled the generation of 1787. The slavery issue inevitably called forth constitutional issues of the structure of the political system and the jurisdiction of national and state authorities, issues that the framers had left ambiguous in the expectation that as a source of controversy, the issues would be, in addition, an inducement to compromise.

These later discussions of compromise, especially in 1819–21, 1832–33, 1846–50, and finally in the secession winter of 1860–61, also reflected current tensions created by the rapidly changing political universe of the early nineteenth century. If the defense of compromise is at bottom a defense of process, then alterations in the political process naturally affect the meaning and justification of compromise. The political culture of the early Republic placed much emphasis on statesmanship as the guiding force of public decision making; as a number of historians have pointed out, despite the emergence of an inchoate defense of party as a legitimate arm of republican governance, antiparty feelings were rampant in the eighteenth century and remained a strong undercurrent well into the nineteenth century. Understandably, many Americans would view compromise within the context of statesmanship and remain skeptical that parties could cultivate working compromises by reconciling interests and principles among majorities and minorities. Indeed, it is arguable that the urge for sectional compromise rested on the instinctive need to *circumvent* party conflict rather than to strengthen it as a counterweight to sectional strife.

The association between compromise and the Constitution blended with concurrent conceptions of how to prevent sections and parties from destroying the Union and produced a series of legislative compromises in 1820–21, 1833, and 1850 that themselves could be seen as extensions of the Constitution's compromises—indeed, as quasi-constitutional compacts reaffirming the compact of 1787. By 1850, Americans had become accustomed to thinking of two kinds of compromise—the normal logrolling and bargaining in daily legislative business and the grand compromise reconciling major interests, principles, and sections. This type of thinking was at work elsewhere in the evolution of American constitutionalism. For example, the American innovation in constitutional law, which distinguished between fundamental constitutional law as constituent power and mere legislative statutory law, was not always honored in practice, even long after the idea was settled in jurisprudence. Organic acts (such as the creation of territories and the admission of new states) were theoretically repealable but in practical terms were permanently interwoven with the Constitution itself, whereas changing interpretations of the Constitution, although theoretically permanent when embodied in case law and accumulating precedent, were subject to the changing whims of legislators and jurists.[29] As we shall see, compromise came to connote the merger of accumulating custom, constitutional law, and statute law, all summarized within the idea that laws, like constitutions, form compacts with the people, imposing sacrifices on rulers and ruled.

But the rise of mass politics and political parties in the late 1820s and 1830s strained the intricate network of assumptions that had shaped the meaning of compromise as it was both articulated in 1787–88 and reaffirmed in subsequent sectional agreements. Compromise can be considered in the abstract as a process of resolving conflicts, but in application it must also be seen as a custom with its own peculiar set of affective associations and ethical imperatives. The common tendency to make this custom a principle of constitutional law through the medium of ordinary legislation created deep contradictions between traditional American notions of popular sovereignty and fundamental, constitutional law.

Political parties shattered the evolving merger of custom, statute law, and constitutional law by substituting their own rules and customs for harmonizing their internal conflicts. As the new media of civic action, the parties developed conceptions of the political process at odds with older notions of how to settle political disputes. Parties legitimized interest-group political action, a development that challenged earlier suspicions that parties might undermine the citizen's willingness to accept concessions for the public good. Politicians who grappled with the sectional conflict also had to grapple with the changing methods of dealing with it and found themselves undermining the traditional view of sectional compromise.

Sectionalism, slavery, constitutional unionism, statesmanship, and parties: all of these forces greatly affected how Americans viewed the actual workings of their political order. As James Farr has pointed out, the process of conceptual change operates at least in part through the exposure of theoretical and practical contradictions in existing political arrangements, forcing the alteration of practices and beliefs to accommodate or suppress those contradictions. The juxtaposition of freedom and slavery, self and community, unitary and divided sovereignty, was supposed to have been bridged by the Constitution's compromises.[30]

By tracing the public treatments of the concept of compromise within the context of sectional compromises and constitutional unionism, we can follow the changing civic culture of the young Republic. Beginning in 1787, the rhetoric of compromise mixed the ritualistic call for mutual sacrifice with the politics of pluralism and interest-group conflict. It reflected the prevailing belief that the new order could survive only by building concurring majorities over time through the process of mutual concession and the creation of a common interest in constitutional stability. It deprecated partisanship and offered statesmanlike conciliation as an antidote to sectionalism and partyism. Compromisers stressed its affective qualities and its aura of constitutional respectability in their attempts to use compromise to prevent the need for further compromise. There was something ritualistic about sectional compromise before the 1840s; the patchwork fabric of compromise legislation, the temporary weakening of party and sectional allegiances, the cycle of denunciation, negotiation, and amicable reconciliation, all contributed to popular feelings about how government in this Union was supposed to work.

But the advent of mass democratic politics and the intensification of sectional strife shifted the context of sectional compromise. Sectionalism and conscience politics eroded the affective, conciliatory qualities of earlier compromises (such as the Missouri Compromise) as betrayals of eternal principles. In response, party politicians used the old rhetoric of compromise as a device to solidify their national coalitions against sectional pressures while they tried to substitute new compromises (usually devised and enforced within their parties) for the old ones. A device used to dampen party and sectional animosities became a weapon in sectional and party warfare. The Compromise of 1850 was, in this sense, a transitional event that transferred compromise from a cultural context in which compromise was an escape from partisanship to a new context in which the settlement required strong party loyalties both for passage and for acceptance. This struggle over compromise revealed not only the newer contours of mass democratic styles but also the extent to which Americans still had yet to reconcile a two-party system with compromise and unionism.

My subject, then, is the position taken by the "defendants" of compromise, who in the end did indeed wind up among the "losers" in the sectional quarrel in 1861. By focusing on their ideas about the Constitution and compromise, I hope to correct the historiographical preoccupation with the failure of compromise and with the clashing ideological and sectional extremes that helped to undermine compromise, and thereby to reveal why many Americans expected the tactic to succeed.

To accomplish my task, I have sought the meaning of compromise on several levels within the civic culture. This required me to adopt two methods of developing the subject. I pursue a brief narrative of sectional compromise in the first, third, and fifth chapters. In the intervening chapters I pause to examine contemporary dimensions of compromise: its relationship to civic training and constitutional education (chapter two) and its role in the statesmanship of Henry Clay (chapter four). All of these chapters try to carry the thematic threads of the relationship among compromise, constitutional unionism, and civic culture along each of several levels of civic life. One level concerns the interaction of formal political ideas and less constrained civic attitudes. My examination of the ratification debates in chapter one sketches the template of compromise arguments and their connection to the creation of a national civic culture under a loose federal union. The struggle over the Constitution did not create a generation of compromisers; it merely fashioned a rhetoric of conciliation that in future sectional and party conflicts served as a historical referent for conciliators anxious to justify current expedients. In addition, the civics literature of the early Republic, discussed in chapter two, offers a striking picture of the "virtues of moderation" that defined the civic attitudes about political participation and procedure during the early Republic. In the civics manuals and schoolbooks as well as the writings on political ethics, one finds a remarkable continuity of thought about the Constitution's relationship to statesmanship, sectionalism, parties, and compromise.

I have also approached the meaning of compromise by looking at how politicians and public moralists explained sectional compromises during the antebellum period. My objective here is not to offer new interpretations of specific compromises but to suggest how the defense of compromise reflected the nation's self-image and its beliefs about constitutional customs. The ongoing sectional debate also revealed the growing influence of political parties in a changing political universe and therefore indicated the extent to which older justifications of compromise as a legitimate outcome of republican politics yielded to the party political culture of a new era. These matters are examined in chapter three, are drawn together with the discussion of statesmanship and politics in chapters four and five, and in chapter six are carried through the Democrats' unsuccessful use of the compromise tradition to the eve of the Civil War.

Finally, I examine the relationship between compromise and statesmanship in an age that simultaneously glorified ideologues and compromisers. The focus of my attention on this matter has been directed at Henry Clay as the foremost articulator of sectional compromise. Clay was not a natural compromiser in the contemporary meaning of the term. He was a restless, impulsive, and often stubborn politician. His advocacy of compromise during sectional crises did not make him a compromiser in all political confrontations, and it is not my intention to turn his defense of compromise into a life's philosophy of compromise. Instead, I think that Clay's views of compromise stemmed from his analysis of the strengths and weaknesses of a constitutional union resting on the shaky consensus that majorities must conciliate minorities instead of simply crushing them in every political contest.

In the forge of experience, Clay learned the blessings and the dangers of compromise, which, fortunately for us, he often spoke and wrote about. Although recent biographies of Clay have rescued some of his political ideas from an undeserved reputation as shallow and inconsistent, they still classify him as a stern, nationalistic unionist in the tradition of Daniel Webster. Although he and Webster did agree on many important public issues, Clay's response to the Missouri and nullification crises indicated that he had a greater attachment to Madisonian constitutionalism than did Webster. A close examination of Clay's constitutionalism reveals, I think, the instinctive conservatism of the nation's early political culture.

Clay knew that to win support for compromise, he had to prove that it was distinctly republican and American, as James Shields claimed. He and other compromisers had to offer their own version of American history, appealing to the judgment of the founders by tying the fate of compromise to the creation and perpetuation of "the Union as it is" and claiming that the solution to the conflict over slavery had been pointed out at the very beginning, in Philadelphia, during that hot summer of 1787.

1 Template, 1787
Fashioning a Rhetoric of Conciliation

We were neither the same
Nation nor Different Nations.
—Elbridge Gerry

On July 22, 1850, Henry Clay rose from his seat in the Senate to make a final plea for his comprehensive settlement of the rancorous dispute over the status of slavery in the United States:

> Who are the greatest of parties in that greatest of all compromises—the Constitution of the United States? There were no technical parties to that instrument; but in deliberating upon what was best for the country, and perceiving that there were great and conflicting interests pervading all its parts, they compromised and settled them by ample concession, and in the spirit of true patriotic amity. They adjusted these conflicting opinions, and the Constitution, under which we sit at this moment, is the work of their hands—a great, memorable, magnificent compromise, which indicates to us the course of duty when differences arise which can only be settled by the spirit of mutual concession.[1]

Clay's appeal to history was more than a momentary flourish. It was a calculated stirring of the nation's collective memory to recall and replicate the process of the constitutional union's birth. It also reverberated with the themes that Federalists had repeatedly elaborated throughout the ratification debates of 1787–88: the Constitutional Convention as model legislature, the wisdom of the framers' concord and sacrifice, and the absence of "technical parties" from the deliberations in Philadelphia in 1787. But Clay's firm belief in the finality of his proposed settlement of the crisis in 1850 excluded other themes of the ratification struggle, especially the Federalists' frequent admission that the Constitution's origination in compromise had made it an imperfect document that would require future amendments; to them, compromise was not necessarily final.

Just as significant as the differences between Clay's and the framers' understanding of compromise was the absence from Clay's account of any sense that compromise preexisted the constitutional union. The framers did not invent compromise, yet subsequent sectional compromisers acted as if they had. The country's long tradition of devising constitutions, compacts, covenants, and charters to arrange its diverse colonial and state polities is missing from later discussions of compromise. Nor does one find an appreciation of the pluralist social, sectional, and economic conditions that were rife in the colonial past and that were the great impetus for colonial politicians to practice the arts of compromise long before the Federalists came to admire some of its qualities. When Clay's generation thought of compromise, it was more likely to think of the framers and their work than of the obscure ancestors who had laid the foundations of a constitutional polity.

One reason for this omission is obvious: the framers created a constitutional union, tying compromise to the creation of a national civic culture born in the act of ratification. Compromise would be essential if this political culture, with its customs and its constitutional superstructure, was to break with past failures at union, failures that could be chalked up to an unwillingness by the states to compromise and symbolized in the paralysis of the Articles of Confederation.

Clay's unabashed glorification of compromise rested on a steadier confidence in the practice than that displayed by his distinguished forebears in the late eighteenth century. Even before the Constitutional Convention's adjournment in mid-September 1787, Federalists were reluctant to advertise the extent either of its compromises or of the conflicts that precipitated them. The Convention's accommodation of republican theory to political reality had been necessary but had left open too many questions about its ultimate intent on vital issues such as a bill of rights, federal-state relations, slavery, and representation. In the end, perhaps compromises *on* liberty could become compromises *of* liberty, a sure invitation to tyrants.

And would not compromise signify an admission of error, of flawed principles and a corrupted legacy? People could remember Aristotle's warning that "when one begins with an initial error, it is inevitable that one should end badly." Well might a statesman of the early Republic hesitate before giving compromise the kind of favorable attention that Clay and his ilk lavished upon it.[2]

The critics of the new Constitution seized on the Federalists' apprehensions, which they used to force their opponents to explain and justify the Convention's conduct, including its compromises. The dynamics of the ensuing debate fleshed out a fuller understanding of compromise that firmly connected a conventional technique for adjusting disputes with exceptional, American and republican qualities. By stressing the relationship between interest and sentiment, or more specifically among compromise, sacrifice, statesmanship, and a more perfect union that promoted a common interest, the Federalists etched a template of legends that men like Henry Clay could evoke in subsequent crises of the Union.

ON SEPTEMBER 17, 1787, after nearly four months of intense and relatively secret deliberation, the Constitutional Convention met at the Pennsylvania State House in Philadelphia for the last time. After some last-minute maneuvers, including Benjamin Franklin's brief plea for unanimity read for him by James Wilson and instigated by Gouverneur Morris, the Convention adopted the Constitution and arranged for its transmission to the Confederation Congress in New York City. In explanation of its labors, the Convention also endorsed a letter over the signature of its president, George Washington. Ostensibly to the president of Congress, the letter was really another of Morris's backstage maneuvers to enhance the Convention's public image. This remarkable message outlined a classic justification of compromise, one that would resurface time and again in public discourse and civics literature up to the Civil War.[3]

Washington's letter articulated the basic definition of compromise and connected it to the behavior of the Convention and to the meaning of a constitutional union. The "peculiarity of [the] situation," which Washington attributed to the diverse "extent, habits, and particular interests" of the states, had generated conflicts that had made it "impracticable . . . to secure all rights of independent sovereignty in each, and yet provide for the interest and safety of all." To resolve this conflict, it would be necessary to sacrifice portions of the "liberty," "rights," and "interests" of both states and individuals. The "magnitude of the sacrifice" would depend both on present conditions and on "the object to be obtained."

Furthermore, the concessions made by the delegates were the products of "a spirit of amity, and of . . . mutual deference," the cornerstone of a nation's civil character, the essence of community. This mutuality had overcome the divisions among the states, unlike previous attempts at union. The resulting settlement—the Constitution, and by extension the Union—was necessarily imperfect; it was what the Convention thought "most advisable," Washington observed, and therefore "liable to as few exceptions as could reasonably have been expected."

Washington's letter is also significant for what it did not say. It neither outlined the Constitution's compromises nor specified the issues that had engendered them, even though it admitted that compromises had occurred. Nor was there any ringing appeal either to the Spirit of '76 of such recent memory or to the ancient rights that Americans had paid such a heavy price to secure. Even more remarkable is the letter's silence about precedents, especially in the country's common experience beyond the Revolution, in the institutional bedrock of covenants, compacts, charters, and constitutions upon which Americans had for over 160 years built their political order. And certainly this was no manifesto of the hybrid republican principles and values that many historians believe were the theoretical building blocks of the Constitution. Indeed, the letter mentioned only two prerequisites for forming a more perfect union: that the current unicameral Confederation was inadequate, and that only "a spirit of amity, and of that mutual deference and concession which the peculiarity of our political situation rendered indispensible," could overcome the deficiency.

Given the portentous nature of the Convention's recommendation to Congress and the country, and considering the fateful decision to scrap rather than amend the existing Articles of Confederation, the absence of a convincing defense that marshaled the lessons of history and the intellectual force of republican political theory at the very onset of the ratification campaign is particularly striking. But the reason for this was not far to seek—it lay in the conduct of the Convention itself. Having severely condemned the Articles and the conduct of the state legislatures as utterly incompatible with sound republican theory and as completely inadequate to the practical needs of an infant nation, the framers had quickly discovered in the Convention that their common criticisms of the present offered few practical guidelines for the future. Republicanism, despite its usefulness as an ideological weapon against British tyranny, was not a cohesive enough doctrine to withstand alone the more demanding loyalties of state, section, and pocketbook.[4]

The result was a long summer of struggle and compromise among conflicting groups and ideas in the Convention, which eventually produced an unintended frame of government that faced an uncertain reception by the waiting public. Almost as soon as the delegates had assembled in Philadelphia in late May, they began quarreling about the history of republics, sectional issues such as slavery and foreign commerce, the relationship between the existing states and the proposed national government, and the very nature of representation, itself the cardinal principle of republican thinking about government. Some issues provoked sharp debate but comparatively simple adjustment, whereas others fused ideological and material elements so firmly that only extended negotiation on the floor, in committee, and under the table broke the deadlock. These conflicts produced the compromises of the Constitution with which we are so familiar.

The great compromise of July 16, which coupled a lower house apportioned by population to an indirectly elected upper house in which the states had equal suffrage, is the most important and enduring of these agreements. The compromise originated in a dispute between small and large states over representation in a bicameral legislature, but this conflict quickly ranged into the issue of counting property or population in the apportionment of representatives and tax quotas. Because slaves could be considered as both property and human, this second issue produced a sectional alignment that superseded the earlier division. This mixture of complex ideological, material, and regional issues required a number of subsidiary agreements in order to satisfy a majority in the Convention. The three-fifths rule, the connection between direct taxes and representation, the provision for a decennial census of population, the origination in the House of all revenue bills (which were amendable by the Senate), and the apportionment of representatives to the First Congress all were parts of this larger compromise. A hodgepodge of interlocking agreements, the great compromise was a microcosm of early republican legislative statecraft.[5]

Each piece of the great compromise rested on a network of ideological and practical arguments. The three-fifths rule, the census, and the apportionment of representatives to the First Congress all sparked fusillades of opposing theoretical and practical arguments drawn from essentially the same reservoir of political theorists and historians. As Forrest McDonald has observed, this early debate in the Convention indicated that the delegates "did not derive their positions from systems of political theory. Rather, they used political theorists to justify positions that they had taken for nontheoretical reasons."[6]

This pattern of debate, deadlock, and compromise held throughout the summer. In mid-August, the delegates hit another logjam over the future of the slave trade and the power of Congress over commerce regulations. And in late August to early September, another deadlock set in over the mode of electing the president. Each of these conflicts required a realignment of opposing forces in the Convention and eventuated in a major compromise.[7]

The manner of decision making, as William E. Nelson has recently observed, suggested a form of compromise that sought the conciliation of minorities and the building of concurring majorities. Through what Nelson calls "instrumental reasoning," the delegates did not merely recombine conflicting interests but tried to define a common interest that answered as much of the minority's demands as possible.[8] Nelson misses the point, however, that the development of concurring majorities within the Convention was itself a suitable template for popular decision making outside the Convention. The delegates realized that a new constitution simply could not survive the continued abrasions of slim majorities and large minorities.

There is little evidence that this kind of thinking was new to the Convention or even consciously introduced into the deliberations. Even a brief reading of the delegates' arguments on behalf of major compromises discloses few references to republican theories about the concept of compromise or to model compromises of the past. The debate over the great compromise, especially over the composition of Congress, offers abundant illustration of the delegates' thinking. Defenders of a bicameral structure initially tried to argue that the two forms of voting and representation were compatible. "We were partly national; partly federal," Oliver Ellsworth of Connecticut told the Convention on June 29. "The proportional representation in the first branch was conformable to the national principle & would secure the large states agst. the small. An equality of voices was conformable to the federal principle and was necessary to secure the Small states agst. the large." Ellsworth expected that "on this middle ground a compromise would take place." James Madison immediately countered Ellsworth with an argument that would later haunt the Virginian in the ratification struggle. "I would always exclude inconsistent principles in framing a system of government," he said. If the delegates were to be consistent, they had to choose one form or another, but not both.[9]

To counter this charge of inconsistency, the advocates of the compromise were left with patriotism, self-interest, and pure necessity in their dwindling arsenal of arguments. If the great compromise substantively reconciled opposing viewpoints through "instrumental reasoning," then attempts to create a common interest in the passage of a compromise, by appealing to the delegates' fears that deadlock and dissolution would bring personal and national misfortune, linked individual ambition for fame with the future of the Union. Caleb Strong of Massachusetts reviewed the history of the compromise, and although he disliked the concession of equality in the upper house, he feared disunion more and therefore "was compelled to give his vote for the [compromise] taken all together." With the Confederation "nearly at an end," he observed, the "Union itself must soon be dissolved" if no accommodation occurred. Other delegates echoed this thinking. Compromise was the prerequisite for an enduring union and also for the grateful remembrance of many future generations. Madison reported in his notes that Ellsworth did not regard himself to be "a halfway man, yet he preferred doing half the good we could, rather than do nothing at all."[10]

At those crucial points when adjournment seemed imminent, only forceful reminders of the consequences of failure could reconcile the delegates to accepting half a loaf instead of none. These were desperate arguments to pitch at a divided audience, but they reflected the necessity of appealing to both ambition and virtue when seeking compromise, a tactic that would figure prominently in future attempts at sectional compromise. Naturally, the delegates became very disappointed with the Convention's slow progress, ceaseless bickering, and constant equivocation. By the time the Convention wound up its business in mid-September, eleven of the original fifty-five attending delegates had already left for more pressing matters elsewhere, another two had bolted the Convention in protest against its centralizing tendencies, and three influential members (Elbridge Gerry of Massachusetts, and George Mason and Governor Edmund Randolph of Virginia) had refused to sign the instrument on the last day.[11]

Little wonder that an assembly convened with such grave purposes and high aspirations would find little to say about the patchwork of agreements so laboriously cobbled together into the new Constitution. "It is the best that could meet the unanimous concurrence of the states in Convention," Nicholas Gilman sighed to his brother on the day after adjournment; "it was done by bargain and Compromise, yet not withstanding its imperfections, on the adoption of it depends (in my feeble judgment) whether we shall become a respectable nation, or a people torn to pieces by intestine commotions, and rendered contemptible for ages." The early letters of many of the delegates mirrored Gilman's ambivalence.[12]

The Convention's letter to Congress, then, capped a long, hard summer and marked a strange beginning to the campaign for ratification of the Constitution. Apparently the Convention lacked a single comprehensive historical or theoretical model on which it could ground a defense of the Constitution that would not offend popular sensibilities. Many of the delegates would not risk venting in public their reviving respect for the British Constitution;[13] the Articles of Confederation were in widespread disrepute, especially among the advocates of the Constitution. The state constitutions had offered many important precedents for the Constitution and would indeed serve as convenient referents on specific issues, but the Convention's innovations—especially its rejection of the Articles outside the amending process provided therein, its provision for ratification by state conventions presumably lacking the power of amendment, and its design for an invigorated executive branch—were a departure from Revolutionary state frames that had been enacted by conventions without final popular approval and that had hobbled their respective executives.

The waiting Antifederalist opposition would seize quickly on these and other weaknesses suggested by the Convention's apparent lack of enthusiasm or precedent for the Constitution. Only brilliant innovative analysis of the nature of American pluralism and its relationship to the diffuse republicanism that shaped much popular thinking about government could adequately answer Antifederalists' objections; the Federalists, especially Madison and Hamilton, would measure up to this task.

But the Convention's letter also pointed another way out for Federalists under attack for their compromises. Although the Convention had been a real departure in the history of American constitutionalism, in at least one important respect it had remained firmly within the American political tradition: unlike the Congress currently sitting in New York, the Convention was a legislative body that had overcome the deep-seated conflicts of sections, interests, and interpretations of republican ideas to arrive at a comprehensive settlement of the crisis of the Union. Here was an object lesson in civic conduct, a model for citizen and politician. "Let it be remembered," the Federalist New York *Daily Advertiser* stated a week after the Convention's adjournment, "that 'the *mutual deference and concession*,' from which this Constitution has resulted, ought to have a strong operation on the minds of all generous Americans, and have due influence with every *State Convention*, when they come to deliberate upon its adoption."[14] In the upcoming struggle, Federalists would transform the ambivalence born of compromise into a quintessential quality of both republican statesmanship and American Union.

THE DIALECTIC OF the ratification debate refined and enlarged Washington's preliminary statements about compromise by placing the concept within the context of history and theory that had been absent from the Convention's discussions of the subject. The debate did not occur in neat stages but instead conformed to the sequence of the ratifying conventions and to the rough patterns of the fragmented circulation of information in this period. The chorus of verbal warfare ebbed and peaked as the Constitution passed from state to state for deliberation, yet it is instructive to view the struggle as an extended conversation about the nature of republican government and its relationship to the special circumstances of American politics, economy, and society.[15]

And a rough division in the progress of the debate did appear. From mid-September until late 1787, Federalists argued mainly by evoking the reputations of famous Convention delegates and by pointing to their unprecedented "unanimity" as a model of republican behavior. By early 1788, the mounting Antifederalist opposition, evidenced by close margins in the Massachusetts convention and the multiplying number of influential newspaper criticisms, had forced the Federalists to supplement their early emphasis on patriotism and concord with specific discussions of the conditions under which compromise did and should occur.

Several events dispelled the delegates' ambivalence of mid-September and gave the campaign for ratification strong momentum by the end of the year. On September 26 the Constitution swept through the Confederation Congress with short, sharp debate, a few shenanigans by its advocates, and a unanimous vote of the states attending. Before the end of October, five states (Pennsylvania, New Jersey, Georgia, Connecticut, and Massachusetts) called special conventions to consider the proposed constitution. Four states (Delaware, Pennsylvania, New Jersey, and Georgia) voted to ratify before the new year dawned, three of them unanimously. Federalists exulted over Congress's "apparent unanimity," which, according to Washington, would "have its effect": the masses, "too often deceived by externals," need not "peep behind the Curtain" at the backstage bickering over the instrument.[16]

Indeed, much of the early Federalist campaign reflected this belief in the public's gullibility, for it emphasized not the substance of the Convention's compromises but the congeniality that had fostered them. Federalist essays often featured patriotic calls for the public somehow to match the Convention's unanimity, and they freely used Washington's letter to drive home the point. "Curtius" summarized the unfolding Federalist argument in an "Address to All Federalists" printed in the New York *Daily Advertiser* soon after the Convention. After praising "the sources of *energy, wisdom,* and *Virtue,* delicately combined" in the Constitution, Curtius exhorted his readers to "behold the greatest concessions made by the strongest; and if any partiality is shewn, it is in favor of the weak." The Convention's entire demeanor had been exceptional for its "most perfect unanimity." Other Federalist papers echoed these sentiments.[17]

The Federalists tried to defend their flawed product by highlighting the novelty of simply arriving at an agreement. "A Correspondent" to the *United States Chronicle* in Providence remarked that "it would hardly have been credible in Europe, or in any Part of the old World, that States so different in their Situation, Extent, Habits, and particular Interests, would have so far divested themselves of all jealousy and Apprehensions of mischievous Consequences" as to write a constitution to be sent to the people for approval. And the states' concord in the Convention could be contrasted easily with their quarreling in Congress. For the Convention's wonderful cordiality seemed a major departure from the factious animosities that plagued the state governments and paralyzed national politics in the Confederation period. The Convention had found a way out of pluralism's maze; compromise had created unity in diversity.[18]

Throughout the ratification struggle, Federalist statements, both public and private, teemed with awestruck allusions to the Convention's unprecedented ability to resolve conflict while they simultaneously described the Constitution as the imperfect product of compromise. In a widely published and influential speech, James Wilson claimed that the "evidence of mutual concession and accommodation" in the great compromise was an asset that "ought rather to command a generous applause, than to excite jealousy and reproach."[19]

According to the historian Peter Onuf, Federalists apotheosized the Convention's compromises in order to obtain legitimacy for the Convention's work: the "miracle" of compromise distinguished it from previous attempts at union while narrowing the options for saving the Union to the one solution offered by the Convention. Thus the appeal to great names, when joined with rhetorical excesses about unanimity and compromise, gave what Clinton Rossiter calls a "compelling tone of authenticity" to the statesmanship of the framers.[20] This emphasis on tactics misses the way that Federalists incorporated the ideas of unanimity and compromise into their conception of civic behavior. Statesmen were supposed to reconcile interests; minorities must acquiesce in decisions by the majority; and citizens must exercise restraint when participating in politics.

The Federalists' bombast about great names and unanimity belied the weak basis for national union that the Constitution was supposed to address. Federalists strained the definition of *unanimity* beyond the absence of dissent, to include a united *amiability*, a wholesome civility and toleration, a welcome and necessary prelude to building national affections to bind the Union. Clearly there were degrees of unanimity that coexisted with imperfect compromise. True unanimity required the minority's acquiescence in defeat. Here again, the Convention provided useful models for civic conduct. Franklin's famous speech on the Convention's last day, in which he confessed his dissatisfaction with the Constitution on some points yet pledged to support it in order to enhance its chances of passage by the states, became an object lesson in proper relations between dissenters and the majority. The speech, along with similar episodes of gracious defeat and acquiescence by Antifederalists in other states, was widely reprinted and praised by Federalists.[21]

As a contrast, Federalists pointed to what they believed to be the obstructionist behavior of Antifederalists in Pennsylvania and Rhode Island. The Pennsylvania Antifederalists' attempts to prevent the general assembly from calling elections for the state ratifying convention, their obstinate refusal to acquiesce in the state's ratification, plus Rhode Island's refusal to attend the Convention or cooperate in the public debate seemed to many Federalists to be uncivil, unrepublican conduct, a direct defiance of "the great principle of society that a part should submit to the whole."[22]

To the Federalists, the misconduct of obstinate minorities proved their point: the improved Union had to rest on compromise, and compromise required appropriate conduct—mutual affections. "Fixed principles and settled habits are necessary for the stability of Republics," argued "Foreign Spectator" in his "Essay on the Means of Promoting Federal Sentiments in the United States." But because virtue was at the heart of republicanism, and because the new government had "no power to maintain the Union" against the people's will, it was crucial that the states practice a politics of conciliation, encourage mutual regard, "scan mutual infirmities with a sister's eye; and generally sacrifice particular advantage for the common glory and happiness." Here was the germ of early republican compromise sentiment, whose implicit majoritarianism weakened the Union's intrinsic power to sustain itself. The Union must conciliate the people or collapse; a coerced union was no union at all (a point with which Antifederalists would wryly agree).[23]

As the Federalist campaign unfolded, the outlines of a strategy appeared. Certainly there would be much substantive argument about the specifics of the new Constitution, but because the Federalists lacked a working model of the instrument, they needed to convey a sense of how it *should* work and of how the nation *would* suffer if the Constitution failed of adoption. Furthermore, the Federalists' own doubts about the Constitution's prospects prompted them to locate the source of possible failure in the character and behavior of citizens and not in some defect in the amendable structure of a new government. The operators, not the machine, would be to blame—thus the intensive Federalist effort to inculcate a national civics lesson in republican ethics, with the Convention as model and its famous personages as civic educators in the practice of statesmanlike compromise. This emphasis on character, of both citizen and leader, bridged the gap between the nationalists' fearful diagnoses of the Confederation's ills and their need to justify the halfway solution created in Philadelphia. Nationality was prospective, still only partly conceived, incomplete. Ratification was not just a legal process, it was part of nation building.[24]

ALTHOUGH THE OPPONENTS of ratification had been active before the Convention adjourned, they were effectively prevented by the delegates' vow of secrecy from making efficient advance preparations for the contest. As the Federalist argument emerged in the public press, Antifederalists mounted an increasingly effective attack against its weakest points and forced the Federalists to refine even further their defense of the Convention's compromises.[25]

In general, the Antifederalists struck at the Federalists' version of concord in the Convention, contrasted the substance of the compromises to the prevailing doctrines of Whig political science, and used the Federalists' admission of the Constitution's imperfection to argue for a second convention to consider amendments. At the core of the Antifederalist attack was the belief that the Constitution was neither the product nor the promoter of public harmony. The instrument had been born in a secret, factious assembly and therefore would perpetuate discord and conflict rather than the peaceful preservation of ordered liberty. The people would "discover in it the seeds of disorder" a Pennsylvania Antifederalist warned, "and sooner or later it must yield to an incurable distemper, fatal to the liberties of their posterity." The vehemence of the Federalists' reply testified to the power of these arguments, diverse as their origins may have been.[26]

It is important to understand that the Antifederalists rarely attacked the strategy of compromise as intrinsically dangerous to republicanism. Republican theorists offered no guidance on when compromise crossed the boundary between a practical statecraft and a declension from first principles, so Antifederalists, like their opponents, had no ideological weaponry for or against compromise. The debate was about the inconsistency and ambiguity in certain compromises, not the morality of compromise itself. But by criticizing the framers' compromises, the Antifederalists forced their opponents to choose between a more specific defense of controversial bargains that would not bear close scrutiny and a broader defense of compromise as a symbol of nascent national identity. Therefore, the Antifederalists did not force their opponents to redefine the concept of compromise but to explain it more fully and to wield it on behalf of the legitimacy of the proposed regime. The Antifederalists could exploit the double meaning of compromise—its implication that the parties had lost something in the bargain—to ridicule the principled credentials of the framers and their work.[27]

The Federalists' glowing depictions of the Convention's unanimity came under withering criticism, especially with the mounting evidence of the Convention's internal quarrels. The revelations, both public and private, of Convention dissenters and nonsigners, plus other early Antifederalist criticisms, punctured Gouverneur Morris's public relations stratagem. As one writer put it, "We KNOW, and the long sitting of the Convention tells us, that (as it is endeavored to persuade us), concord and unanimity did not reign exclusively among them."[28]

Luther Martin's widely published disclosure of the conflict within the Convention blasted the Federalists' claim of unanimity. Combined with the growing Antifederalist declamations that the public should not be swayed by "the authority of names," Martin's revelations deeply wounded the Federalists' depiction of the Convention's compromises as patriotic gestures by disinterested republican statesmen.[29] In his "Genuine Information," the peppery Marylander went to the very heart of the great compromise, portraying it not as a product of concord and unanimity but as a fallback position extorted by a beleaguered minority against a consolidationist juggernaut. Because the Articles of Confederation already provided equal state representation, why, Martin asked, should the small states give it up if not under duress? And would this new "solemn compact" be any more durable than the one that Federalists had overthrown in Philadelphia?[30]

This eyewitness testimony of angry confrontation within the Convention encouraged the public to disregard "externals" and "peep behind the Curtain" at the Constitution's compromises and their real sources. "The unanimity of the federal convention, and the sanction of great names, can be no further urged as an argument after [Martin's] exposition," a prominent Antifederalist wrote. "He has opened such a scene of discord and accommodation of republicanism to despotism as [to] excite the most serious apprehensions in every patriotic mind." "Plebeian," a New York Antifederalist, put this most succinctly: "Let the Constitution stand on its own merits. If it be good, it stands not in need of great men's names to support it. If it be bad, their names ought not to sanction it." And the Federalists' admission that the document was imperfect just worsened matters. A correspondent to the *Pennsylvania Herald* noted Franklin's ambivalence and asked, "If general Washington's reason for signing this federal work was the same, what becomes of the great argument founded upon the approbation of these illustrious patriots?" Antifederalists had found the weak link in Federalist appeals to "mutual affections" and "unanimity": compromise signified ambivalence about nationhood, not confidence in its success or in the existence of popular support for a stronger federal union.[31]

Critics also looked closely at the compromises and found them ambiguous, unbalanced, and unfair, a cloak for secret personal and sectional ambitions. Wherever the Constitution was clear on sectional questions, as in the three-fifths rule, northerners and southerners alike complained that they were doomed to permanent minority status. And wherever the Constitution was ambiguous, as in the "necessary and proper" clause, Antifederalists in general feared consolidation, oppression, and ruin at the hands of a distant, uncaring elite possessing the sole power of expounding and enforcing the fundamental law of the land.[32]

In addition to claiming that the new Constitution betrayed local interests, Antifederalists attacked the Federalists' belief that national union could pacify conflicting states, regions, and interests. As Peter Onuf has pointed out, the Antifederalists' famous argument that the Constitution could not encompass and adjust the clashing interests of an extended republic revealed a static conception of the Union in which one state's gain was another's loss. By this view, compromise as simple adjustment of conflicting, shifting majorities and minorities over time could not occur under the hybrid structure erected at Philadelphia.[33] "In a republic," explained "Brutus," "the manners, sentiments, and interests of the people should be similar. If this not be the case, there will be a constant clashing of opinions; and the representatives of one party will be continually striving against those of the other. This will retard the operations of government, and prevent such conclusions as will promote the public good." "Cato" noted that the future Congress, "composed of interests opposite and dissimilar in their nature," would "in its exercise, emphatically be, like a house divided against itself." A national government would threaten liberty because it would require a standing army to accomplish what a divided legislature could not.[34]

The Constitution would intensify, not harmonize, these conflicts because ambitious leaders would exploit popular divisions in order to obtain ratification and retain power. And the provision for concurrent powers of state and federal governments guaranteed perpetual discord among all components of the system. The Antifederalists denounced Federalist scare stories about disunion as an attempt to stampede a frightened public, and they pointed to the Constitution's radical innovations as the real source of discord and danger. Indeed, the Constitution did not protect those liberties and privileges that the states shared, but instead its ambiguity endangered them. "What was this wonder working concession and accommodation?" "Cincinnatus" asked of James Wilson. "If they consisted in giving up, or hazarding any of the . . . fundamental principles of liberty" on demand of the "more furious spirits in the convention . . . , [then] it will command a general execration."[35]

The Antifederalists' frequent declaration that bicameralism and the new federalism embodied irreconcilable contradictions in the structure of government did not mean that they opposed the idea of checks and balances. Instead, they argued that because such contradictions were hidden within the Constitution's ambiguity at important points, subsequent reconciliation of clashes between rival authorities would rest in the hands of ambitious national leaders remote from popular control.

The Antifederalists' solution was to demand a second constitutional convention to consider amendments offered by the state conventions. Informed by the people's real opinions, as determined in the current debate, the new assembly would address Edmund Randolph's demand that "all ambiguities . . . be precisely explained." The new convention would delineate congressional and state powers "so as to leave no clashing of jurisdictions nor dangerous disputes; and to prevent the one from being swallowed up by the other, under the cover of general words, and implication." This meant not only specifying the powers of state and federal governments but also incorporating a bill of rights; both of these modifications would reduce the probability of future conflicts over liberties that the Federalists' Constitution had jeopardized in its ambiguous language and sectional bargains.[36]

Clearly, the thrust of Antifederalist objections to the Constitution rested on the conclusion that the climate of "mutual amity" was not strong enough either in the Constitutional Convention or in the country at large—or, for that matter, in the human condition itself—to warrant granting vaguely defined powers to an unbalanced national government. It would be much better to leave the resolution of conflicts to local agencies more familiar with the customs, manners, and practices of their constituents and to build into any general government the specific terms under which compromise might occur.

The Antifederalists' counterattack demonstrated that the Federalists' hero worship had failed to conceal the simple fact that compromise, especially ambiguous compromise, still demanded explanation. The Convention's compromises and the Federalists' hyperbole of the miracle of unanimity and concord screened a shaky foundation for a perpetual union. Even more to the point, the Federalists' reluctance to incorporate a bill of rights signified a fundamental misreading of what *American* really meant. As Donald Lutz has pointed out, bills of rights not only were designed to limit government but also were acts of self-definition that described, often in lengthy detail, what made a people unique. The Federalists entirely missed this essential point and unconvincingly argued that necessary protections already existed in the state constitutions. If Americans were going to create a new union, the Antifederalists argued, then its founding charter must make more enduring affirmations than that this would be a nation of complacent compromisers.[37]

BECAUSE THE Antifederalists had skillfully used both the Federalists' confessions of the Constitution's imperfections and eyewitness accounts of the Convention's squabbles to refute the Federalists' claim that patriotic unanimity had reigned in the Philadelphia Convention, a more convincing explanation of the Constitution's compromises would be necessary. Furthermore, the Antifederalists' criticisms of particulars of the compromise necessitated a broader defense of compromise. Otherwise the public debate might completely shift over to the terms established by the Antifederalists and descend into a rancorous dissection of the Constitution clause by clause, burying its general advantages under an avalanche of local grievances and intensifying the clamor for a second convention. To the Federalists, a second convention occurring amid particularist demands for further limitations on the proposed government would be a disaster. "Let every American be permitted to expunge what *he* judges exceptionable," went the common Federalist refrain, "and not a sentence of the system will survive the scrutiny."[38]

Practical questions demanded practical answers. Enlightenment political science would be of limited use in this stage of the debate. To answer Antifederalists' criticisms, Federalists firmly steered discussion to the question of union or disunion, setting a precedent for future advocates of national compromise who entertained similar fears that the social order would crumble without an overarching constitutional process for managing conflict. Federalists elaborated a history of American politics from the Articles of Confederation through the present, arguing that in the face of clear evidence of the decay natural to republican governments, the Convention had created a unique opportunity to overcome divisive conflicts and create a stable national union. And of course the delegates' willingness to shake hands and accept an admittedly imperfect Constitution truly set this Convention apart from previous attempts at union. The opposition's arguments had still failed to pose an effective answer to what one Federalist believed was the essential question facing the country: "Shall we rise into one respectable nation, or sink into thirteen factions?"[39] This position contained many exaggerations and a few gaps, but it was flexible enough to meet the barrage of often conflicting charges leveled by the Antifederalists at the Constitution.

So the Federalists set about explaining what unique conditions had fostered the disposition to conciliate and what implications this attitude would have for the new nation under the Constitution. They argued that, unlike the Confederation government, the proposed frame contained institutional restraints that steered the nation toward the political center, encouraged moderate conduct, and therefore avoided the extremes of anarchy and consolidation. Although Federalists continued to stress the importance of giving leaders the discretion to adjust policy according to changing circumstance, they softened their early patriotic appeals to "unanimity" in favor of a more practical examination of the ways the Constitution minimized the potential for abuses of power.

In keeping with their desire to avoid troublesome specifics, the Federalists sidestepped the Antifederalists' criticisms of the substance of the compromises, preferring instead to shield the Convention's sectional bargains behind the disinterested spirit of the great compromise. Finally, the Federalists persistently argued that the amending process left open a "Constitutional door" for future adjustments as time and circumstance might dictate. The Union created by the Constitution could endure only if two qualifications were met: change must be directed by the orderly form prescribed in the instrument, and it must be guided by a spirit of conciliation. In fine, the Federalists' elaborate argument transformed a strategy of compromise into a symbol of the Union.[40]

The Federalists claimed that their opponents preferred disunion because the Antifederalists overlooked the possibility of compromise as an acceptable way to reconcile minorities and majorities. As Noah Webster put it, "In civil society, political liberty consists in *acting conformably to a sense of a majority* of a society." And that "sense" could be peaceably determined only in a conciliatory spirit. Antifederalists who argued that the Constitution did not sufficiently accommodate their local interests were apparently unwilling to make sacrifices in order to accommodate others. And Antifederalists who claimed that America's jarring interests and sections could not find common ground under a national government were too dependent on a zero-sum analysis of politics in which only winners and losers inhabited the political community.[41]

Both Antifederalist viewpoints were disunionist because they were not conciliatory. According to Washington, the Antifederalists "do not consider that for every sacrifice which they make they receive an ample compensation by the sacrifices which are made by other states for their benefit; and that those very things which they give up operate to their advantage through the medium of the general interest." In his view, the issue was self-evident: "There must be reciprocity or no Union[;] which is preferable will not become a question in the Mind of any true patriot." Union was not just patriotic; it was practical.[42]

Federalists cited the paralysis of the Confederation as proof that without such reciprocity, union was impossible. They recited in excruciating detail their many criticisms of the Confederation, reminding Americans how partisan animosities had exploited the Articles' structural defects and had frozen the deliberative process, leaving unresolved a multitude of economic, sectional, and diplomatic issues, from the disposition of western lands to the problem of state laws that abrogated contracts. "The great fault of the existing Confederacy," James Wilson had told the Philadelphia Convention, "is its inactivity."[43]

Of course, most Antifederalists had granted that the Confederation was defective, but they had also challenged their opponents to explain how a new Congress could cope with issues, like the status of jury trials in civil cases, that the Convention had intentionally left to posterity to decide. "What sense is there," "Cincinnatus" asked Wilson, "in supposing, that what . . . was impracticable with the Convention, will be practicable with the Congress? What faculty can the one body have more than the other, of reconciling contradictions?" The Federalists responded by predicting that Congress, acting within a frame that encouraged compromise, would avoid the Confederation's turmoil by further emulating a Convention that had reconciled contradictions.[44]

In Federalist eyes, the Convention's circumstances clearly contrasted not only with the Confederation Congress but also with the behavior of the Antifederalists. The Convention was nonpartisan, they claimed. As "Publius" pointed out, the Confederation Congress acted much like previous assemblies, troubled by "factions, contentions, and disappointments" that blocked what "the republican principle demands, that the deliberate sense of the community should govern the conduct of those to whom they entrust the management of their affairs."[45] Why had the Convention been immune from "the pestilential influence of party animosities"? He answered, "[All] the deputations composing the Convention were either satisfactorily accommodated by the final act; or were induced to accede to it, by a deep conviction of the necessity of sacrificing private opinions and partial interests to the public good, and by a despair of seeing this necessity diminished by delays or by new experiments."[46]

Even though "Publius" accepted the inevitability of parties, he nonetheless denounced them and spared little praise. It was one thing to realize how differences of opinions could lead citizens into opposing camps, but quite another to celebrate the polarization of society as supportive of the public good. But why had the Convention been free of partisanship? "An extinction of parties necessarily implies either a universal alarm for the public safety, or an absolute extinction of liberty," "Publius" observed. The latter condition had not yet occurred, even if the Union's current misfortunes invited it. But the former, the framers' "alarm for the public safety," brought on by a crisis of the Union, had muted partisanship in Philadelphia and paved the way for mutual concessions. This was the fundamental prerequisite for grand compromise, for tempering the passions and acting in concord, as Albert Furtwangler has put it.[47] In sum, compromise had been a reprieve from party conflict, an alternative to pitting large, closely matched minorities against each other.

By stressing concord instead of a false unanimity, Federalists like "Publius" were trying to explain the conditions that had led to pragmatic accommodation or to "instrumental reasoning" on difficult issues. Having conceded that the Convention had experienced deep divisions, the Federalists would go no further; Luther Martin's disclosures notwithstanding, they insisted that the Convention's compromises had occurred in a nonpartisan atmosphere. In the Virginia Convention, Madison discussed this disposition to conciliate, pointing out that compromise had occurred because the delegates had been "calm and dispassionate," free of party restraints, and flexible in their opinions—and even then, he admitted, it had been "extremely difficult, to agree to any general system."[48]

In the crucial struggle over ratification in New York, leading Federalists often resorted to such arguments. John Jay devoted almost all of his *Address to the People of New-York* to a discussion of the unprecedented conditions leading to compromise in the Convention. Because the delegates had been "perfectly unprejudiced in favour of any particular plan," he rather disingenuously claimed, a "spirit of candour, of calm enquiry, of mutual accommodation, and mutual respect . . . [had] regulated their debates and proceedings." Concord permitted reasoned argument and amiable compromise—the hallmarks of civic propriety.[49]

What implications did the Convention's exceptional moderation have for the new government? It prescribed the brand of leadership necessary to avoid the Confederation's ills. Federalists proclaimed the virtues of moderation, restraint, and conciliation as the essence of wise, paternal leadership. Alexander Hamilton reassured the New York Convention that despite the difference of interests that might "create some difficulty, and apparent partiality, in the first operations of government, yet the same spirit of accommodation, which produced the [Constitution], would be exercised in lessening the weight of unequal burdens." Prudence and paternalism, the touchstones of Federalist political ethics in America's early national period, went hand in hand with this notion of compromise. During the ratification struggle, these qualities replaced the nationalists' earlier demands for a "power of coercing" fractious states and were the basis of Federalists' predictions that moderation would govern future federal-state relations.[50]

How did the Constitution reinforce this behavior? The framers fashioned a government whose many divisions were supposed to undermine the effects of partisanship. The unwieldy electoral college, for instance, was designed to weaken party coalitions by extending the balloting across the states. And other provisions aimed at fostering the kind of statesmanship that resisted party intrigue. Checks and balances would cultivate the deliberate sense of the political community over time while restraining popular passions and the temptations to abuse power. The system of representation would filter the nation's leadership without entirely divorcing it from the general conditions of the electorate. The staggered election of senators, a Federalist noted, would "sufficiently" prevent "all combination. . . . What scheme of iniquity could ripen in two years?" "A Mechanic" flatly predicted, "The Federal Constitution will no doubt put an end to all parties, if it is adopted, as it clearly will."[51]

Nor would simple majorities be a sufficient safeguard of the public interest. The Constitution would cultivate concurrent majorities through stages of debate and deliberation, to minimize the frustrations of disgruntled minorities by conciliating their interests and opinions. The Federalists assumed that the formation of a concurrent majority would reduce the risk of partisanship, which seemed to be most acute in unicameral governments or large assemblies and in any case when the legislature was either closely divided or completely deadlocked on an issue.[52]

The separation of powers was another inducement to deliberation and compromise in the Constitution; the legislature in particular, "where promptitude of decision is oftener an evil that a benefit," concentrated the necessary incentives. "Good constitutions are formed upon a comparison of the liberty of the individual with the strength of government: if the tone of either be too high, the other will be weakened too much," Hamilton explained. "It is the happiest possible mode of conciliating these objects, to institute one branch peculiarly endowed with sensibility, another with knowledge and firmness." As one Federalist argued, although majority rule is the best possible alternative to an impossible unanimity, "men are ever running into extremes." Unlike unicameral systems (such as Pennsylvania's), where "party spirit" creates violence, disorder, and extremism, bicameralism preserves deliberation, prevents rashness, and balances wisdom and age with innovation and youth.[53]

The requirement of a two-thirds majority for critical decisions helped to bring out the deliberate sense of a concurring majority. James Wilson explained that the necessity of a large majority to override the veto would caution the legislature against passing bills by simple majorities. Hamilton noted that the requirement of two-thirds of the senators present to concur in treaties was designed to reconcile the energy of the executive with the goal of "a reasonable regard to the major sense of the community." A bare majority would "embarrass the operations of the government" and "subject the sense of the majority to that of the minority."[54]

Having accorded compromise an integral place in the character of the new government's leadership and structure, the Federalists were able both to answer Antifederalists' criticisms of the specific bargains made by the Convention and to quiet the call for a second convention. At first glance, it appears that the Federalists tailored their defense of the slavery compromises to suit the needs of local audiences. James Wilson and Tench Coxe claimed that the slave trade clause augured the eventual abolition of slavery, whereas C. C. Pinckney and James Madison claimed that slavery would be perfectly secure under the Constitution. Historians have cited these conflicting interpretations as evidence of what Donald Robinson calls "two completely different worlds of discourse on this issue. . . . It was not long before men were interpreting these ambiguities according to their own interests or commitments."[55]

There was a third world of discourse, which justified these slavery compromises as necessarily ambiguous. The point was not that the Constitution should or should not endanger the peculiar institution, but that the creation of a process to manage this particular conflict without immediately resolving it was a step forward, no matter what the future would decide.[56] Madison's ambivalence typified this attitude. Only in the Virginia Convention did he argue that the Constitution did not sanction abolition. But his discussion of the issue in Federalist nos. 42 and 54 was a masterpiece of evasion, which, when coupled with his remarkable essay on ambiguity in no. 37, makes the apparent thrust of the Federalist position more intelligible: like the problem of federal-state relations, this was one of many issues that would require future adjustments. For the present, denunciations of the entire document by an opposition too divided to propose a coherent alternative only threatened to destroy any possibility of union.[57]

Madison defied his opponents to define exactly the boundaries of government. If "the faculties of the mind itself have never yet been distinguished and defined with satisfactory precision" and "remain a pregnant source of ingenious disquisition and controversy," it would be impossible to delineate "the institutions of man, in which the obscurity arises as well from the object itself, as from the organ by which it is contemplated." Even more difficult would be the problem of shaping legislation to avoid ambiguities "until their meaning be liquidated and ascertained by a series of particular discussions and adjudications." But our own ideas are subject to such wide variability that the problem worsens, especially since "no language is so copious as to supply words and phrases for every complex idea, or so correct as not to include many equivocally denoting different ideas." Given these "sources of vague and incorrect definitions," it was hardly surprising that the Convention compromised on so many important issues.[58]

After describing the great compromise as a realistic accommodation to circumstance, Madison, the reflective philosopher and historian, cut loose from republican ideology. Considering the Convention's sharp conflicts over a multitude of issues, was it not "wonderful," he asked, that it had been "forced into some deviations from that artificial structure and regular symmetry, which an abstract view of the subject might lead an ingenious theorist of the subject to bestow on a Constitution planned in his closet or his imagination?" As Madison put it in a later paper, "It is superfluous to try by the standard of theory, a part of the Constitution which is allowed on all hands to be the result not of theory, but 'of a spirit of amity, and that mutual deference and concession which the peculiarity of our situation rendered indispensable.'" Madison's divided mind on the nature of human institutions was leading him to a defense of ambiguity based on his hope that the persistent clash of extremes would generate a stable constitutional mean. By such arguments, Madison turned the science of government into the art of compromise.[59]

Other Federalists pursued the tactic of burying the slavery compromises within the larger spirit of the Convention. Slavery was one of a number of issues dividing the Convention, which, Hamilton explained, experienced "very different combinations of the parts upon different points." Thus, in the commercial clauses, the sectional issues, and the conflict between large and small states, "a delicate and difficult contest arose." The three-fifths rule was part of a larger accommodation, and "without this indulgence no union could possibly have been formed." The rule resulted from mature deliberation and not caprice or desperation, a Connecticut writer added. And the slave trade clause was "neither dark nor mysterious"; its "meaning and intention" was "obvious." Although slavery was an evil and was unpopular, he claimed, it was also firmly established, so that it could not "be got rid of at one stroke." The writer noted: "In this circumstance, the Constitution does everything which a Constitution could reasonably do. It provides for the interest of the Southern States, and, at the same time, manifests to the world that slavery is inconsistent with the views and sentiments of this country, which error will be reformed as soon as it can be done consistent with the interest of the people."[60]

These opinions apparently had a popular base because the ratification struggle featured a lot of talk and no action on the Constitution's slavery compromises. Of all the recommended amendments accompanying the states' ratifications of the Constitution, only one of them, Virginia's call for a two-thirds vote on commercial laws, threatened to disturb the compromises on slavery. The Massachusetts Convention heard a number of denunciations of the slave trade, but in the end it was silent on the subject. So was Pennsylvania's Convention, despite a vigorous debate in the press among Quakers angry at the Constitution's tolerance of slavery.[61]

The weight of the entire Federalist response to initial criticisms by the

Antifederalists also bore heavily against the call for a second convention. The Antifederalists had argued that if, as their opponents claimed, wisdom, moderation, and deliberation had marked the Philadelphia Convention's proceedings, then why not hold another convention composed of delegates even more informed and therefore wiser than the first? The Federalists replied that a second convention comprising members attached to local interests would not accomplish what the Constitutional Convention had done: it would not compromise.

Federalists declared that the Antifederalists were displaying the pointless partisanship that had paralyzed the Confederation Congress. How could there be a true meeting of minds under such circumstances? As Madison warned Governor Randolph, a second convention would sap the public's confidence in the delegates "and give a loose to human opinions; which must be as various and irreconcilable concerning theories of Government, as doctrines of Religion." Washington agreed, citing the tremendous divisions within the Antifederalist ranks.[62]

Another convention, John Dickinson argued in his "Fabius" essays, could not duplicate the Constitutional Convention's "temper of conciliation" and "satisfactory harmony of decisions" because "minds" were "agitated with disgusts and disappointments" during the ratification debate. Responding to Antifederalist attacks, John Jay declared that even if new delegates had wisdom and information equal to that of the old, it did not follow "that they would be equally *disposed to agree*." The raging partisanship of the current struggle would invade the new convention, and a new frame would therefore be "forcibly carried by a slender majority," leaving a large and disgruntled minority in its wake. Although severe, close conflicts sometimes produce lasting agreements, Jay continued, to expect "that discord and animosity should produce the fruits of confidence and agreement, is to expect 'grapes from thorns, and figs from thistles.' "[63]

The Convention's exceptionalism also precluded preratification amendments. Considering the difficulty of reaching the existing compromises, new changes would multiply the problem, Hamilton explained in Federalist no. 85. A Philadelphia Federalist predicted that at a new convention, the small and large states would immediately rip the great compromise apart; "upon this rock the Constitution would be wrecked, and all its parts would be scattered in a hurricane of anarchy." He continued in another article: "The most artful logic in the world cannot show another line of compromise than the one adopted, and it would be nothing short of madness to hazard the salvation of our country on a bare chance of its repetition. Where is the man, who after having drawn a prize, would put his ticket into the wheel again?—If such a man could be found, would you suppose him to be in his senses?"[64]

But the Federalists' admission that the Constitution was imperfect cast some doubt on the value of this "prize" and left them little alternative to supporting eventual changes in the instrument. In fact, they argued persistently that the Convention's work was not the last word on the Constitution but was a prelude to the expected adaptations that must arise when "the spirit of America" required them. "Conciliator" urged that the First Congress be considered as another "Federal Convention" that would inscribe the states' consensus on amendments into the Constitution. "Thus, you see, that the government is but a trial, and all governments are progressive things, which can never be made compleat till judged of by experiment; in the mean time remedies are constantly in our power, unless we voluntarily destroy that power, by becoming too corrupt to deserve to be free." Dickinson approved of advisory amendments before ratification to provide "the undoubted sense of every state, collected in the coollest manner, not the sense of individuals." The new Congress could then compose any differences and "adopt such alterations as . . . recommended by general unanimity."[65]

This position implied the unthinkable to many Americans: the Constitution would never rest on a solid foundation if subjected to constant amendments. The Federalists' arguments against a national bill of rights and in favor of making future alterations sacrificed too much power to domestic diplomats trained in the art of compromise. The constitutional settlement would *never* be final but instead an endless series of usurpations by corrupt politicians. "Is it not an acknowledged principle, in all legislative bodies, that whatever law is enacted at one session, may be repealed at any succeeding one?" an "Honest American" asked "Conciliator." His opponent replied by repeating the Constitution's amending clause and pointed out that a concurrent majority would be an adequate check on the whims of politicians. But other Federalists, especially Noah Webster, claimed that there was no such thing as an unalterable form of government; the Constitution's compromises would forever be open to negotiation. Federalists just could not escape the unsettling conclusion that popular sovereignty, even when filtered through a complex system of representation and internal checks, enthroned the collective prejudices and passions, as well as the reason, of the multitude.[66]

Compromise, ambiguity, and amendability: the implication was clear. No structure of government would be a perfect guarantee of ordered liberty; only the character of the citizens (from whom republican leaders must be drawn) could preserve the rights of the people. Compromise, which had made the Constitution, was the only way to hold on to it.

THE GREAT POLITICAL conversation about the nature of America's constitutional order had ranged over an impressive array of deep and possibly unsolvable political and social problems in 1787–88. The framers of the Constitution had quickly realized in Philadelphia that adapting republican ideas to American reality required much compromise and even more frustration and disappointment. Once they had emerged from the Convention, the delegates and their Federalist allies had to explain their conduct in terms that the electorate could readily understand. When it came to answering the simple question "How is this new order going to work?" the Federalists fell back on the behavior of the framers as the model for future citizens and leaders in the new Republic.

The Federalists' portrayal of the Convention's congeniality defied both common sense and Antifederalist eyewitnesses' multiplying testimony that unanimity had not reigned supreme in Philadelphia. But the Federalists did continue to claim that this model assembly had been devoid of the cancers that had plagued recent republican experiments—its compromises had been nonpartisan if not unanimous.

The fundamental role of compromise in the creation and preservation of the Constitution and the Union has dominated histories of the Convention. As James Hutson has recently pointed out, the "triple compromise" paradigm (the three-fifths compromise, the great compromise, and the slave trade–commerce compromise) was a particularly useful organizing theme for early whig and nationalist historians such as Richard Hildreth and Timothy Pitkin. And few modern historians have passed up the opportunity to examine these and other compromises, treating them either as case studies in realistic, democratic statecraft that exemplified the nonideological, pluralist politics of a republic or as evasions either of moral responsibility or of the unbridgeable ideological conflicts seething beneath the surface of early republican politics. And each agreement's quality as a compromise has been severely questioned by one or more historians, who claim that on closer inspection, the agreement was no compromise at all.[67]

Yet the contemporary evidence that Federalists defended the Constitution as a compromise cannot be gainsaid by later analysts looking for a deeper message in the ratification debates. The new system incorporated compromise as a conservative instrument of ordered change by requiring multiple steps and concurrent majorities in order to alter the balance of power. As Willmoore Kendall has argued, the system put the advocates of drastic change on notice that "even if they have a majority out in the country . . . [they] must cool their heels in the ante-room of our politics until they can achieve a consensus among the three branches and so, since the branches represent different constituencies out among the people, a popular consensus as well." Forrest McDonald wrote, "The untidiness of the system necessitated that the operation of American government would forever recapitulate its process of birth." Compromises, "some arrived at openly and some under the table," created American government, but "it could only be made to work through similar methods." Such a system greatly enhanced the power of a minority to obtain significant concessions, and considering the framers' intense reaction to the turmoil in the states during the Confederation period, this result was clearly intended to bind the largest number of people as close to the new system as possible.[68]

The Federalists' arguments for the exceptionalism of the Convention's and the Constitution's compromises provided a ready stable of legends, a few truths, and some comforting evasions for later sectional compromisers seeking to prevent the rising tide of political conflict from overwhelming the process that had managed it in 1787. The many themes of this compromise argument—its bias against abstract theory, its premise that parties intensify rather than mute conflict, its recognition that conflict requires flexibility and mutual respect if it is to be a source of strength to the Union, its open reliance on the politics of moderate and prudent statecraft, and its combination of liberal sentiment with a conservative regard for continuity—merged in the debates over the Constitution's compromises.

There were practical problems with the compromise tradition as it was established by 1788. The Federalist argument that compromise requires the muting of partisanship implied that parties undermine the moderate temperament necessary for statesmen to act for the public good. And because compromise created the Union, partisanship could destroy it. The Federalists were trying to exile certain Union-threatening issues from the arena of party combat. Such assumptions would die hard as the new nation began to fill the constitutional blanks in the first Congresses of the early national period. Political parties were just around the corner, and although Federalists became resigned to their existence, the ambivalence about their effects would linger until the Civil War and would influence future compromisers' opinions about how to use these informal national institutions in the sectional struggle.

As the first Congresses constructed a new government and began to implement the Constitution, the weaknesses of this outlook began to emerge. The formation of political parties and the possibility of sectional allegiances among them suggested a dangerous division in the polity that a fragile union might not be able to overcome. Washington's Farewell Address, with its explicit warning against geographical parties, reflected the basic Federalist beliefs that parties and local allegiances were a dangerous combination and that only disinterested statesmanship and willing sacrifice by the people could possibly avert such a domestic calamity as sectional parties. The Farewell Address joined Washington's conciliatory letter to the president of Congress as a kind of technical manual of Federalist political science, prescribing a politics of conciliation and a policy of avoiding sectional parties in the interest of preserving a constitutional union. Understandably, these founding documents became important tools in the training of citizens during the early national period.

The Federalists' defense of compromise had some troubling implications. The Antifederalists, however ineffective some of their arguments were, had at least tried to force their opponents to face the essential question of the purpose of the Union—and therefore of the compromises. To many Federalists, the formation of the Union was an act of self-definition that would require "time and experience" to mature. But within the broad objective of promoting ordered liberty, a purpose on which all could agree, lay intractable questions about whose liberty measured against how much order. Slavery, an issue that the debaters were quick to treat as roughly similar to the many other conflicts natural to the American scene, would force future advocates of compromise to confront such formidable questions.

The Federalists' alarm for the safety of the Union led them to claim that compromise was the nation's best refuge. While they reassured Americans that the Constitution's compromises could be amended in the future, they hoped to minimize the danger of instability and extremism by employing compromise as a standard of behavior. This tactic bound together three types of association that were within the larger conception of *compromise* and that were not really interchangeable: compromises of the Constitution, compromises for the Union, and compromises of the social compact.

The compromises of the Constitution were the explicit bargains negotiated by the framers and incorporated into the pact. The great compromise (including the three-fifths clause), the slave trade–commerce power compromise, and the electoral college compromise are the most famous of these. Like any other clause in the document, such compromises were open to interpretation, but their presence in the Constitution and the consensus that they had indeed been the product of compromise provided a starting point for discussion, just as the amending clause offered a final resort to end any controversy.

The compromises for the Union were implicit, mutual restraints by the members of the Union (states, citizens, regions, interests), restraints that permitted different social and economic systems to tolerate each other and live peaceably. These compromises were unwritten; nowhere could anyone find a real pact between these diffuse groupings, and certainly the attempts of states, citizens, regions, and interests to specify these unwritten understandings would provoke serious dispute. The compromises for the Union were deducible from tradition and therefore were affective in the attachments they fostered, symbolic in their meaning, and cumulative in their force. They implied a stronger and broader mutual restraint than the legal force of a limited Constitution because sacrifice for the sake of the Union was what had created the Constitution.

Perhaps the most significant illustration of this ethic of restraint was the clause (in Article V) restricting amendments of the slavery and representation compromises, a direct contradiction to the principle of popular sovereignty and an unexplained assumption that the parties to the Constitution had agreed to place these questions outside the immediate province of concurring majorities over time. Simply put, men who could not establish a consensus on the future of slavery ended up establishing a consensus on mutual restraint, signified by the temporary exile of this dangerous issue beyond the jurisdiction of constitutional amendment for at least twenty years.

Furthermore, these compromises for the Union were not sets of interlocking agreements that exchanged concessions; any unilateral concession could be compared to any other unilateral concession made at another time and place. The fugitive slave clause, which the Convention passed unanimously and with little debate, was not one of the compromises of the Constitution, but it could be seen as a compromise for the Union: a sign of northern conciliation that the South would have to match. The implications were obvious: compromises for the Union were vague and open to the most violent controversy, forming a fragile and unreliable foundation for the national experiment in ordered liberty.[69]

A third category comprised the compromises of the social compact, or the implied exchange of a portion of one's liberty for a modicum of social order as the price of entry into political society. "I see not how my utmost wishes are to be gratified until I can withdraw from society," a Virginia Federalist remarked. "So long as I find it necessary to combine my strength and interests with others, I must be satisfied to make some sacrifices to the general accommodation." This was not idle or abstract speculation. Many Americans believed that the separation from England had left them in a state of political and social limbo that might at any moment explode into anarchic violence. Only the sacrifice of some individual liberty would preserve the rest, and the ratification of the Constitution represented just such a deliberate decision.[70]

These types of association mirrored the variations on social contract theory that had been inherited from the Middle Ages and refined in the Enlightenment. Contract theory, as J. W. Gough has pointed out, emerged from a basic distinction between nature and convention, natural law and civil polity, from a distinction between a historical contract among the people to form a specific type of government and a logical, yet unhistorical social contract for mutual protection and governance. But Americans found ways to merge these distinctions, speaking in the same breath of the Constitution as a compact or contract that imposed on liberty what Justice Joseph Story called "wholesome restraints"; a violation of the Constitution could therefore let loose a social holocaust. Compromise, compact, and contract were closely interwoven. The importance of a constitution as the embodiment of fundamental law firmly tied these conceptions together and offered future generations a set of basic assumptions about the Constitution and civic duty that few reflective men could ignore.[71]

The problem was that anyone seeking to alter the compromises of the Constitution appeared to be disturbing the compromises for the Union, which, if accomplished, would tear the social fabric asunder. Technically this was not inevitable; the Federalists' argument that the Constitution was imperfect and amendable left the door open to renegotiate those compromises without automatically endangering the larger compact of which they were a part. But the self-interested bargains in the Constitution were protected by the larger, unchanging imperative of maintaining the Union. This raised the possibility that *any* compromise could achieve the status of a compromise for the Union if it reaffirmed the communal restraints that had marked the nation's birth. Compromise could become an end in itself, an ethical imperative, if the Union and, by extension, the social compact were to survive.

2 The Virtues of Moderation
Compromise and Civics

Gentlemen must give way a little. It does not become a republican to say, "I will not submit to this," or "I will have that,"—his great duty is to regard the general good and suffer the majority to govern.
—Hezekiah Niles

The adoption of the Constitution and the formation of a new national government established the context in which Americans considered the problem of political compromise. This was to be a constitutional union, partly federal, partly national; the harmonizing of its parts was to be left to "time and experience" and wise statesmanship. Compromise, no longer a justification for launching a risky experiment in republican government, became a conservative tool for preserving the new system. A structure of divided powers and federal responsibilities was a standing invitation to compromise, bargaining, and the accommodation of conflicting interests. But the Constitution not only rested on the fundamental institutional heritage of British and colonial polities; it also reified a political culture. The Federalists not only explained and predicted the operation of the new system but also appealed to what they thought were common assumptions and expectations about the proper *temperament* of citizens in a republic. Their call for the cultivation of a common interest based on "mutual affections" delineated the path of future civic educators: by studying, understanding, and implementing the Constitution, good citizens, acting in a conciliatory spirit, would preserve, improve, and strengthen it.

Of course, a long period of conflict and adjustment lay ahead as politicians scrambled to improvise settlements to outstanding issues and as the people became more accustomed to the new order of things. To begin with, serious conflicts about federal and state relations, conflicts that had surfaced during the ratification struggle, continued to divide the nation's leadership up to the Civil War. Joseph Story, the great jurist, warned in 1840:

> Some peculiar habits, interests, opinions, attachments, and even prejudices, which may still be traced in the actual jurisprudence of each State, and are openly or silently referred to in some of the provisions of the Constitution [sparked controversies in 1787 that] have since immeasurably increased in concentration and vigor. The very inequities of a government, confessedly founded in a compromise, were then felt with a strong sensibility; and every new source of discontent, whether accidental or permanent, has since added increased activity to the painful sense of these inequities.

Should the strife between sections continue, he warned, disunion would occur and destroy the Constitution. "Our very animosities will, like those of other kindred nations, become more deadly, because our lineage, our laws, and our language are the same."[1]

Moreover, the emergence of a party system that, according to most historians and civics writers before the Civil War, divided the community between advocates of states' rights and supporters of a stronger federal government ensured that the final settlement of most constitutional questions would be put off long into the future. James Madison remarked in 1824 that any constitution, especially a system based on federal principles, "whether written or prescriptive, . . . must be an unfailing source of party distinctions." He added:

> There is nevertheless sufficient scope for combating the spirit of party, as far as it may not be necessary to fan the flame of liberty, in efforts to divert it from the more noxious channels; to moderate its violence, especially in the ascendant party; to elucidate the policy which harmonizes jealous interests; and particularly to give to the Constitution that just construction, which, *with the aid of time and habit*, may put an end to the more dangerous schisms otherwise growing out of it.[2]

Madison's argument was consistent with his frequent declaration that only time and experience—"the early, deliberate & continued practice under the Constitution, as preferable to constructions adopted on the spur of occasions, and subject to the vicissitudes of party or personal ascendancies"—coupled with close scrutiny of "the comments prevailing at the time it was adopted" and an awareness of "the evils & defects for curing which the Constitution was called for & introduced," could settle conflicts of interpretation. The system, it bears repeating, was designed to cultivate the deliberate sense of the political community over time, but how much time would be required? And how would the new order survive major crises in the meantime? As the historian John McCulloch observed in 1813, "Time is the parent of wisdom, but its instructions are communicated slowly."[3]

The founding generation's experience with political parties did not affirm that they were compatible with the stability of the constitutional order. The fact that parties had organized around differing interpretations of the instrument merely encouraged Federalists and Republicans to regard each other as subversive. If parties were supposed to be dedicated to "measures, not men," and were to reflect eternal, abstract principles of government, how would it be possible for them to compete peacefully, rotate in power, and at the same time foster a continuous constitutional tradition? Was it possible for Republicans to compromise with a party they universally believed had abandoned reason for force and appealed to the worst side of human nature? If it was impossible to compromise conflicting principles, and if parties sought to implement their respective principles through a party program, then party conflict had yet to make its accommodations with the constitutional tradition of disinterested compromise.[4]

Considering this tradition of constitutional and party conflict, doubts lingered about the security of the Republic's foundations. "It is yet a problem, whether united representative republics will continue to diffuse their blessings through a prosperous and grateful community," William Sullivan wrote in the introduction to the 1831 edition of his civics text, *The Political Class Book*. Eminent statesmen were still arguing about whether this was a nation of states or of citizens or of both. (Sullivan discussed all three and opted for the last as the current favorite.) Who would respect a fundamental law that was still a matter of controversy? Who would obey it? What if a state should defy the national government, Sullivan asked. "Such cases are not to be supposed, and consequently are not provided for," he answered uneasily. "If they happen, consequences must take care of themselves." Civics writers were by no means unanimous on the nature of the constitutional union.[5]

For many citizens, compromise in the tradition of the founders was the only way to deal with such unsettling questions because compromise signified restraint, sacrifice, and moderation. It substituted civility for substance in an age still struggling to determine the meaning of its growing political institutions. Thus, the condition of the citizen's temperament lay at the heart of the antebellum civic ideal. As Sullivan put it, echoing a legion of educators, ethicists, editors, historians, and politicians, "the solution" to the republic's dilemma may have depended, "in no small degree, on the veneration which the young carry into manhood, for the institutions of their fathers; and not less on their ability to distinguish between the unprincipled contrivances of politicians, and the manly actions of statesmen."[6] This was no prescription for unquestioning obedience to the nation's leaders but instead was a call for faith in civil and social institutions.

Much of the extensive political commentary about compromise and the condition of the Constitution during the severe national crises that punctuated American history before the Civil War viewed compromise not only within the historical context of the founding but also in terms of the duties of citizens in a republic. Henry Clay declared, "Compromise is peculiarly appropriate among the members of a Republic, as of one family." He cradled the process in a powerful, comforting metaphor that blended sacrifice and platonic intimacy—important, cherished sentiments that many Americans regarded as the cornerstones of civic life. In this context, compromise was not an abstract doctrine of bartering the claims of rival interests; it was a form of association requiring mutual deference and sacrifice.[7]

Great compromises exhibited personal and social traits—mutuality, self-restraint, and an intense reverence for the Union, the highest symbol of order—that were greatly valued by Americans. As Michael Lienesch has observed, Americans recognized soon after ratification that "effective government relies not on written rules only, but on an unwritten ethic, the shared expectations that make government necessary, the conventions that make it acceptable, the agreements that make it work." To Clay, it was a matter of plain common sense: "All legislation, all government, all society, is formed on the principle of mutual concession, politeness, comity, courtesy, upon these everything is based. I bow to you today because you bow to me. You are respectful to me because I am respectful to you."[8]

This relationship among compromise, temperament, and duty can be traced in a number of contemporary sources, including election-day sermons, political oratory, and newspaper commentary. But nowhere did history and ethics merge into civic ideals with such clarity and force as in the civics literature—schoolbook and popular histories, civics manuals, and works on political ethics—that directly confronted the difficult task of explaining America to future citizens. The absence of consensus on whether this was a nation of states or of citizens heightened the value both of civic education in the deliberative process (public debate, the daily routines of governance, and the proper behavior of voters, jurors, magistrates, and statesmen) and of the temperaments most conducive to consensus (reasonableness, moderation, and a reflective attachment to existing social and political institutions). Americans were obsessively conscious of both the unprecedentedness of their experiment in liberty and the uncertainty of its future. The greatest danger to a republic still forming its habits and customs was not bad ideas but bad character. "It may be an easy thing to make a republic, but it is a very laborious thing to make republicans," the common-school reformer Horace Mann remarked. In America, good citizens had to be made; they were not born to the role.[9]

Writers on political ethics, particularly, confronted the challenge of describing the relationship between compromise and civic ideals. The most comprehensive works on this subject were those of Francis Lieber, the foremost exponent of what the historian Wilson Smith calls the "Whiggish ethics" of the emergent middle class. By applying Common Sense moral philosophy and the scientific method to historical materials, Lieber tried to fashion a science of civics applicable in a limited range of institutional settings and based on his conclusion that the good society cultivates "mutual moderation," the ethical foundation of compromise.[10]

Although Lieber hoped that his work would be of practical use in training citizens, his immediate scholarly and occupational objectives limited its influence on a mass audience. His early work used few American sources, suffered from a stilted and pedantic style, and gingerly sidestepped sensitive issues like slavery. But the schoolbook histories and civics manuals did directly address compromise in its American setting; they could ignore neither the equivocal character of the Constitution nor the persistence of sectional and party conflict since its framing. They fused the moral and civic categories outlined by Lieber with the still powerful political science of the Federalists to explain the citizen's duties under the Constitution.

Taken together, the historical and ethical foundations of compromise fostered a doctrine of civic responsibility that aimed at the conservation of existing social and political institutions as the anchors of a new and untried constitutional order. Civics writers and ethicists used history and ethics to argue that mutual concessions, which preserve the process of deliberation and cultivate the mutual attachments that maintained its legitimacy, were the proper response to severe conflicts of principles and interests.

"MODERATION IN ALL THINGS is the perfection of human wisdom," the Baltimore editor Hezekiah Niles intoned in the summer of 1828 as southern protests over high tariff rates became more radical and threatening in tone. The indefatigable Niles had been reprinting nullification editorials in his influential *Weekly Register* and responding to them with minute sermons and homespun homilies like "truth is a victor without violence," and "error of opinion may be safely tolerated where reason is left free to combat it." But South Carolinians were not calmed by quotations from Jefferson and lessons from Aesop. In their minds, moderation signified weakness and meant capitulation. "This word *moderation* savors of slavery—not freedom," "Cassius" told readers of the *Charleston City Gazette* in the early summer of 1830. "In the present state of things, it is another name for toryism and timidity." These were fighting words to Niles, a protectionist and inveterate Anglophobe. "The manner and language of these men, is horrible," he sputtered. "The bottom of the whole business is a pitiful jealousy or meanness of mind, that hates an increase of population and wealth, except to its own limited sphere of action, and for itself."[11]

Niles's reaction to the South Carolina hotspurs (similar to his response to the nation's polarization over Missouri in 1820) exemplified the importance in antebellum America of the manner, style, and temper of political discourse. Mutual concessions required mutual respect: compromise rested on civility. As Niles put it during the Missouri controversy, "We may differ on principles and wrangle about practices, but there are certain great points of moderation and forbearance—mutual respect and good will, on which *all* should agree." Recoiling from the realization that the Missouri question seemed "already to have made a *moral* separation" among people who "had begun to love each other," Niles expostulated: "Frenzy to the brain that shall plot to disturb the happy progress of these things! But mutual forbearance and moderation is indispensably necessary to their preservation, and the indiscrete [*sic*] may destroy all which the coolest heads and best hearts have built up, as the asylum of the afflicted, the hope of humanity, and home of liberty."[12]

The dominant moral philosophy of the early Republic justified and strengthened the importance of moderation as a virtue that regulated the operation of the individual's "moral sense." Americans liked to think that republics ran on reason and not instinct, but their political ethics valued demeanor more than the substance of ideas in the political marketplace. The ethical milieu of the early nineteenth century was shaped by Scottish Common Sense moral philosophy, the seedbed of the genteel tradition that, as Henry May has observed, nicely suited the country's complacency about political reform and its Enlightenment justifications. Although other ethical systems, religious ideas, and cultural styles—from transcendentalism to backcountry communitarianism—challenged the emotional and logical underpinnings of Common Sense philosophy, this didactic ethic defined the mainstream of American ethics right up to the 1850s.[13]

Common Sense moral philosophy argued that evidence of objective moral laws can be found and sifted by consulting our intuitions and applying reason to experience. Man has a moral sense, a rational faculty for knowing good from evil. According to Thomas Reid, a leading exponent of this school, experience, consensus, and necessity offer overwhelming evidence that our intuitions about morality permit us to make basic assumptions about our conduct in life without having to engage in a Socratic exploration of the motives for every important decision. Theorists might fancy that they have refuted "principles which irresistibly govern the belief and the conduct of all mankind in the common concerns of life," Reid pointed out, but in the end, they must yield to these principles anyway.[14]

The moral sense, like other rational faculties, could be trained and improved. Because the first duty of man was to uncover the operation of moral laws through reason—to seek rectitude—education and experience together could sharpen the moral sense. The clearer our sense of right and wrong, the more accurate will be our application of moral laws in practical affairs. The Eighth Commandment never stopped a burglar from entering a house, Francis Lieber observed, but it enables us to catch and punish him and to protect private property in general by instilling at home and at school "the tradition of that rule."[15] Common Sense thought attempted to combine and refine the intellectual tools men employed to blaze a pathway through life. It stood between the abstract rationalism of the Enlightenment and the reflexive faith of revealed religion by entertaining a strong skepticism of both.

Common Sense philosophy found a fertile environment in America after its arrival in the mid-eighteenth century. As May notes, "It was enlightened, moderate, practical, and easy to teach." In a nation preoccupied with creating institutions and instilling the habits that perpetuate them, Common Sense thought was a convenient reference point for ethical instruction at the faculties of divinity and moral philosophy at Harvard, Princeton, William and Mary, and the University of Virginia, where books by the Scottish authors Dugald Stewart, Thomas Reid, and James Beattie had become standard texts by the 1820s. Eventually these were replaced by homegrown varieties, such as Francis Wayland's best-selling *Elements of Moral Science*, first published in 1835. This flexible, practical ethical system "could be used to sustain or validate any set of ideas," May notes, "but was in fact associated with the Moderate Enlightenment and moderate Calvinism," the twin pillars of the Constitution and the Protestant mainstream.[16]

By the 1830s, Common Sense philosophy had become the basis for the "Whiggish ethics" of the American middle class. Unlike Enlightenment ethics, Whiggish ethics did not define people's rights and protect them against encroachments of power. Instead, it sought to confine liberty within a ring of obligations that would bind people to each other and to the existing social order. More a style of thought than a doctrine, Whiggish ethics emphasized the idea of a "respectful citizenry" trained, through experience in a wide variety of civic, religious, and business associations, to act with mutual deference and a sense of duty toward self and society.

Outward comportment, shaped in the forge of experience, reflected a trained inner psyche and was the measure of one's fidelity to the social and political order; it revealed the individual's intentions instead of disguising them. Whiggish ethics used faculty psychology to assess the relative distribution of one's inner passions and rational faculties. A number of behaviors could be traced, identified, and encouraged or suppressed according to the degree they exhibited the mental tension between passion and reason.[17]

Temperament (the current condition of one's rational and emotional faculties), and not ideology or social class, was the badge of moral worth, the window into one's intentions. And the most valued temperament in the antebellum world was the classical virtue of moderation, a state of mental equipoise in which the higher rational faculties, unobstructed by baser passions, regulate the practical limits of one's abilities and influence. The essence of moderation was realism, an awareness of the plurality and mutual limitations of moral ends. Political ethics was not for dreamers and utopians; it was supposed to promote, and indeed it idolized, practicality. In sum, the political ethics of antebellum America prized reasonableness as much as reason.[18]

The most comprehensive theorist of the "respectful citizenry"—and therefore of the relationship among temperament, politics, and compromise—was Francis Lieber (1800–1872). Lieber centered much of his political theory on the importance of mutuality, the communal attachments it fostered, and the myriad of associations and institutions thus generated. Lieber, America's first formal political scientist, blended Scottish Common Sense moral philosophy with comparative, empirical observations of political behavior in Europe and America to create a unified science of civics.

Lieber's works on ethics, history, and political science reveal not only the contours of antebellum civic ideals but also the way compromise undergirded civic institutions and attitudes. The distinctiveness of Lieber's work on this subject lay first in its comparative scientific methodology and second in its utter conventionality, which to a great degree made it a barometer of current thinking on political ethics. Unlike such teachers of moral philosophy as William Paley and John Witherspoon, Lieber was not affiliated with a specific religious denomination or sect and had few theological axes to grind. Instead of trying to demonstrate the practical evidence of God's laws on earth, Lieber assumed the existence of objective ethical standards and focused on developing practical guidelines for civic conduct. He employed the scientific method and a wide reading of European sources to construct a theory of institutional development as the setting for civic action. He was a comprehensive if not innovative thinker.[19]

Lieber's comparative approach stemmed from his training and experience. He earned a doctorate in mathematics at Jena in 1820 but never practiced the discipline. A political refugee from Prussian persecution in the early 1820s, he had studied history in the household of the Roman historian Barthold Georg Niebuhr. Lieber absorbed his tutor's strong appreciation for the stabilizing effects of social and political institutions, especially the law, where custom, reason, and justice intersected. He became fascinated with the nature of the social bond, the strands of habit, affection, and prejudice that tame the appetite and yet animate the network, the formal and informal associations that make up social life. Lieber's blend of Niebuhr's conservative historicism and his own liberal views enriched and balanced his outlook on politics. Deeply frustrated by the petty factionalism, bureaucratic obscurantism, and popular indifference that continued to prevent the unification of Germany, Lieber became an admirer of the integrated constitutional systems rooted in English soil and blossoming in the United States.

In America, a laboratory of institutional evolution, the plentiful supply of materials for study far outstripped the supply of academics to tap it. Lieber's eccentric personality delighted Brahmin society in Boston and Philadelphia, but his ambition to obtain a prestigious post at a major eastern college went unfulfilled for thirty years after his arrival in 1827. Serving a restive term as professor of history and political economy at Charleston's South Carolina College from 1835 to 1855, he felt like an exile in a land of overbearing plantation nabobs and warring Presbyterians. Their demands that Lieber pledge allegiance to slavery were all too reminiscent of the Prussian censors who had driven him out of his homeland. Fleeing north in 1855, he finally settled at Columbia College Law School in 1857 as professor of history and political science.[20]

Lieber's roving intellect touched an awesome array of subjects and produced many works of broad scope and uneven quality. He had an opinion on everything from penal reform, international law, economics, and guerrilla warfare to hermeneutics and history. But his books on political theory, *Manual of Political Ethics* (1838) and *On Civil Liberty and Self Government* (1859), broke little new ground and instead summarized and filtered contemporary political ethics through a sieve of obscure and famous European authorities. Lieber's antebellum political theories were remarkable not for their originality or controversiality but for their eclecticism. He endowed a variety of conventional ideas with intellectual respectability by expounding their internal logic and searching out their historical sources.[21]

Lieber believed that politics is a science, the science of securing rights defined by moral law. The political scientist must study past politics and political institutions and "ought to be a manly and profound observer and construer" who spurns "fantastic theories or empty velleities" as nothing more than historical oddities. In addition, because the state exists for moral ends, "politics is a moral science," a branch of ethics that applies abstract principles to practical political life to determine "the wisest course for the conscientious citizen." How far should a citizen go in opposition to the government? Should he join a party? What are the proper limits of political action? The political scientist uses the facts of political life to prescribe answers to these questions about civic duty.[22]

Lieber grounded his view of civics in an examination of the web of affections that define social man. All social organization rests on mutual sympathies, he argued, and not on enlightened self-interest (which he considered to be a fragile bond open to the highest bidder). "There is no imaginable force that can keep a body of men united, be it for whatever purpose, if they are not first morally united, be this upon habit, prejudice, or even for criminal purposes; the union must be mental in origin," he thought. What is the essence of this moral tie? Reciprocal obligations or "mutuality, if we consider it in an ethical point of view; that of reciprocity, if we view it in the light of natural law." And mutuality, instilled within the family (the "nursery of patriotism"), is the basis of friendship, "a ramified bond of society, a tie of good-will between individuals, who might otherwise remain insulated." "Let sympathy and disinterested affection come whence it may," Lieber declared, "so that we have it—a refreshing dew upon the arid fields of practical life."[23]

Friendship produces "mutual moderation," Lieber's favorite social trait, which when it becomes "habitual" prevents political "excitement." Moderation, or temperance, consisted in "the keeping of the proper mean between extremes, and the tempering of excitement or passion." The only way to achieve moderation was through social intercourse and an "honest daily repeated endeavor to temper our appetites and impulses."[24]

The accretion of mutual associations over time spawns institutions, Lieber reasoned; the oldest institutions, as the products of generations of interactive sympathies, are therefore the most valuable. The churches, educational systems, corporations, and many other forms of association are the foundation of the state, "the chiefest of human unions, . . . the sacred institution [that] deserves each man's faithful devotion, to serve where it is right, to improve where wrong." Lieber was no statist but instead was an analyst and advocate of what Robert Nisbet calls "mediating institutions," private preserves of privilege that resist the intrusion of political conflict, cushion the shocks of change, and anchor men to society by providing a sense of continuity with the past.[25]

So far, Lieber's analysis was neither new nor original; his theory of institutional evolution mixed feudal conceptions of mutual social obligations with historicist and scientific ideas drawn from Burke, Kant, Hegel, and a host of German romantic and historical writers. But unlike feudal institutions inhabited by classes of people frozen into social ranks, Lieber's institutions were populated by a common citizenry. The ideal civic man was a jack-of-all-public-trades, equally comfortable in the mayor's chair, the church pew, the jury box, and the countinghouse. Trained by institutional experience, this civic man displayed an inner balance and outward calmness—moderation—that qualified him to deliberate on public affairs.[26]

Intellect and polity merged in Lieber's theory of institutions; moderate citizens lived in a moderate polity, both guarded by a friendly matrix of evolving institutions. But this was not an abstract polity of permanently peaceful citizens, for conflict is inevitable.[27] Conflict stemmed from rival temperaments in the polity. Competing ideologies, interests, and beliefs can peacefully coexist in society, but conflicting passions cannot. Lieber accepted the popular contemporary analogy between human and political systems and assumed that the vices and virtues of the former determined those of the latter. It was merely a matter of scientific observation and historical study to differentiate between those human (and therefore political) characteristics that were most amenable to the survival of institutions and those that were not. The citizen's duty was to avoid those attitudes inimical to institutional health. Lieber listed a number of those traits ("obstinacy" and "fretfulness") that thrive in the absence of "calmness of soul," but he pointed to "fanaticism" as the most dangerous temperament in politics because of its power to erode the emotional cement of institutional life.[28]

Fanaticism is moderation's evil twin. A fanatic "is actuated by a false zeal for some general principle or truth, real or supposed, so far that he commits wrong," usually by obtruding "principles and standards of action into spheres which ought to remain entirely foreign to them."[29] Fanaticism is obsession with one idea, one aim, one interest; moderation is expansive reflection on a multiplicity of partially achievable ends. Fanaticism lures us away from reality and into the dreamworld of the abstract; moderation directs sincere wishes to realizable ends. Fanaticism thrives on conflict; moderation promotes platonic intimacy. Most important, fanaticism alienates people from each other because it undermines mutuality, the communal prop of institutional order.

Lieber considered religious fanaticism to be the most dangerous form of this temperament, but he devoted more attention to fanaticism's most common guise: party zeal. Lieber could not help but appreciate the benefits of party activity, and he applauded the evolution of a legitimate opposition in England as a great forward stride in institutional evolution. But his endorsement of parties was greatly qualified by his belief that "parties foment the spirit of dissension, while it is the duty of every citizen to assuage discord and allay civil strife as much as possible." His outlook on parties admired Britain's "historical" parties while it equivocated between treating America's parties as temporary coalitions or as mere factions.[30] In any case, "all party excitements are liable to the danger of political fanaticism," which turns concessive friends into uncompromising enemies and causes the ultimate alienation when "the greatest link and tie of humanity, language, loses its very essence, and people cease to understand one another." As an example of such party distortion, Lieber deplored the manner in which the term *friends* had cloaked *favorites* in party conversation where the word was "abusively extended to followers, adherents and adherents' adherents."[31]

Lieber's solution to the problem of emotional excess in politics accepted the current wisdom. Patriotism, the highest form of moderation in the institutional setting, will subsume temporary passions under the imperative of permanent public interest. Genuine patriotism "enlarges instead of narrowing our views" because it acknowledges "a general union of civilization." Without it, "factious spirit and selfishness united with boldness must be rife."[32]

The greatest problem facing the modern state, Lieber claimed, is "to last long—to last with liberty and wealth."[33] How can the patriotic citizen promote this end? He must hold fast to institutional government and avoid extremes because only through representative government "can we safely steer between the fanaticism of theorists and unprincipled expediency—one of the great objects of good government."[34] The first duty of the citizen and the statesman is to preserve evolving institutions because a "social being owes his social, human relation to the continuity of society."[35] Lieber's conception of proper civic behavior favored the middle ground between ideological rigidity and pragmatic amorality.

The statesman, as a model of good citizenship, must demonstrate moderate qualities in extra measure, for the art of ruling devolves on the ability to reconcile contrasts and to make "all parts, however opposed to one another, march toward the same great and common end."[36] Lieber ticked off a long list of the statesman's traits, including "purity of soul," "fervent religious veneration," "good health," and "exactness of mind."[37] An assembly of statesmen must multiply these characteristics for practical legislation to emerge from the welter of conflicting interests and ideas in the polity. For the unavoidable conflicts that shape policy must be contained at least by moderate temperaments: conciliation promotes compromise. Parliamentary tactics and rules should encourage conciliation and mutual moderation. Thus, Lieber endorsed the use of intraparty coalitions as long as their necessary compromises rested on affective mutuality. It is useless, he believed, to try to compromise with an enemy who cannot be conciliated.[38] Compromise with "friends" is natural and occasionally desirable; compromise with an enemy—the opposing party, in this instance—emerges only after conciliation has tempered passions and reminded common citizens that they are "friends." Given Lieber's stress on conflicting passions as the chief danger to the social order, the problem of compromise resolved itself into a matter of temperament first and foremost.[39]

More than any other political observer in his day, Lieber outlined the political and ethical context of compromise. The upshot of Lieber's thinking was that conflict, although inevitable, is unpleasant, undesirable, and ultimately dangerous when in the form of emotional fanaticism; that platonic mutuality is the foundation of the social order and requires moderation for its continuance and for any resistance to fanaticism; and that patriotism is the ultimate form of mutual moderation to which all statesmen should aspire.[40] These ideas formed the underpinning of constitutional unionist thought, for they celebrated the diversity of a decentralized polity united through the balancing of principles, institutions, and interests.

LIEBER'S CONCEPT of civic duty in the institutional setting revealed how little civics had changed since the nation's foremost civic educators—the Federalists of 1787—had offered their example as the model of republican conduct. Lieber's elaboration of civic responsibilities and his depiction of the citizen's proper character would have found few critics in Philadelphia in 1787. And none of the framers would have quarreled with Lieber's premise that representative government is "a real government *of* self, as well as *by* self."[41]

Although Lieber had composed the most comprehensive treatment of civics before the Civil War, few Americans endeavored to unravel his tangled prose and chaotic organization.[42] Instead, the common man's civic instruction came, if at all, from political parties, the press, and the schools, instruction that included a legion of civics manuals and school and popular histories that began to appear by the late 1790s and attained a wide readership by the 1830s and 1840s.[43] Whereas Lieber had constructed his paradigm mostly from European materials, popular historians and civics writers found plenty of worthwhile prescriptions for proper civic conduct in the history, provisions, and practice of the Constitution. But their agenda—to perpetuate the Republic by teaching Americans to be "respectful citizens"—differed from Lieber's scholarly purpose; theirs was more urgent, immediate, and focused.

Because the founding of the nation was too fundamental an event to ignore, civics manuals and American histories invariably narrated the causes, course, and consequences of the framing of the Constitution and, in doing so, came face to face with the inconsistencies buried under the instrument's compromises. Civics educators did not shrink from the task of explaining these compromises—indeed, they cited the controversial nature of the subject as the most important reason for writing about it. As the most systematic survey of constitutional history and practice for the common reader and perhaps the first formal exposure for many future citizens to this important subject, the civics literature of the early Republic provides a remarkably coherent picture of civic ideals and changing political culture before the Civil War.

Modern historians have frequently overlooked contemporary civics literature when studying the popular constitutionalism of the antebellum period. Of greater interest to them is the important and more mature work of such contemporary scholars and legal specialists as Joseph Story, Chancellor James Kent, Timothy Pitkin, Richard Hildreth, George Bancroft, and George Ticknor Curtis, who at least acknowledged their sources and hitched their prejudices to a plausible methodology. But these histories and commentaries were too massive and densely written to appeal to a popular audience. The civics literature, on the other hand, distilled these scholars' works into simple, sermonic narratives designed to implant in young and untutored minds a permanent appreciation of the American constitutional heritage.[44] The primary objective of civics education was to create model citizens, public people of moderate comportment, social amiability, and political integrity, warmly attached to fellow citizens and to the institutions that shaped their daily lives. It tried to explain the nation's often divided and equivocal constitutional heritage in such a way as to cultivate sturdy patriotic sentiments that would cherish vital institutions, the basic framework of constitutional government, and especially the processes of deliberation, and therefore guard them from the divisive, corrupting forces of sectional and party spirit that Americans believed were the twin threats to the stability of the political order.

Invigorated with an optimistic, progressive view of historical development, republican education aimed ultimately to avert the suicidal streak in the history of republics: their tendency to succumb to the vices of their citizens. Educators and schoolbook writers uniformly agreed that the most direct and effective route to this ambitious goal was the study of the principles, provisions, and history of the Constitution. Civics manuals and a large number of popular and schoolbook histories invariably contained the text of the Constitution (frequently accompanied by extensive, clause-by-clause commentary), plus the Declaration of Independence, Washington's Farewell Address, the Articles of Confederation, and frequently Washington's compromise letter to the Confederation Congress. Therefore, civics education in the early nineteenth century was mainly constitutional education very broadly conceived. It drew within its orbit a legion of political scientists, politicians, historians, and informal commentators as interpreters and transmitters of the country's constitutional tradition.[45]

These writers viewed civil institutions, and especially the Constitution, as the bulwark of social order and therefore as the proper focus of civic education. In his 1847 civics text, Washington McCartney argued that the Republic's future would rest not on "fine-spun, logical deductions" but on "a Bible, a church, a school-house, and a printing-press; these are real, positive, powerful bodily things—actual existences whose operation upon the character of our country can be relied upon with certainty." Such "republican institutions," he stated, "are restraints—palliatives—correctives" that "repress rather than to give a loose rein" to one's sinful nature.[46]

The great jurist Joseph Story simplified his learned constitutional *Commentaries* for family reference in the hope that it would kindle warm sentiments for the Union and the Constitution. Mordecai McKinney, the author of the *Constitutional Manual* (1845), believed that a proper understanding of our civil institutions could "induce strong and settled attachment to their principles and impart ability for their maintenance; compared with which all other impulses or sentiments in regard to them are as nothing."[47] Joseph Burleigh designed his *American Manual* (1848) to promote "a knowledge of the nature and necessity of political wisdom—the paramount importance of the Constitution of the United States," fidelity to the Union, and "the perpetuity of its institutions."[48] Education in republican civics, then, was part of a larger cultural impulse in the antebellum period, which venerated the Constitution and its framers as civic ideals against which Americans should measure their political conduct.[49]

Politicians applauded this emphasis on the Constitution. Knowledge of the Constitution, "which is for the most part plain and simple in its provisions" according to Senator John M. Berrien of Georgia, would broaden civic awareness and help the student "realize more cordially the intimate relation in which he stands to every other citizen; and thus its tendency would be to draw closer the fraternal bond which unites us as one people." Berrien's remark reveals the heavy reliance that Americans placed on the Constitution as the alpha and omega of their republican order. "Yield away the Constitution and the Union, and where are we?" George Dallas asked. "Frittered into fragments, and not able to claim one portion of the past as peculiarly our own! . . . Our liberties could not endure the incessant conflicts of civil and conterminous strife; our independence would be an unreal mockery, our very memories would turn to bitterness."[50]

This awesome role assigned to the Constitution broadened the scope of civic education, for the ideal citizen must understand two mutually dependent "constitutions"—the nation's and the citizen's. Civic educators believed, in the words of the historian Michael Lienesch, that just as the Constitution balanced power and liberty, "constitutional self-government introduced in turn a balance between psychological states, a medium of personal moderation."[51] Thus, civics manuals frequently combined moral science, history, and constitutional exegesis into an integrated course in political behavior. And standard schoolbook histories frequently drew important lessons from the exemplary behavior of the framers. "The citizen must become a statesman," was the common refrain among the civics writers. Within this framework of study, compromise was not a theory of conflict resolution but a symbol of forbearance, mutuality, consensus, and practicality.[52]

Some modern historians have viewed the antebellum civics agenda as an attempt by a New England–dominated educational elite to create an unending line of mediocre, obedient, republican "machines," unwilling to challenge the existing order. By apotheosizing the Constitution, deifying its creators, and declaring the perfection and the superiority of American culture and political virtue over European and primitive cultures, authors hoped to stunt the political ambitions of future citizens by proclaiming that the great work of reform was over and that the citizens should direct their energies toward expanding the nation's prosperity and exploiting its resources.[53]

My survey of antebellum history and civics books does not fully support this interpretation. Although a large number of civics writers did come from New England, these were generally the earlier authors, active between about 1800 and the mid-1830s. A growing number of authors came from Pennsylvania, New York, and Ohio as the publishing industry expanded into the West and as the potential profit of selling texts to newly formed school districts attracted local lawyers, jurists, and teachers to the textbook business.[54] Moreover, civics writers pointed out that the Constitution was not perfect and that the virtue of the framers lay in their commonsense ability to reconcile differences.[55] It is easy to distort the meaning of language that now appears strident but that our ancestors generally regarded as mild, moderate, and effective when addressed to a semiliterate, rough-hewn population.

The authors and publishers of most civics books, then as now, took great pains to appeal to the widest possible audience and to avoid controversy while encouraging citizens to be vigilant of their rights. According to the superintendent of the New York common schools, "If the political fabric cannot find in the public intelligence, a basis broad and firm enough to uphold it, it cannot long resist the shocks to which, through the collision of contending interests, it is continually exposed." Thus, citizens should be upright and conscientious in defending their rights and show an "independence and discretion" and "sound and enlightened discrimination" that would keep them from becoming "the dupes of artful leaders, and their country a prey to internal discord."[56] By encouraging youth to judge the behavior of politicians according to the standard set by the Founding Fathers, these authors distinguished between moderation and mediocrity and made the scrutiny of public officials one of the hallmarks of the republican citizen.[57]

In keeping with its emphasis on moderation and restraint, the civics literature portrayed the Constitution's compromises as mutual sacrifices for the sake of the Union. Schoolbook histories simplified the Convention's conflicts and praised its compromise spirit, occasionally attributing this to divine inspiration. The 1833 edition of the Reverend Charles A. Goodrich's *History of the United States of America* admitted the necessity of compromise and then dated the Convention's mutuality from Benjamin Franklin's (unsuccessful) motion for daily prayers to help break the deadlock of early July. After that point, "the guidance of divine wisdom was daily sought," and "the spirit of concession pervaded the Convention," prompting the framers "to sacrifice local interests on the altar of the publick good."[58]

Most popular histories and civics manuals stressed the intractable nature of the conflicts that plagued the Convention, the necessity of making compromises to overcome them, and the patriotic spirit of concession that prompted the framers to do so. While discussing the Constitution's purpose of creating a more perfect union, Joseph Burleigh urged his readers to remember that during the founding period, "sectional jealousies and prejudices then existed as they do now—but [the framers] went to their duties with pure hearts and enlightened and liberal views." The "political state of society" and the "force of circumstances" necessitated "numerous and liberal concessions. He continued, "Now, for the people to disregard the injunctions of the Constitution, and cast it aside, would denote political insanity."[59]

The Articles of Confederation came in for particular censure as a prime example of the dangers of disunion. Story concluded that the Confederation's "utter unfitness, as a frame of government, for a free, enterprising, and industrious people" made reform imperative. And the people apparently did not appreciate the "great difficulties and sacrifices of opinion" experienced by the framers, for the ratification ordeal, Story continued, became a "humiliating lesson . . . of the evils of disunited councils, and of the pernicious influence of State jealousies, and local interests." Liberty, in sum, requires "wholesome restraints."[60] After excluding the Articles from the first two editions of his Constitution manual, William Hickey decided to incorporate it in the third "*merely as matter of history*, as it were out of place to mingle that inefficient form of government with the present approved and successful system, which has stood the test of more than half a century." Hickey had his political agenda too—to discourage southern disunionism, which portended "relapsing into the enfeebled condition of the General Government before the adoption of the Constitution."[61]

Although most civics writers discussed the conflicts over interstate commerce, debts and taxes, and the threat of rebellion in the backcountry, they usually viewed the Convention's debates as arguments over means, not ends, and as expressions of party spirit and sectional rancor. Michael Lienesch's argument that the postfounding generation "rewrote the history of the Convention," portraying this "intense and partisan congress . . . as a dispassioned philosophical gathering" and depicting the Constitution as "the product not of expediency and compromise but theory and philosophy" is wide of the mark. Civics writers did not try to obscure conflicts in the Convention but meant to highlight them all the more to praise the framers' achievement. Americans could admire the framers as statesmen willing to compromise for the public good, and not as philosopher-kings.[62]

Party spirit arose from differences of opinion about the strength of the new government, and in the minds of the civics writers, party spirit was a major obstacle to the spirit of conciliation and compromise. Contemporary historians often observed that the Convention's conflicts boiled down to a single one between states' rights and federalism, a clash that became the foundation for enduring party divisions.[63] According to John Lord, slavery was the most emotional of the Convention's issues, making it "impossible" to achieve unanimity on topics of intense interest to particular states "or [which] were likely to touch the balance of power between the North and the South."[64] "Much honest difference of opinion existed, in particular, where the strength of the new government came into question," Emma Willard noted in her famous *Abridged History* (1857). "Other points of dispute arose, which were still more dangerous, because they divided parties by geographical lines." The most difficult of these was the struggle over the ratio of representation.[65]

Mary Howitt's dramatic account depicted a Convention rife with deep conflict:

> Months went on in discussion and deliberation; the soundness and wisdom of purely democratic and republican governments were questioned; committees sat; adjournments took place; causes of dispute occurred; rival parties contended, federalists and anti-federalists; slaveholding and free states, difficulties having arisen even then between the slaveholding and nonslaveholding states as regarding representation, and every other interest. But if difficulty and doubt and discord arose, they were met and overcome. Nor can any greater argument be advanced in favour of the sound wisdom and the true patriotism of every party, than that all opposing interests and all questions of contention were gradually compromised.[66]

How great seemed compromise's victory over such collisions! It "holds up this convention," Willard rhapsodized, "as an example to future times of the triumph of strong patriotism and honest zeal for the public welfare, over party feeling and sectional prejudice."[67]

The great compromise attracted much praise. "This arrangement," Joseph Story observed, "so vital to the peace of the Union, and to the preservation of the separate existence of the States, is at the same time, full of wisdom, and sound political policy [because it] introduces and perpetuates, in the different branches of the legislature, different elements, which make the theoretical check contemplated by the division of the legislative power, more efficient and constant in its operation." According to John Holmes, the compromise found a way "to guard against [the] extremes" of anarchy and consolidation. "By this provision," he wrote, "as well the dictate of compromise as of profound wisdom, the balance was preserved, and conflicting interests were settled and adjusted."[68]

Historians and civics writers often adopted the Federalists' tactic of associating unpleasant compromises of the Constitution with compromises for the Union. The three-fifths clause, for instance, occasioned little direct praise yet remained as a prime example of disinterested sacrifice for the Union. Edward D. Mansfield's civics manual, *Political Grammar of the United States*, first published in 1834, admitted that the clause was unfair to the free states but nevertheless warned them "not to complain, as it was the *necessary result* of the *compromise*, without which it is probable the Union never could have been formed." William Sullivan conceded that the absence of direct taxes worsened the inequity of the clause, but then he reminded his readers that the clause was "part of the national contract, . . . as binding on all the nation as any other part of it."[69]

Joseph Story depicted the three-fifths and fugitive slave clauses as northern sacrifices to the South in the interest of the Union. The three-fifths clause "was seen to be unequal in its operation," he explained, "but was a necessary sacrifice to that spirit of conciliation, in which the Union was founded." When "viewed as a matter of compromise," it "is entitled to great praise, for its moderation, its aim at practical utility, and its tendency to satisfy the people [of all the states] that the Constitution ought to be dear to all, by the privileges which it confers" and the "blessings it secures."[70] As the three-fifths rule lost any intrinsic support from its origin as a sectional compromise, civics writers sought refuge in an expansive, sentimental explanation of it as a patriotic sacrifice for the Union. In sum, northerners who restrained their indignation about it were acting patriotically.

The Constitution's distasteful bargains faded into the compromise spirit of the work. In his renowned lectures on the Constitution, William Duer praised mutuality's victory over discord in the Constitutional Convention as "a signal example of the benignant influence of peaceful deliberation and calm decision, combined with a spirit of moderation and conciliation, not only beyond all precedent, but [when compared with other nations], . . . beyond the hope of imitation." And even if the republican experiment should assemble the ingredients of success, he warned, the "madness and folly" of the Founding Fathers' sons could wreck that success if they forgot these simple and important lessons. Edward Mansfield, sensitive to the growth of sectional feeling by the mid-1850s, added to later editions of his *Political Grammar* both the Northwest Ordinance (as a warning to southerners) and Washington's Farewell Address (which he regarded as practically a part of the Constitution itself).[71]

Mordecai McKinney's constitutional catechism, written in 1845, succinctly summarized this history lesson:

> Is the federal constitution to be regarded as the result of concession and compromise?
>
> Yes. It was the act of the people of the original States, voluntarily uniting, through mutual concession and compromise in relation to various local interests and other matters, in establishing a government for the Union. And such is it, always, to be considered, in its nature as to its obligation upon the people, and their allegiance to it.
>
> This variety of interests arose from, principally, the actual difference in the extent and situation of the territories of the several States, the number of their inhabitants, their agricultural productions, the existence of slavery in some of the States, and their peculiar laws and institutions.[72]

Washington McCartney saw the Constitution's compromises as its defining characteristic. The instrument was "a compromise of all interest, and of all theories," he argued. "From this compromise it derived an originality, a character of its own, and also a dissimilarity from other known forms of government." In his opinion, the debate about the nature of the Union ignored the peculiar circumstances surrounding its creation, "for, viewed in the light of the compromise which gave it existence, the Constitution is neither a compact of States, nor a directly popular government, but it is the *Constitution of the United States*."[73] Here was a constitutional and ultimately an ethical foundation for constitutional unionism: the peculiarity of a constitution founded on compromise rooted an otherwise legal framework of government to the national character and the social bond itself.

IT WAS ONLY NATURAL for the promoters of America's civic ideals to transfer the logic of past compromises to the present and urge new citizens to cultivate a temperament like that of the framers. They argued that any issue, and not just those that troubled the founding generation, should be approached in a spirit of compromise. John Holmes, attempting in 1840 to explain in his statesman's manual the "seeming paradox" of federalism even though he was "almost entirely without a model," listed those "great and momentous subjects growing out of our complex relations . . . which are perplexing to ourselves, and in which our wisest and profoundest statesmen have entertained contrary opinions." At the top of his list was the problem of dual allegiance to state and nation, followed by questions of territorial policy, the treaty power, "the method and means of determining a contested election of the President," and slavery. These "and many others equally grave and important, are still left, perhaps to distract and divide us, but, as we hope and trust, to be determined by the same wisdom and forbearance which influenced and effected the adoption of the Federal Constitution."[74] Any discussion of the dispute over the nature of the Union should be conducted cautiously, Andrew Young advised his readers. It was important to avoid "a spirit of controversy" on such delicate topics. Concord had created this marvelous system of government, he noted, and must continue to regulate the spirit of its creators' sons as well.[75]

So the schoolbook and popular histories, as well as the manuals of civics instruction, concentrated on trying to nurture a conservative ethic resistant to extremism yet pliant enough to permit new citizens to decide ultimate questions for themselves in the full knowledge that final, settled answers rarely emerge from public debate. The result was a remarkable mixture of individualism and communal spirit; writers tried to harness the reader's ambition to the larger public good, especially as the emergence of mass politics in the 1830s rendered irrelevant older appeals to disinterested mutual sacrifice. "Let every citizen feel himself individually responsible for his moral and political influence, and act with reference to the general good," Andrew Young argued, "and our republican institutions are safe. . . . MANKIND CAN BE GOVERNED AND YET BE FREE." William Sullivan devoted a chapter to instructing his young readers in moral science and "the common rules of conduct" (which included "*courtesy, complaisance, and politeness*"). "Modest self-respect; the suggestions of common sense are safe guides in personal deportment," he advised. We should not always say what we feel, or "society would be intolerable." Only by practicing self-restraint and moderation could the citizen successfully resist the guiles of party demagogues.[76]

The Constitution's stormy history could be used in the battle against fanaticism in party or sectional form; the framers' great achievement served as a standing lesson in moderation. Thus, the emergence and survival of a party system provoked a mixed reaction from civics writers because of the country's ambivalent attitude toward parties. The founding generation had warned against parties at the same time that it had divided into rival parties over the interpretation of the Constitution. The idea that a permanent division of the polity could result in consensus seemed to defy common sense. Parties thrived on conflict by stirring up emotions and diverting the loyalties of voters away from the public good and toward the ambitious plans of party leaders.[77]

Yet it was also clear that a legitimate opposition could strengthen liberty by fostering popular vigilance of the government and providing an outlet for dissent. The line between antipartyism and the acceptance of a party system, so easily drawn by modern historians, was often difficult to determine because the boundaries of party activity—the range of issues and emotions that parties encompassed—were amorphous and unpredictable until the mid-1850s. Not surprisingly, civics instructors and historians routinely combined praise and condemnation when touching the subject, always careful to remind their readers that parties are another of liberty's dangerous temptations, capable of much good but more often abused than directed to the public welfare. Antebellum political science accepted the principle of a legitimate opposition but frequently denounced the practice.[78]

Although historians differed on the chronology of party development, they generally agreed that American political parties represented continually clashing principles that dated back to the Convention. Henry C. Watson wrote in his *History of the United States of America* (1853), "Before the Convention . . . met, the two great parties, which afterwards assumed the names of Federalists and Democrats, arose, and commenced the contest which afterwards became so violent as to endanger the union."[79] Washington McCartney argued in 1847 that the historical roots of American parties lay in the Constitutional Convention's debate over the distribution of federal and state powers. The delegates had tried to resolve this through an "amalgamation of theories," which left neither party fully satisfied. The conflict continued outside the Convention during the ratification struggle and, under different party labels, up to the present day.[80]

If party conflict seemed inevitable, if not desirable, then civics writers found it more useful to discourage party spirit in order to prevent fanaticism. Andrew Young, for instance, criticized the idea that parties are a "salutary check on each other":

> But it must be evident to all who have observed the effects of party spirit among us, that the evils flowing from it overbalance all the good which it can produce. Where freedom of opinion and of speech is tolerated, parties must necessarily exist to some extent; but their existence should be founded upon differing of opinion merely.
>
> But party spirit, when unrestrained, becomes intemperate and revengeful; and it is then that its pernicious effects are seen. Parties, while contending for power, forget right, and lose sight of the public good. The rights of the minority are disregarded. Men, for difference of opinion, are made the subjects of proscription and persecution. In this state of things the strife is for men, without regard to principle.[81]

Washington McCartney devoted a chapter of his civics manual to showing that the "bloodless warfare" of parties in fact "demonstrated that democracy on an extended scale is practicable in these United States," as long as the parties "stand on the common platform of republicanism, and fire a common artillery upon the diminishing ranks of legitimacy." McCartney then backtracked. "We do not wish to be understood as defending or encouraging the spirit of partyism," he hedged, quoting Washington's Farewell Address in support. Parties are preferable to "despotic silence" and have temporary missions that, once fulfilled, no longer justify the parties' existence. McCartney prayed that the Constitution would "never find worse enemies than the old Federalists and Democrats."[82]

Joseph Burleigh reminded future voters that their "uncommon liberty" made them "subject to more sudden and intense discussions than any other people on the globe." In this state of affairs, "almost everyone is a politician, warmly attached to his party; and the opposite views and interests of parties engender controversies [that] may endanger the tranquillity of the nation by a struggle for power among ambitious leaders." Politics therefore tests the "virtue and intelligence of the people, and the discretion, moderation, and integrity of American politicians." Succeeding generations must prepare themselves for this, Burleigh advised, by becoming familiar not only with the principles of the Constitution but also with "the causes, the motives, the forbearance, the unwearied labor in its production, and the unparalleled wisdom and sagacity of its framers." Such knowledge would produce "harmony and union" among a people inspired by "*an ardent* desire" to perform their civic duties and would teach the ordinary citizen to "use much caution and inquiry" when "making political statements," being sure to avoid "angry words, or imputations of bad motives."[83]

Benson Lossing applied the same formula to the slavery issue. Noting that the recognition of slavery in the Constitution "by fair implication" was "one of the important compromises which the framers found necessary" to secure ratification, Lossing urged the readers of his *Pictorial History of the United States* to discuss "all of the perplexing lineaments of the question" with "candor and forbearance." Avoid harsh words that impair the reign of reason, he advised. "Mutual recriminations, ungenerous expressions, and flippant censures, only tend to alienate the affections of those who ought to live as brothers, conceding to each other sincerity of feeling and honesty of motives."[84]

The highly qualified acceptance of parties by the civics writers suggests that some thoughtful observers of the practical operations of American government still sought to reconcile compromise and the new politics of party. Time and personal political commitments might affect this judgment; later editions of some civics manuals deleted or diluted antiparty statements, retaining formulaic warnings about fanaticism and partyism.[85] In the 1840s, some civics writers emphasized the distinction between faction and party as a way of admitting that honorable party competition could coincide with a constitution above parties. Constitutional compromise—across branches of government or between sectional interests—offered a respite from party conflict, helping to remind citizens of the limits of parties. The sectional conflict of the late 1840s and the 1850s would intrude on this increasingly favorable outlook on parties and would send some civics educators (such as Emma Willard) scurrying back to the safety of the old statesmanship as the antidote to political polarization.[86]

Several important themes emerged from this popular civics literature. First, in the hands of civics writers, a formal, dry, legal document obtained a distinctive personality from its creators; their patriotic sacrifices could be discerned in its provisions and held out as permanent, written testimony to the power of mutual sacrifice as the cement of the Union. Second, civics writers and historians made compromise a moral act, justified both by its higher purposes and by its intrinsic quality of sacrifice, two reasons amply supported by the practical, Common Sense ethics that dominated ethical thought in the early Republic.

Indeed, the very strength of the Constitution rested on this important convergence of ethics and the human personality. As the historian George Ticknor Curtis observed in 1850, the "moral completeness" of character needed for making a constitution "does not consist solely in devising schemes, or creating offices, or parcelling out jurisdictions and powers. There must be adaptation, adjustment of conflicting interests, reconciliation of conflicting claims. There must be recognition and admission of great expedients, and the sacrifice, often of darling objects of ambition, or of local policy, to the vast central purpose of the greatest happiness of all." The framers, he continued, displayed "a high sense of justice; a power of concession; the qualities of magnanimity and patriotism; and the broad moral sanity of the intellect, which is farthest removed from fanaticism, intolerance, or selfish adhesion to either interest or opinion."[87]

Third, by urging ordinary citizens to emulate the framers, civics writers obscured any differences between citizenship in an individual state and citizenship in the Union, for both required the same qualities of moderation and disinterested public spirit. Although the framers came to Philadelphia as delegates of states and as representatives of diverse economic and social interests, their compromises simultaneously preserved and subsumed those differences and tied their accomplishments to the creation of a single nation. Civics writers helped to forge a chain of association among compromise, duty, and the Union, thus encouraging Americans to regard compromise as the act of living statesmen, not of abstract, inanimate states. The thrust of this literature was deliberately national, to help incorporate a loose population of restless individuals into a national civic culture. Compromise and constitutionalism provided the text for such an effort.

Finally, the writers' willingness to tolerate the contradictions behind the Constitution's compromises suggested the continuing theme of constitutional unionist analysis: that a union of freedom and slavery was tolerable until deliberate, concurring majorities successfully conciliated enough dissenters to resolve the slavery question. By appealing to readers as independent, rational citizens, the civics writers tried to promote a detachment from local prejudices and an appreciation of the system's fine balances, both characteristic of the Madisonian heritage that supported constitutional unionism.

The spirit of compromise—defined in an antiparty age, reinforced by Common Sense ethics, and invigorated by the powerful cultural urge to judge the performance of one's civic duty by the standard set in 1787—exerted a strong appeal throughout the first half of the nineteenth century. Politicians recognized its magnetic force. Composing his endorsement of William Hickey's fact-book on the Constitution a month after Congress passed the final compromise measures of 1850, Michigan Senator Lewis Cass urged the manual's readers to reflect upon "the blessings which the Constitution has brought, and upon the difficulties it encountered before it received the sanction of the American States and people."

> If we were now separated, as we were in 1787, no mortal power could bring us together. Whether, with all the experience of our

> dangers and our blessings, we can be kept together, must depend upon the spirit with which we come up to the work. Whether the feelings of concession and compromise which animated our fathers will continue to animate their sons, or enough of them to preserve and perpetuate this precious heritage . . . is the great question of the day, which events are fast hastening to a solution, under circumstances as imposing as they are portentous.[88]

Cass assumed that the moral dimensions of the slavery issue were less important than the moral imperative of maintaining the Union. But sectional crisis pitted the "feelings of concession and compromise" against the urgings of conscience as the nation struggled with its great moral paradox. Politicians like Cass would have the difficult task of applying the framers' civics lesson to the intractable problem of slavery in a republic. And they would rediscover what the framers had already warned against: sectionalism and party strife would tax the virtues of moderation to the very limit.

3 Constitutional Rituals

1820 and 1833

Our Federal Union—It Must Be Preserved
—Andrew Jackson

The Union: Next To Our Liberty, Most Dear
—John C. Calhoun

Mutual forbearance and reciprocal concessions, thro' their agency the Union was established—the patriotic spirit from which they emanated will forever sustain it.
—Martin Van Buren

Civic educators outlined and refined a rhetoric of conciliation that they applied to the entire range of civic involvements; the language of moderation, mutuality, and reciprocity was a standing admonition that the citizen's duty must always be executed within certain psychological restraints. But were their admonitions heeded? Was the political science of American civics—the understanding of how the Constitution and its institutions were designed to operate—in any sense applied by the public? This question is very hard to answer. We know, for instance, that school attendance rates in the North and particularly in the Northeast were high enough by the 1830s to support the conclusion that at least some formal civics instruction did filter down to part of the school-age population.[1] Perhaps we are limited to uncovering in contemporary public discourse a similar set of assumptions about constitutional duties, even though we cannot pinpoint whether they originated with formal civics instruction or with one of the other mediators of civic culture (such as political parties).

Public moralists, as David Hollinger has reminded us, needed an audience and tried to couch their policy prescriptions and diagnoses of the body politic in terms the common citizen could understand and in part appreciate. In a sense, just as civic educators had incorporated compromise into Americans' civic ideals, so did statesmen try to enact it into law. As several historians have noted, the second generation of American politicians—the men in power from the mid-1820s to the early 1850s—was acutely conscious of its position in the marching order of American history.[2] The fathers had embedded fundamental principles of republican government in a new constitution and through their statesmanship had secured it against foreign intervention and domestic turmoil. The sons now had the difficult task of applying those principles to public policy while preserving the constitutional heritage, a mission that they took seriously and that compromise served well.

In the early Republic, many statesmen adapted the Federalists' political science and the civics ideal to a politics of conciliation, making familiar arguments drawn from history and reinforced by a political culture that valued statesmen who reconciled deep conflicts of principles and interests. "The art of compromise," Merrill Peterson has pointed out, "became a conserving force, cushioning the shocks of change, mediating between reason and violence, vindicating institutions at the expense of interests or doctrines; and when this art failed, the Union was dissolved."[3]

The politics of conciliation coupled image with ideology in the service of a conservative policy. As Daniel Webster remarked, "My object has been, and is, to preserve the Institutions of our Fathers; and I feel, deeply, that those institutions can only be preserved by conciliation, and the cultivation of friendly sentiments between the different parts of the country." The politics of conciliation offered Americans a bridge from a political present confused by constitutional and partisan controversy to a past that was rapidly fading into the mists of legend.[4]

Although reasons of policy and of ambition might justify pursuing a politics of conciliation, other objectives and consequences might also be influential. The template established by the founding generation was in many ways predictive; according to the Federalists' descriptions of the conditions tending to require grand, disinterested, statesmanlike compromise, a definable set of circumstances must be present. As we saw in chapter one, their analysis of politics argued that severe conflict between closely matched forces would invariably create a crisis that could be resolved only if local allegiances were subordinated to the common good.

The Federalists had used this argument to deflect Antifederalists' criticisms of the Constitution's ambiguous compromises, and George Washington had elaborated on the most dangerous form of such conflicts in his Farewell Address. The durability of this outlook throughout the early Republic suggests that Federalist political science did rest on verifiable observations about pluralism, party politics, human ambition, and the basic operation of a system centered on rule by deliberate majorities over time.

Is it possible to test the Federalists' predictions? Certainly we can find evidence that a later generation saw the emergence of parties and the recurrence of sectional quarrels as evidence that the Federalists' premonitions were coming true, and that grand compromise along the old model was the best way to prevent disunion. This is not to say that later generations uniformly regarded sectionalism and party politics as intrinsic evils but merely to point out that an age determined to preserve the "Union as it is" had to reconcile the transformations of American politics with the original understanding of politics outlined by the Founding Fathers. Many Americans could be ardent sectionalists and happy party warriors while retaining their faith in the old Constitution. But many could not. They might pursue the politics of conciliation as one of several ways to convince the electorate that the defense of the "Union as it is" need only return to the "first principles" of the founding generation, especially to the successful processes for resolving deep conflict, and therefore to resort to grand, nonpartisan compromises designed to restrain passions and permit the public business to go forward.

The spread of party activity and the growth of party organizations in the middle years of the nineteenth century offered convincing proof that parties could devise workable compromises on most policy issues. But sectional questions invariably raised the problem of sectional parties and sent politicians and citizens back to the founding period for guidance. Crises of the Union seemed to demand the suspension of partisanship and a return to the old statesmanship of compromise.

Under these circumstances, sectional compromise can be seen as a kind of constitutional ritual: an unfolding drama about old and new styles of politics. The ritual lay in the customary, predictable behaviors and rhetoric of compromisers—the ways they shaped debate, formulated issues, appealed to the public, and portrayed themselves as successors to the framers' statesmanship. The histrionics of a Henry Clay or a Daniel Webster might entertain or enrage the watching public, but it might also enlighten the country about how these men thought the system was designed to work. And if the rhetoric of conciliation seemed incredible when coming from an avowed partisan like Clay, it nonetheless expressed political perceptions that an audience might verify through the unfolding sectional drama.

It is instructive, then, to examine the course of sectional and party politics through the lens of the Federalist political science that underlay constitutional unionism. In fact, there is a striking concurrence between, on the one hand, the rhetoric and behavior of compromisers during sectional crises and, on the other, the Federalists' predictions and perceptions about the Constitution's operation. Sectional crises did tend to crop up when the existing party system was either decaying or in the process of realignment. And when national parties failed to manage sectional tensions, antiparty rhetoric resurfaced along with its associated sentiments about the Constitution, statesmanship, and fears of corruption.

The great divide between compromisers and their forebears would eventually appear over the nature of the settlement: Federalists expected that the growth of concurring majorities on sectional questions would permit the country to resort to the amending process to resolve these questions. But it was clear up to the Civil War that such concurring majorities had not yet formed; compromisers had to devise immediate legislative settlements in the hope that someday such majorities might emerge to resolve sectional questions. This was a dangerous practice, for it tended to conflate temporary legislative compromise with constitutional law as a way to insulate the bargain from tampering by future Congresses.

Under these circumstances the advocates of conciliation tried to replay the drama of 1787, recalling older arguments and appealing to increasingly dated values. Their successes in 1820–21, 1833, and 1850 reinforced the identification of grand compromise with constitutionalism. Any sectional compromise that survived the test of parties and elections and therefore obtained the acquiescence of the deliberate sense of the political community over time attained a special significance in the public mind because it had satisfied the Madisonian criterion for settling questions of constitutionality. Compromise in this context settled issues by "removing" them from party strife, thereby answering what most politicians believed was the crying need to settle the Republic's foundations upon a firm bedrock of constitutional precedent. Americans came to invest great hopes in grand compromise and its kindred policies of sectional conciliation and evolutionary constitutionalism.

The major compromises of 1820–21 and 1833 revealed the workings of this constitutional ritual of sectional compromise. In each case, the intensity of sectional confrontation made a negotiated settlement imperative, and, predictably, because each conflict intertwined controversies over slavery and the nature of the Union, compromise in the tradition of the framers seemed the proper answer. Furthermore, the bitter memory of such deep sectional divisions combined with their peaceful aftermath to help give compromise an important and unique place in Americans' vision of their past and present. Indeed, there is some evidence that legislative compromises were deemed akin to constitutional compacts, bargains not strictly immune to repeal yet clearly more important than ordinary legislation. Finally, these compromises highlighted the standard of statesmanship among the second generation. Henry Clay's experience (explored more deeply in the next chapter) illustrates how Americans celebrated compromise as an attribute of statesmanship. The reconciliation of interests and principles was the ultimate aim of creative statesmanship. Compromise had a legacy, and when that legacy began to unravel in the mid-1840s, reflective people sensed the end of an era.

SECTIONAL AND PARTY tensions had coexisted since the founding of the Republic, but for several reasons they rarely threatened the political order before the 1850s. One of the primary objectives of the early Republic's statesmen had been to avert the formation of geographical parties. Their limited success in this was due mainly to the structure of American politics and the deferential political culture of the day. For one thing, the federal government's small sphere of action lowered the stakes of sectional confrontations and interposed barriers to united sectional interests. Much of the early conflict over slavery, for instance, occurred in the state courts that addressed the problem of state reciprocity over fugitive and sojourning slaves in the North and northern free blacks traveling in the South. Through an intricate set of precedents built up through the 1820s, the courts established a tradition of accommodating various state laws so that, within limits, blacks traveling in the North or the South temporarily carried their home state's definition of their status with them.[5]

Although sectional alignments had roughly coincided with party positions in the first party system, the small size of the electorate, the wide variety of state electoral systems, and the localistic orientation of most citizens helped to stunt the growth of parties and to limit their ability to consolidate sectional interests. Furthermore, the constitutionalism of northerners strengthened their disinclination to make slavery the focus of national debate over sectional issues. Slavery was considered a property matter, and if Congress or the courts moved against it, then everyone's property could be endangered. Individuals could instead place the slavery issue within the context of state action. By abolishing slavery in their own states without demanding federal action, many northerners reconciled two different values: their dislike of slavery and their love for a union that required fellowship with slaveholders. With the ultimate disposition of slavery's status left to the states, Americans could discuss it at the national level with considerably less rancor than in later years.[6]

Within this context, slavery could enter national debate before 1819 without automatically provoking a crippling confrontation. It is tempting to treat southern alarms at every mention of slavery as the sign of impending crisis. But it would be difficult to find an issue that was not hotly discussed or treated as a harbinger of declension from the wisdom of the framers. Compared with the debates over fiscal policy, for instance, Congress's voluble discussions of slavery blend easily into the day's clamorous political discourse. Quaker petitions in 1790 for the abolition of the slave trade drew strong southern reactions but did not set off a crisis. The colonization movement was very active at the national level, petitioning Congress in 1827 for a share of land revenues and recruiting prominent politicians and presidents to lend their reputations to the advancement of its work. Congress also peacefully debated and passed a fugitive slave law in 1793, inserted fugitive slave provisions in all organic territorial legislation (including the reenacted Northwest Ordinance and the Missouri Compromise), and in 1804 banned the slave trade into or out of Louisiana (Orleans) Territory. And the federal government's failure to carry through with the direct-tax side of the three-fifths rule prompted northern complaints about the rule's inequity, but without any serious threats to domestic tranquillity.[7] The Supreme Court frequently handled slave cases and sometimes made controversial decisions, but few Americans before the mid-1850s feared that these actions endangered the Union. The Court was widely regarded as detached from the emotional roller coaster of party politics. In fact, as Don Fehrenbacher has pointed out, the direction of public debate inevitably pushed the issue before the Court as it became increasingly clear that the parties and Congress were worsening matters and were unable to reach a peaceful solution.[8] So the problem for political leaders was not to keep slavery from becoming a national issue but to keep it from becoming a party issue. The convergence of sectional and party lines haunted the dreams of national politicians before the Civil War, for these allegiances had a combined effect that they lacked separately.

When placed against a background of limited party activity and relatively effective constitutional and cultural checks on sectional extremes, the crises and consequent compromises of 1820–21 and 1833 assume a unique significance. Both crises acutely defined sectional positions that had already been apparent in national politics. The danger lay in the relationship of the crises to the condition of the party system and the cluster of attitudes about party beneath it. Both crises occurred when national parties were in disarray. The first came with the dying gasps of Federalism and the second with the birth pangs of the Whig opposition. In fact, the two compromises that ended these controversies stemmed in part from an attempt to check the alignment of sectional and party animosities. The Missouri Compromise was partly an attempt by the dominant Republican party to prevent a Federalist resurgence, whereas the Compromise of 1833 was in part an attempt by a weak opposition to build an intersectional coalition. And in a sense, those compromises were the natural product of an older, Madisonian constitutionalism that admitted the recurrence of sectional conflict and supported "nonpartisan" compromise as a way to avert the formation of geographical parties.

The Missouri controversy, which convulsed Congress and to some extent the nation between 1819 and 1821, built on these patterns just as it rehearsed the sectional conflict of thirty years later. This debate firmly fixed national compromise as a compact binding in faith and honor, a peaceful, practical, and patriotic continuation of the civics lesson begun in 1787. It also echoed the conflict, confusion, and ambivalence over slavery that had disturbed the Constitutional Convention, and it exposed the yawning gap that the slavery issue opened between the rhetoric and the reality of compromise. The settlement of 1820–21 continued the civic tradition of conflating the compromises of the Constitution with the compromises for the Union, for the severity of the conflict exposed the raw, unprocessed materials of American nationality, creating fears for the social order. Therefore the real objective of this settlement was to remove a divisive issue from Congress and party politics and to diffuse slavery's emotional impact over a broad, decentralized political system.

In 1818, Missouri Territory requested Congress's permission to form a constitution and seek admission as a slave state. Because Missouri's exposed geographical position pushed slavery's limits far above the Ohio River, which was the informal partition between freedom and slavery, a coalition of northern Republicans and former Federalists tried to impose a restriction gradually ending slavery there. Debate over this restriction deadlocked the House and the Senate as each chamber became a sectional stronghold. The Senate removed the restriction, amended the proposed Missouri Enabling Act to include a ban on slavery in the territory north and west of the proposed state's southern border, and grafted the package onto a bill for the admission of Maine, as a lever to force concessions from the House. In March 1820, Congress compromised the issue; it separated the Missouri Enabling Act from the Maine bill, removed the proposed restriction on Missouri, and drew a line between freedom and nonintervention from Missouri's southern border across the rest of the Louisiana Purchase.[9]

The controversy occurred against a backdrop of economic dislocation and adjustment to the postwar era of expansion, settlement, and commercial growth. Sectional tensions had always provided a counterpoint to the ebullient national feelings that pervaded the postwar era, but in 1819 they received stronger impetus from a sharp banking and currency depression that westerners and some southerners blamed on the pro-East financiers who ran the Bank of the United States. The crisis also occurred at the ebb of the Federalist party's fortunes. Federalism had lost its early appeal to a limited number of southern aristocrats and had become generally a northern organization with a pronounced antislavery bias and a tone of effete disdain for the hard-boiled western and southern interests that controlled the Jeffersonian Republicans. The Missouri controversy offered the Federalists an issue with which to divide southern Republicans from their northern allies and revive the Federalist party. In sum, the danger of sectional parties elevated the conflict over Missouri to a Union-threatening issue, and the alarm for the Union was the great prerequisite for subsuming party feelings and reconciling clashing interests and opinions.

The tendency to view the compromises of the Constitution as binding sectional pacts created by and radiating a spirit of conciliation that reached from the Convention to the present hour often surfaced in the debates. While defending his amendment to restrict the further spread of slavery into Missouri, Representative John W. Taylor of New York quoted Washington's compromise letter to Congress and tried to reassure southerners that he entertained no intention of altering the Constitution's foundation of compromise. "The bond has been executed," he stated in a common metaphor, "and we will faithfully perform all its conditions; we yield, without grudging, to the slaveholding States all the political advantages, they have a right to demand."[10] Arguing in favor of compromising the issue, Representative James Stevens of Connecticut reminded his colleagues that they held their seats "by the tenure of compromise" that sacrificed "something like particular rights" in the interest of "the general welfare." Present leaders must realize what the framers had recognized, he urged. "And now, after thirty years' successful experience, who dare arraign their wisdom or their patriotism?"[11]

Who indeed? For once darkened by the shadow of the framers' wisdom, the debate narrowed and descended into a dense thicket of confusing, hair-splitting arguments about just what those compromises really contained, arguments that only reinforced the tendency to speak in abstractions about the "spirit" of the framers and the Constitution. If any consensus was to emerge from this debate, it had to be at least a reaffirmation of the decision in 1787 that the Union was more important than fixing a policy on the future of slavery. Everyone agreed that the Constitution's compromises "touched" slavery, but after that point each side tried to hitch the sentiment of compromise to its own sectional interests, and given the common understanding of compromise as conciliation, mutuality, and patriotic sacrifice, there was more at stake here than the winning of a few debating points.

In arguing that the compromises of the Constitution mandated either the restriction or the protection of slavery, the debaters were setting the conciliatory spirit of these compromises against an avowedly sectional interpretation of them—a most difficult position for any politician in an age of youthful nationalism. "The *landmarks* that belong to the issue are not clearly laid down," Hezekiah Niles observed in August 1819, "and seem to depend more than could be wished for, on the *feelings* or *interests* of persons, than the written law."[12]

But written law and unwritten custom imposed a special burden on northerners in this quarrel. Because the Constitution's compromises tolerated slavery, restrictionists felt compelled to acknowledge past wisdom while seeking to limit its present force. They argued that the compromises exempted the original thirteen states from the broad definition of republican government contained in the Declaration of Independence; any new state, in order to comply with the Constitution's guarantee of republican government, must secure to all inhabitants the rights to life, liberty, and property. And any new state created out of federally owned territory was particularly bound by the guarantee clause.[13]

Under this interpretation, the three-fifths clause (which the restrictionist Rufus King described as "an ancient settlement" that "faith and honor stand pledged not to disturb") applied only to the original thirteen states and did not hold out a blanket recognition of slavery in lands acquired thereafter.[14] Instead, the clause merely recognized an existing balance of power between the sections. And when northerners considered this compromise in connection with the slave trade ban, an antislavery intent seemed apparent in the minds of the framers. In sum, the three-fifths rule was a temporary concession to slavery, while the slave trade ban was a permanent restriction on the institution; together, they signaled the Convention's antislavery intent, forming a "silent compact," as Pennsylvania's John Sergeant put it, "with an afflicting necessity."[15]

Opponents of restriction argued that the compromises of the Constitution sought to limit not slavery but the federal government's jurisdiction over it through a series of sectional trade-offs. "The Constitution was a compromise as to slaves," North Carolina Senator Nathaniel Macon responded, "but not a compromise to emancipate."[16] Pointing to other, nonslavery compromises in the instrument, P. P. Barbour of Virginia claimed that if the three-fifths rule did not apply to new states, then neither did the great compromise, so that new states would not be entitled to two senators![17] John Holmes of Maine District told the House that the three-fifths *ratio* was the real compromise, a middle ground between full enumeration and entire exclusion of slaves from representation. "It was a compact," he stated, "and we are bound by it; and if it was a bad or a good bargain, I will never complain of it on the one hand, nor boast of it on the other."[18]

The problem that both sides faced (and that eventually worked to the antirestrictionists' favor) was that the Constitution's compromises interlocked enough to make nonslavery provisions hostage to those touching slavery, so that questions about one provision awakened fears of attacks on the whole. James Madison observed at the onset of the crisis that the clauses on representation and taxation, commerce and navigation, and the slave trade "had such a complicated influence on each other which alone would have justified the remark that the Constitution was 'the result of mutual deference & concession.' " Thus, the restrictionists' attempts to circumscribe the jurisdiction of the slavery compromises exposed them to the charge of trying, in the opinion of the Virginia legislature, "to weaken the strong cement of mutual concession and confidence, in which the foundation" of the Union had been set.[19]

The compromise that emerged from the debate during 1819 and early 1820 did not reflect any significant alteration of northern opinion on the constitutionality of restricting slavery either in Missouri or in the Louisiana Purchase. It was simply that the restrictionists' resolve temporarily cracked under the unremitting strain of the controversy. By March the agitation had gone on for over a year, distracting attention from pressing public business and subjecting the Union to mounting sectional stresses. The extremely close divisions in Congress presented a classic case of legislative paralysis, prompting familiar apprehensions of geographical parties. The South's intransigence made it apparent to some northerners that a free Missouri was not worth the threat of disunion and that a compromise preserving some free territory to the North would be acceptable.[20]

One of the most eloquent calls for compromise came from Hezekiah Niles, who had become convinced by late January that this was now a question of compromise or disunion. A staunch advocate of an entrepreneurial economy based on free labor and domestic manufactures under federal sponsorship, the Baltimore editor detected that southern apprehensions over slavery lay at the bottom of the crisis. Although he lived in slave country, Niles was a restrictionist. The bulk of his readership lived in the mercantile centers of the Northeast and the thriving commercial towns of the Ohio and the Mississippi river valleys, areas receptive to his Franklinesque journalism. Niles had concluded that slavery's doom was already sealed by its inefficiency, a fact he frequently documented with masses of comparative economic statistics, so it was understandable that he preferred making concessions to a weakening South rather than sticking to restrictionist demands at the expense of public peace.[21]

Niles's greatest fear was the erosion of mutuality and the breakdown of rational discussion portended in the threats of disunion and violence that frequently echoed through Congress and the press. Niles "severely opposed" drawing lines that marked sectional distinctions and therefore encouraged sectional parties, but he suggested that what had worked for the Constitutional Convention should be useful now as well. Whatever the solution, he thought, it was "the *reason* of the nation" that should be appealed to. Urging the country to " 'keep cool' and have respect for each other's judgment," Niles predicted: "If the proper temper prevails, there is no doubt that we shall get through the momentous question now before congress in peace and harmony. . . . It is now that the *patriot* should come forth, balance contending interests by the public good, and give stability to the Republic." Once he had pronounced this theme of conciliation, Niles never left it.[22]

Would the compromise of March 1820 survive for long? Was it final? Like sectional compromises before and after it, the first Missouri Compromise in 1820 did not satisfy everyone. Several congressmen believed that it was not a compromise at all, especially considering the South's reluctance to admit that the law confirmed Congress's power to legislate on slavery in a territory. Men on both sides realized that the Compromise paired an immediate concession to slavery with a prospective concession to freedom. The Louisiana Territory covered by the Missouri Compromise ban was "uninhabited," leading restrictionists to wonder if the South would be ready to concede any meaningful implementation of the ban once settlers actually entered the area. Some antirestrictionists who were backing the Missouri Compromise line disclaimed such a concession. If settlers south of the line had "vested rights" immune from congressional interference, as South Carolina's William Lowndes maintained, then what about the "vested rights" of future settlers north of the line? If they should desire to introduce slavery, would southerners stand by the decision of 1820 and enforce a ban? Lowndes's interpretation of the compromise, Representative Timothy Fuller of Massachusetts claimed, left "the compromise a shadow." He added, "All is yielded by one party and nothing by the other."[23]

Even more unsettling, considering the critical matter of timing, was the fact that the organic act admitting Missouri was practically irrevocable, whereas the provision banning slavery above thirty-six degrees thirty minutes latitude could be excised in the future. Kentucky Representative Ben Hardin's claim—"the faith of the nation is pledged to the people of that Territory"—did not mollify northerners like Representative Joseph Hemphill of Pennsylvania, who saw this as "an ordinary act of legislation" and wondered what would prevent another Congress from repealing this portion of the Compromise.[24]

Niles conceded Hemphill's point but nonetheless argued: "The circumstances of the case give to this law a *moral force* equal to that of a positive provision of the Constitution; and we do not hazard any thing by saying, that the Constitution exists in its observance. Both parties have sacrificed much to conciliation—we wish to see the *compact* kept in good faith." Like many northerners who accepted the Compromise, Niles believed that it would permit the nation's silent antislavery majority to emerge when "political power" rested where "the effective population" was located. Others offered more pragmatic explanations for its permanence. John Holmes believed that the preponderance of free states in the House of Representatives and of slave states in the Senate afforded "each party a security" that the Compromise would be permanent.[25]

The question of permanence arose again in November 1820 when Missouri proposed a constitution mandating the exclusion of free blacks and mulattoes from the state, much along the lines of Kentucky's constitution.[26] Northerners denounced the exclusion as a brazen violation of the privileges and immunities clause, and they mustered enough votes in the House to defeat several compromise proposals from the Senate and to stall Missouri's admission. Southerners argued that the citizenship of free blacks was so variously defined and restricted by individual states that no uniform "privileges and immunities" could possibly be inferred from the status of free blacks. They urged that Missouri be admitted and the issue left to the courts.

This second Missouri debate was more dangerous to the Union than the first. It occurred in the midst of a presidential election; only a hasty compromise, improvised by Kentucky Representative Henry Clay and Virginia Senator James Barbour and rammed through the House by devious methods, prevented the debate over Missouri from blocking the tabulation of electoral votes.[27] The debate also revealed a clearer delineation of sectional animosities. Gone now were the South's ritual apologies for slavery's intrinsic evils and the North's pacific assurances of preserving constitutional guarantees for slavery. Many northern congressmen, referring to this controversy as a sectional "contest for power," had returned to Washington in the late fall intent on undermining the first Compromise and delaying Missouri's admission until the offending clause could be removed.[28] The restrictionists disingenuously denounced the first Compromise as inequitable and nonbinding while simultaneously claiming that Missouri's defiance had violated the Compromise's conciliatory spirit. They then reintroduced the restriction on slavery in Missouri, supporting it by a two-to-one margin.[29]

Southerners argued that the initial concession to freedom north of Missouri's southern border bound Congress to admit Missouri promptly and that any delay constituted a violation of what South Carolina Representative Charles Pinckney called "the compact of the last year." The first Compromise, southerners believed, had forever settled this dispute in a compact "binding in honor on every part of the Union." They understood, Pinckney said, that in the extended American empire, encompassing so many different interests and opinions, "every thing must be done by compromise" just as the Constitution had been. And just as the Constitution's compromises on slavery had permitted southerners to keep their slaves, they could "see no reason why on the same subject the compromise of the last session" should not be adhered to. Kentucky Representative William Brown moved to repeal the ban on slavery because "the consideration promised for this restriction" had not been paid and "the plighted faith of Congress for the admission of Missouri" had been violated. Other southerners threatened secession and civil war if Missouri's admission was stopped.[30] In sum, the debate over black citizenship merged with the continuing argument about the first Missouri Compromise, complicating both issues and introducing a sense of frustration, weariness, and mutual betrayal as each side toted up lists of broken promises and accused the other of violating the original agreement. Expressing a sentiment common among moderates of both sections, Niles wrote that he had become "so wearied and disgusted with the *pro and con* of this question, as to have nearly resolved never to mention it again, except in a simple record of facts as they occurred."[31]

It is in this context—the reopened attack on the first Missouri Compromise and the intensified sense of frustration in Congress—that the second Missouri Compromise in 1821 should be understood. A small group of moderates led by Henry Clay defused the crisis by arranging for the passage of a resolution requiring Missouri to declare that nothing in the state's constitution or laws would be construed to impair the privileges and immunities of citizens of other states.[32] Everyone understood that this resolution was substantively meaningless; it ignored the crucial questions both of Congress's power to impose conditions on a prospective state's constitution and of the nature of state and federal citizenship. And although it allowed a court challenge to Missouri's constitution, the state could, and eventually did, ban free blacks and mulattoes after admission, claiming that the proviso did not bind Missouri as a state.

But the resolution also revealed how much importance both sides attached to Congress's role as an interpreter of the Constitution: restrictionists feared that Missouri's admission would entail a congressional endorsement of an unconstitutional state charter, a precedent they did not want to establish. And Clay, who later referred to this resolution as a declaration of an "incontested principle of Constitutional law," viewed it also as a significant precedent.[33]

The real objective of the resolution was to absolve northern congressmen of complicity in Missouri's action and thereby to split up a potentially permanent coalition of mild and strong restrictionists. Supporters of the resolution argued that the debatable constitutionality of Missouri's anti-black clause was less important than the clear and present danger of sectional violence. For even if the citizenship issue was not related to the previous question of slavery in Missouri, the second debate did renew and intensify the agitation that had marked the first debate. Thus, this link with the first Missouri Compromise—a chain of fears of disunion, of geographical parties, and of civil war—prompted many weary congressmen to accept any reasonable way out of the conflict. "Hard words will never obtain a victory in a matter like this," Niles pleaded. "Railing begets railing, and opposition produces opposition."[34]

Some restrictionists supported the resolution in order to protect their gains in the first Compromise. By ending the agitation, they effectively enforced the immediate concession to slavery in Missouri while pledging to preserve the ban on the institution in the northern Louisiana Purchase. Niles, again taking up the cause of conciliation, frequently admitted that the first Compromise was flawed but that he had nonetheless submitted to it because it had upheld the principle he "had contended for"—the reiteration of congressional power over slavery in a territory. Although Niles "had no doubt of the *right* of the matter," he thought that the public welfare required first and foremost "a compromise of *feeling*" on it. And that "principle of compromise, though possessing only the authority of a law, had become, from its nature, as a part of the Constitution."[35]

Such a principle was worth defending, and many participants proceeded to employ their reasons for accepting the first Compromise in the service of negotiating a second. "The harmony of the union, and the peace and prosperity of the white population most excited our sympathies [in 1820]," Niles argued. Although some people had exaggerated the danger to the Union, the new debate revived earlier fears of sectional parties, of "Hartford men" and "Virginia influence." In settling the issue by opting for a middle course against the "sectional or party-like stand of extremes," Congress had proved that the peace and prosperity of the Republic could be protected only by forbearance, moderation, and mutual respect. The Monroe administration organ, the *National Intelligencer*, agreed with Niles's analysis. It attacked the Missouri constitution as unnecessary and provocative, but seeing the continued congressional paralysis as far worse, it welcomed the resolution's passage as a sign of restored harmony.[36]

According to Don Fehrenbacher, the most important legacy of this struggle was the "bitter memory" of it. Accurate in the sense that the acrimony was unpleasant for Americans to recall, this observation needs clarification, for if many Americans thought the crisis unfortunate, many others were happy that it closed with a compromise instead of with the majority's imposition of a settlement on a large, bitter minority. Henry Clay was quite content to take more than his share of the credit for the outcome—his title of "great compromiser" issued from this struggle, and he never disowned it out of fear for his reputation.[37]

Furthermore, the Missouri Compromise repeated the older patterns in the politics of conciliation. The advocates of compromise, whatever their sectional loyalties, readily adopted the template of ideas molded in the ratification struggle and emphasized in the civics literature. Compromise was patriotic and peaceful and was a reaffirmation of the mutual affections that made America a nation. It was a unique response to unique circumstances, especially to the country's wide dissimilarities of geography and economy.

But the Missouri Compromise left some unfinished business. Part of the pledge was vulnerable to congressional action, a hostage to changing circumstances and altered states of mind. Not so the Compromise of 1833, which, after a much longer and in some ways more dangerous struggle, demonstrated to many Americans that sectional issues could best be settled by quasi-constitutional compacts.

IF THE MISSOURI COMPROMISE revealed how the 1787 paradigm of compromise could help dampen tensions arising from the paradox of slavery in a free republic, the nullification crisis of 1828–33 indicated how broadly such notions about compacts and compromise could be conceived and applied in politics. Although slavery lurked behind each of the major crises that threatened the Union before the Civil War, it is important to understand that *any* issue with the potential of disrupting the Union brought forth the rhetoric of compromise. It was not always clear what issue would sunder the Union, for politicians discovered threats to liberty and union in any of a number of conflicts, from the public lands to the tariff.[38] The custom of drawing one's diagnosis of any current conflict to its abstract, extreme conclusion—to the disruption of the Union—had the effect of obscuring real dangers and of exaggerating minor ones.

South Carolina's challenge to the country in 1832 certainly elevated the tariff controversy to a first-class crisis of the Union, but by placing the question of a tariff within the larger context of majority rule and minority rights, the state raised much broader and more immediate questions about the relationship between policy formulation and the nature of the Union than had the Missouri controversy. For even though the two crises threatened to break up the Union, they did so in fundamentally different ways that aptly illustrated the strengths and weaknesses of the developing compromise tradition. In 1819, the problem of territorial expansion became confused with the politically unresolvable issue of slavery's morality. But in 1832, the immediate question of a tariff became entangled with the familiar conflict over majorities and minorities. The latter issue was at the heart of republican government, and despite the intensity of the debate over it, politicians could find more guidance on it in the writings of the framers than they could on the question of slavery. Despite South Carolina's attempt to convince southerners that protectionism threatened slavery, most Americans agreed that a compromise on the tariff seemed a natural response to a clash of economic interests over taxation.

The protective tariff was the immediate issue in 1832–33. It had become the focus of a broader public conflict between the national economic policies of the postwar administrations of Madison, Monroe, and Adams and the resurgent states' rights movement spurred by the Missouri controversy and intensified by the nationwide depression that had begun in 1819. After the War of 1812, the Republican party had sought to complement the nation's commercial and political independence from Europe by enacting a comprehensive national system of economic development designed to create a home market and strengthen the Union by harmonizing its separate and frequently opposing regional economies. By 1824, most of the pillars of this "American System"—a national bank, a federally supported transportation network, and especially a protective tariff—were on the statute books, further strengthened by a series of Supreme Court decisions that undermined state barriers to the flow of capital and favored federal promotion of economic growth through an expanded construction of the Constitution's commerce and contract clauses.[39]

These policies stimulated strong opposition, which began to congeal in the Democratic party under the leadership of the charismatic war hero

Andrew Jackson. The activist political culture of the Jackson period, which encouraged mass agitation to remove barriers to economic growth and political expression, altered popular attitudes about parties and their relationship to the Union. Paradoxically, parties could be seen both as defenders of the Union and as agents of sectional interests. The trick was to keep sectional tensions quietly subsumed within the larger needs of a national coalition. In particular, the Missouri crisis had prompted important politicians like Martin Van Buren of New York and Thomas Ritchie of Virginia to consider using parties to mute sectional tensions and fortify the federal system's resistance to sectional divisions. The long deadlock between the House and the Senate was, to these men, evidence enough of a fundamental weakness in the bicameral system, one that party loyalties might overcome. And a national coalition of various sectional interests could promote the cause of conciliation and keep the slavery issue out of Congress and presidential politics.

From its inception in the mid-1820s, the Democratic party saw its fundamental duty as the preservation of the Union through intraparty sectional conciliation. By gathering the plain republicans of the North and the planters of the South under a broad platform of states' rights and strict construction, the party could manage and confine explosive sectional issues. "Party confidence is the strongest bond of the Union," the *Democratic Review* declared in 1835. "Like the relation between husband and wife, it destroys individualities," substitutes "a general interest" for sectional loyalties, "and makes the election of every President, a triumph not of a section, but of the whole."[40]

Between 1824 and 1832, Van Buren and his allies in Virginia and Tennessee diligently and successfully constructed the essential elements of this national coalition, but it was some time before the new party's effectiveness as an intersectional stabilizer could be demonstrated. The nullification crisis, for instance, was an in-house dispute that got out of control; it began over a tariff passed in part as a party-building tactic, was intensified by the personal alienation of John Calhoun from Andrew Jackson, and was settled only with a major defection of southern Democrats into the nascent Whig coalition, a process that continued well into the late 1830s. Furthermore, the party faced a revolt of Madisonian conservatives uneasy about Van Buren's unabashed glorification of mass party politics.[41]

In order for Van Buren's idea to work, a strong party organization unified by an efficient press, by a network of state and local committees, and most important by unshakable partisan attachments among the electorate would be needed. But it took many years for the legal reforms in the states to expand the electorate sufficiently to make mass political campaigning and uniform, professionalized organization a strong antidote to sectional pressures. As Richard P. McCormick has demonstrated, the second party system did not fully manifest its distinctive, mass political character until the election of 1840, when the Whig party finally united behind an attractive candidate supported by a nationwide political organization.[42]

The confusing, transitory party situation in the mid-1830s actually contributed to the negotiation of a grand compromise over the tariff because the adjustment from deferential to mass political styles still left room for the interplay of statesmen as yet unfettered by party discipline and able to appeal to the familiar, nonpartisan tradition of compromise. "Parties have arisen *'less generous in their nature'* than the old ones were," Hezekiah Niles sighed in an 1823 editorial that lamented the passing of the "old landmarks" of party. Time brought no relief either. Nine years later, at the peak of the nullification crisis, Niles expressed his frustration with confusing divisions over "tariff and anti-tariff, Jackson, Clay, Calhoun, or Wirt—for the supreme court or against the supreme court, for nullification or anti-nullification—for the bank or against the bank, for internal improvements or anti-internal improvements, *and so forth, and so forth,* the whole making a most curiously conflicting and never-before-heard-of political *compound!*"[43]

The tariff rates enacted in 1828 and Jackson's victory on a reform platform in the momentous election of that year touched off a long conflict over fiscal policy that extended into the 1840s. Not ready to tackle the divisive issue of the tariff until the reduction of the 1812 war debt justified reducing government revenues, Jackson entered office urging caution and appealing to the framers' spirit of compromise for the tariff schedule, which was to come before Congress in 1832.[44] Meanwhile he attacked more exposed targets, including internal improvements and especially the Second Bank of the United States, which his followers blamed for the nation's economic woes.

But many southerners regarded the tariff as the keystone of the American System. In South Carolina, whose postwar bubble of prosperity had burst in the Panic of 1819, the tariff of 1828 and the more moderate (but still protective) rates of 1832 came under fire as unfair, unconstitutional taxes imposed by one section on another. John C. Calhoun, fearing the loss of his power base, sought to manage this outburst of violent opposition by issuing a series of protests and state papers justifying state resistance to unconstitutional federal legislation.

Calhoun's theory of "state interposition," as he preferred to call it, directly challenged the politics of conciliation and the tradition of compromise.[45] Beginning with his "South Carolina Exposition and Protest" (1828) and his "Fort Hill Address" (1831), Calhoun developed a theory of state-federal relations that emphasized the originative role of the states in the making and interpreting of the Constitution. Sovereign states had created a union (not a nation) by temporarily ceding part of their sovereignty to the federal government. As he elaborated on this idea in speeches and eventually in a dense work entitled *A Disquisition on Government* (1853), Calhoun argued that the states could protect their function as the sole intermediaries between the federal government and the people. They could judge the constitutionality of federal laws, and in response to an unconstitutional act, once all redress had proved unavailing, they could interpose their authority, block the enforcement of the law within their borders, and in effect force the other states to call a constitutional convention to resolve the question by a "concurring majority" of at least three-fourths of the states. If the aggrieved states did not succeed in having their complaints redressed, then they could reclaim all of their sovereign powers and legally secede from the Union.[46]

Calhoun frequently argued that his objective was to protect the interests of minorities against a rapacious and oppressive numerical majority and that nullification's real purpose was as a deterrent and not as a routine practice. He denied accusations that he relished disunion, claiming that he sought, through a "suspensive veto," to "compel the installing [of] the highest tribunal provided by the Constitution, to decide on the point in dispute." This would not destroy the Union, he said, but "make it honest."[47]

Calhoun believed that the implementation of his theory would bring compromise between majorities and minorities by wrenching statesmen from their ties to local interests and forcing them to negotiate. In this sense, his assumptions mirrored the constitutional unionist belief that only a disengagement from party politics could enable statesmen to patch up a sectional quarrel. But his theory of concurrent majorities was less about majorities than about a specific minority, and it sought less the common interest than the protection of a minority interest. The operative word in Calhoun's theory was *compel*—this was not conciliation but the deliberate holding of the Union hostage by a disgruntled minority. Although Calhoun tried to minimize the likelihood of secession, his theory nonetheless ruled out the possibility of acquiescence should the dispute fail to go before a constitutional majority for settlement.

Nor did his ideas display the patience that lay behind the Madisonian concept of cultivating concurring majorities *over time*. Calhoun wanted redress *now* on pain of disunion. Unlike the compromise tradition, which drew largely on the divided sovereignty concept underlying Madisonian pluralism, Calhoun's concurrent majorities ultimately appealed to the united will of classes of sovereign states, just as the nationalist theory of Daniel Webster and Joseph Story appealed to the will of a national majority of citizens as the supreme sovereigns in the system.[48]

Calhoun and other nullifiers misunderstood how firmly compromise had become a matter of sentiment as well as of institutional forms and complex checks and balances. Americans had placed the concept within a civic tradition that valued comportment, attitude, and intentions and had identified it with statesmanship. Furthermore, Calhoun's theory made the calling of formal constitutional conventions a much more routine matter than Americans were willing to allow. By the 1830s, the original Constitutional Convention was completely encrusted in layers of patriotic sentiment that placed impossible conditions on any future assemblage or even any future amendment. "The Constitution may need amendment," Niles admitted, "but when the passions are excited, is not the time to amend."[49] Party strife or minority threats of nullification and secession hardly provided the proper circumstances for a convention. The Federalist argument against a second convention remained powerful years later.

No matter how theoretically consistent Calhoun's policy would be, most Americans found it nonsensical and took more notice of the nullifiers' threats ("where we cannot *conciliate* we must *compel*") than of their claims that a new constitutional convention would compromise the tariff issue in a spirit of amity and mutual forbearance. Calhoun's friends frequently warned him that the public did not support forceful resistance as a constitutional remedy for unconstitutional laws. "They see in it all the horrors of war—civil war," a correspondent told him. "They see no difference between the attempt of the Hartford Convention to make a separate peace and the attempt of a single State to have a separate tariff. The question so settled destroys not the [tariff] law but the government."[50]

The nullifiers ignored such warnings, defeated their unionist opposition in South Carolina, and called a state convention in November 1832. That convention then passed an ordinance nullifying the tariffs of 1828 and 1832, setting February 1, 1833, as the date for implementation, and authorizing the state to call up troops to enforce the ordinance and repel any federal attempts to intervene.

South Carolina's action and Calhoun's theory challenged two other theories of the Union's origins: Daniel Webster's argument that a union of citizens preceded the Constitution, and Andrew Jackson's belief that a union of states preceded it. The fact that advocates of both these positions found common cause against nullification tends to blur the differences between and within their viewpoints. Jackson's response to nullification revealed a strong commitment to majority rule, states' rights, and a perpetual union. Emboldened by his resounding victory over Henry Clay in November and angered by South Carolina's refusal to heed his calls for restraint, Jackson began to doff the cloak of moderation and to take a hard line. In his annual message of December 1832, Jackson downplayed compact theory, arguing that the reserved rights of the states were already protected in the Tenth Amendment and through the Constitution's limitations on federal power and did not stem from their undivided, original sovereignty.

His "Proclamation" a week later was more forceful and stepped closer to Webster's interpretation of the Constitution, claiming that the Constitution was a creature of the people acting through their state legislatures and special ratifying conventions. Any attempt by a minority to block enforcement of federal laws therefore was a defiance of a majority will constitutionally expressed and merited severe punishment. In sum, Jackson argued that true Jeffersonian states' rights doctrine supported rule by a constitutional majority, whereas Calhoun's heresy perverted Jefferson into a supporter of minority rule over majority rights.[51]

Webster had already outlined his argument in his famous debate with Robert Y. Hayne in 1830. The Constitution and the Union rested on the ultimate sovereignty of the people, with the states as important but subordinate political communities within the federal system. Outside of the Constitution's restraints on abuses by majorities, Webster pointed to the diffusion of property and to the federally managed balance of class and sectional interests as the sources of moderation and forbearance in cases of severe political conflict. Given his firm belief in the supremacy of federal laws and his ardent protectionism, it is not surprising that he sided with Jackson in this crisis and condemned nullification as extortion, not conciliation. In a speech at a New York antinullification meeting in May 1831, Webster reminded Americans that although the "genuine original spirit" of the government was "of conciliation, of moderation, of candor, and charity, . . . no ground" could be "granted, not an inch, to menace and bluster."[52]

Hezekiah Niles, already throwing fits over rumors of compromise on his beloved protective tariff, agreed with Webster. In a steady stream of increasingly heated editorials, Niles argued that the slavery interest underlay South Carolina's antitariff position, and as in the Missouri crisis, he raised the question of equitable treatment under the three-fifths compromise, as if to drive home the continuing, but waning, restraint of the free states. The lower 1832 rates had already proved that conciliation under a spirit of justice was preferable to concessions forced from a majority by a spirit of defiance. But "CONCESSION, not *conciliation*, was demanded [by the nullifiers], and the 'WE WILL' and 'WE WON'T' substituted for that courtesy which an honest-hearted minority should always extend towards a well-tempered majority. *Passion* was altogether on the side of the weakest."[53] Niles, Webster, and other high protectionists were determined to block any tariff reductions. Webster remained aloof from efforts to mediate the question and instead sought to postpone the tariff to the next session.

Jackson's response to nullification, especially his request that Congress give him sufficient authority and materiel to crush the nullifiers if they resisted enforcement of the tariff laws, appeared to some observers as provocative as Calhoun's theory. His "Proclamation" and the Force Bill that his followers sponsored in January 1833 evoked ambivalent responses from moderates in the crisis, for, as Merrill Peterson has observed, "Jackson terrified: he did not conciliate." Glad that the president was going to stand firm, they nonetheless suspected the tempestuous Old Hero of exploiting the crisis in order to expand his already broad construction of executive power. The growing coalition of anti-Jacksonians could find common cause in opposition to the president's assertion of executive power and could effectively use the politics of conciliation to point up the similarity between Jackson's Force Bill and South Carolina's militant stance.[54]

In fact, Jackson's "Proclamation" sorely divided his followers and eventually helped to isolate him from ongoing efforts at compromise. As Richard Ellis has trenchantly argued, even though the "Proclamation" was a logical extension of the larger views on the nature of the Union outlined in the annual message, most Jacksonians saw it as a radical departure from the presidents's initial moderation on the tariff. They viewed with alarm the wave of applause emanating from old enemies like Webster, Joseph Story, and John Quincy Adams, just as they feared that Jackson's stance would isolate southern moderates and precipitate a major and fatal sectional division of the new Democratic party. Although some southern states had formally condemned nullification by late January 1833, the internal struggles between Jacksonians and Calhounites in Georgia, Alabama, North Carolina, Virginia, and Mississippi prevented endorsements of Jackson's "Proclamation" or of his Force Bill and revealed a good deal of discomfort with the president's willingness to coerce a state to remain in the Union. Nullification and presidential coercion had gone too far in divorcing the spirit of moderation from the arithmetic of majority rule and minority rights.[55]

Little wonder that Martin Van Buren, impresario of the Democratic coalition and a presidential hopeful, urged Jackson to moderate his aggressive statements and called for compromise on the tariff. Administration forces in the House of Representatives responded by devising a bill to reduce tariff rates drastically and quickly over the next two years to the levels of 1816. The bill's sponsor, Gulian Verplanck, a New York free trader, argued that the bill did not completely abandon protection, but it soon became clear that it had little chance against a motley coalition of protectionists and free traders.[56]

With the Democrats facing an internal sectional revolt, with Jackson in an uncompromising temper and drawing closer to Webster, and with Calhoun waiting in anticipation of forcing the government to yield, Henry Clay stepped in to renew a compromise proposal that he had been formulating since December 1832.[57] The situation perfectly suited his talents, ambitions, instincts, and views of policy, subjects to be explored in more detail later. Clay believed that a compromise with Calhoun and the nullifiers was impossible, but his relations with Calhoun were cordial enough to form the basis for an uneasy alliance. More important, Clay detected that moderate southerners, already edgy about Calhoun, shared the Kentuckian's discomfort with Jackson's aggressive handling of the crisis.[58]

Of all the opposition's arguments against Jackson, Clay's attacks against executive usurpation rang particularly true in 1833. Since 1829, Clay had been claiming that Jackson's spoilsmanship and partisanship were subverting legislative prerogatives and overturning settled constitutional policies. In his "Proclamation," Jackson had declared that "the People, . . . and not the States, are represented in the executive branch," just as the members of the House of Representatives are "all representatives of the United States, not . . . of the particular States from which they come." Clay judged these and other assertions "unsound" and "ultra Consolodation," especially when coupled with Jackson's claim, made five months previously in his bank veto message, to an independent executive power of construing the Constitution.[59] And now Clay shuddered at the prospect of Jackson leading an army into South Carolina to dispense the summary justice he had dealt out to Arbuthnot and Ambrister in 1819.

Constitutional doctrine and worries about a marauding Jackson were not the only motives for Clay's action. Because Clay believed that the Union rested on the mutual affections of citizens and states, he feared that any alienation of feelings could lead to dissolution by the common consent of its members. He placed tremendous importance on the policy of conciliation both as preventive and as a first resort in a crisis. Clay worried that Jackson's aggressive language and threatening tone would spread the conflict, not allay it. Already Jackson's support for Georgia's defiance of the Supreme Court over the status of Creek Indians in the state, Clay thought, had encouraged South Carolina, which had "constantly appealed to the successful example of her neighbors," and made the president "the main cause of nullification."[60]

The crisis also gave Clay the opportunity to revive his flagging political fortunes. Soundly beaten in the 1832 presidential election, Clay saw here an opening through which he could regain his support in the South. Clay determined that a sectional pact could be the core of a more powerful and useful opposition party, which he had been trying to build since his days in the Adams administration. Clay believed that the South's opposition to the tariff encouraged northern abolitionists who blamed slavery for the South's refusal to accept protectionism. Clay hoped, in effect, to extend the compromise between northern commerce and southern slavery in the Constitutional Convention by forging a pact that would restrain southerners on the tariff and northerners on slavery while protecting the economic interests of both, as the framers had envisioned. Such an appeal to the moderate men of the North and the South could give Clay the mediated triumph that could elevate him to the presidency, for it would encourage the kind of defections from Jackson's camp that Clay believed would vindicate the exercise of reasoned, statesmanlike conciliation.[61]

Henry Clay's compromise settlement, like his other compromises, offered a package of concessions wrapped in the language of conciliation. His plan made concessions on the tariff while relying on the Force Bill as an incentive for southerners to negotiate. Clay's bill for the distribution of the proceeds of federal land sales also was reintroduced in order, as many procompromise senators thought, to mollify protectionists by keeping up the fiscal pressure to renew protective tariffs once the national debt had been paid.[62] An ardent opponent of nullification and secession, Clay had reluctantly acquiesced in the Force Bill by admitting its necessity while depriving it of his vote in the knowledge that it would pass in tandem with his "olive branch" tariff measure.[63] The plan's centerpiece was a tariff schedule gradually reduced to a flat 20 percent ad valorem rate by 1842 (later changed to home valuation), which could effectively keep protectionism alive in political discourse while making the revenue standard a reality in fiscal policy for the near future.

Clay recognized what high protectionists did not—that to keep the tariff "disenthralled from party political excitements" (as Niles desired), it was necessary to disarm critics of their claims against the tariff's sectional inequities while temporarily suspending the operation of the protective principle. A high tariff was not a stable tariff, he believed, because it provoked disputes that made policy a hostage to changing party fortunes. Stability and predictability were more important to manufacturers *and* planters than extremely high or extremely low tariff rates.[64]

Clay's parliamentary gifts served him well in pushing his plan. He overcame opposition in the House, bested Webster in a verbal duel in the Senate, and cajoled manufacturers and free traders from both parties to obtain passage of the land, tariff, and Force bills on March 1, 1833, which he celebrated as "the most important Congressional day that ever occurred." Jackson signed the Force and tariff acts and pocket vetoed the land bill.[65]

Clay's defense of his plan, both in 1833 and for many years thereafter, was a model of constitutional unionist argumentation that emphasized history, sentiment, mutuality, and honor as the guarantors of what he regarded as sectional compacts that cultivated a deliberate consensus among the people. Admitting that one Congress cannot formally bind another, Clay declared that federal laws nevertheless "created a species of public faith which could not be rashly broken." The public's security against any changes in the compromise "was in the character of the bill—as a compromise," for history would "faithfully record the transaction," narrate the extraordinary nature of the conflict, and point to its peaceful aftermath. Clay asked:

> When all this was known, what Congress, what legislature, would mar the guaranty? What man, who is entitled to deserve the character of an American statesman, would stand up in his place, in either House of Congress, and disturb this treaty of peace and amity? . . . [That] great principle of compromise and concession which lies at the bottom of our institutions [will] remove that alienation of feeling which has so long existed between certain parts of this widely spread confederacy, so as to enable us to transmit to after-times the substantial blessings, as well as the name, of the glorious fabric of wisdom which our fathers bequeathed to us.[66]

Four years later, Clay was repeating these arguments for the distinctive nature of compromise in order to fend off attempts to alter the tariff measure. The Compromise of 1833 had removed the tariff from party strife, he maintained. "There are some things too dear to be dragged into the vortex of political contest, and made the objects of party calculation." Searching for a precedent, Clay put the "much agitated Missouri question" in this class of legislation. "Have not other great interests of this Union been permanently compromised by acts which are equally within the power of Congress with the law of 1833?" he asked. In a remarkable aside, Clay treated the Missouri Compromise not as an unfinished pledge to freedom north of the compromise line but as a continuing pledge of sectional restraint on the slavery issue and therefore as a benefit to southerners now seeking to dismantle the tariff measure. The Missouri law was repealable, Clay reminded the Senate; but those southerners who demanded "a violation of our implied faith" regarding the 1833 compromise in effect endorsed the kind of pledge breaking that would threaten other sectional compacts. "What propriety is there in lending ourselves to a violation of another compromise, while we hold fast to this, which is so dear to them?"[67]

The real value of compromise, he argued, lay not in its details but in its general effects: mutual sacrifices protected rival interests and opinions from harm by locking them into a permanent embrace that only the deliberate sense of a majority could untangle over a long period of time. Just look at the aftermath of the compromise's passage, he urged. Peace and order were proof of its consensual basis. "Do you find here no evidence that it has been the understanding of the American people that that law was to be respected, and was to be held inviolate?"[68]

Clay offered Americans a kind of compromise different from that presented by Calhoun. Whereas Calhoun could trust only constitutional majorities expressed formally through the amending process, Clay's concurring majorities acted through Congress, conciliating minorities and majorities through normal legislation whose unique quality as a compromise binding in honor over time reminded Americans of the dangerous currents just beneath the surface of politics while it simultaneously cinched the cords of union more tightly than before.[69]

IT IS EASY to regard the sectional bargains of 1820–21, 1833, and even 1850 as crisis legislation enacted just as the nation's clock struck midnight. But it is important to realize that none of these crises broke suddenly upon the country, all of them involved familiar issues and old sectional animosities, and in each case Americans chose to settle the controversy through congressional compromises and not through amendments, judicial decisions, or national referenda. The growing tendency to make sectional compromise a constitutional ritual illustrated the thickening web of constitutional custom, of a growing merger among legislative precedent, political culture, and popular perceptions of the constitutional heritage, a merger that united history, ethics, and sentiment within a selective politics of conciliation.

The process of supplementing a written constitution with a prescriptive one based on custom and evolving through deliberative consensus over time was at work in a range of constitutional fields and political issues as well. The constitutionality of a protective tariff was as hotly debated as that of the national bank and of slavery, yet unlike those issues, the protective tariff did not face a judicial test. Instead, a consensus had developed through successive public debates, election campaigns, and congressional enactments and had culminated in the Compromise of 1833, which accepted a middle solution (to acquiesce in the constitutionality—but, for the near future, not in the policy—of protection) and permanently disarmed the tariff as a cause of disunion.[70]

Compromise encompassed broader ground than the slavery issue, then. Declaring a belief common among his fellow politicians, President John Tyler pointed out in 1843: "The prominent interest of every important pursuit of life requires for its success permanency and stability in legislation. These can only be obtained by adopting as the basis of action moderation in all things, which is as indispensably necessary to secure the harmonious action of the political system as of the animal system." Union, he argued, was "the great interest, equally precious to all," and "should be fostered and sustained by mutual concessions and the cultivation of that spirit of compromise from which the Constitution itself proceeded."[71]

Tyler was echoing the messages of other presidents, especially Jackson, Van Buren, and William Henry Harrison, who had appealed to compromise in the spirit of George Washington.[72] Compromise as sentiment naturally emphasized statesmanship, for only great statesmen could cultivate the affections of the citizenry and elevate a divided nation's attention to the Union, as the civics writers had urged. Indeed, the civics literature supported the popular tradition of burying the substance of sectional compromises within their spirit, pointing out that the crises of 1820 and 1833 had been met and settled by great men. The Reverend Charles A. Goodrich told his young readers that the nullification crisis "was a season of peril through which we passed. But the God of our fathers imparted energy & wisdom to our rulers, and the violence of civil discord was allayed—and harmony and peace were restored" by Clay's "act of pacification between the north and the south—a middle course between extremes."[73]

Such complacency ignored the growing influence of party and sectional tensions within the country. These crosscutting pressures emerged in the late 1830s and the 1840s to challenge the compromise tradition's emphasis on stability, sentiment, and statesmanship. The rise of rival, reductionist, pro- and antislavery constitutionalisms pierced the rhetoric of mutuality and began to encroach upon the compromise tradition. Party organizations blurred the distinctive attributes of men like Clay, muting them under the imperatives of "availability" and the necessity of silence on divisive questions.

Historians agree that the new party system offered strong alternatives to sectional pressures and that it generally worked the way Van Buren had envisioned.[74] The parties suppressed sectional tensions by hitching local interests to national economic issues and to accusations of their opponents' corruption and declension and by conforming to the ramshackle federal system that permitted widely divergent platforms in different localities. If the parties ran out of those issues they had found most effective in suppressing sectional pressures, however, then the long-postponed slavery question might reemerge as a party issue. Yet it seems clear that throughout the life of the second party system, sectional tensions challenged and fed on the very partisanship that was supposed to mute them. The nature of partisan campaigning and rhetoric mitigated against a consensus on parties as legitimate bulwarks of the old Union; charges and countercharges of attempting to undermine the Constitution, a staple of party rhetoric, weakened the legitimacy of the system and left it vulnerable to rival sectional constitutionalisms.

The resurgence of the slavery issue in the late 1830s and the 1840s, then, intensified the bitterness of partisan rancor as it simultaneously drove party politicians into a defensive posture. A new generation of party leaders (especially Democrats), confident that the cement of their own parties could contain sectional pressures, saw fewer reasons to be limited by old sectional compromises (like the Missouri Compromise) when searching for ways to soothe sectional feelings. A nervous defensiveness replaced the older, calmer appeals to mutual sacrifice and statesmanlike detachment. James K. Polk remarked at his inauguration in 1845:

> Every lover of his country must shudder at the thought of the possibility of its dissolution, and will be ready to adopt the patriotic sentiment, "Our Federal Union—it must be preserved." To preserve it the compromises which alone enabled our fathers to form a common constitution for the government and protection of so many States and distinct communities, of such diversified habits, interests, and domestic institutions, must be sacredly and religiously observed. Any attempt to disturb or destroy these compromises, being terms of the compact of union, can lead to none other than the most ruinous and disastrous consequences.[75]

A keen observer might have noted the tone of defensiveness here. Unlike the exhortations to the spirit of compromise that had marked previous addresses and speeches by statesmen, Polk's remark anticipated the rigid combination of finality, nonintervention, and arid constitutional literalism that would mark the soulless statecraft of the Democratic party in the 1850s. Indeed, Polk himself would fail to persuade his party to adopt the extension of the Missouri line as an equitable resolution to the conflict over slavery in the West. Democrats would instead add popular sovereignty to their traditional spread-eagle expansionism as the way to heal sectional rifts.

Constitutional unionists acting in the compromise tradition might have accepted the logic but recoiled at the context of Polk's statement. Agreeing with Polk and his followers that sectional compromises ought to stand undisturbed, they nonetheless pointed to the *spirit* of compromise as more important than the substance of compromise, which could be subject to party whims. They observed how sectionalism and party strife seemed to go hand in hand, and they remained skeptical about the ability of a two-party system to contain the two. A compromise tradition that had stressed conciliation and toleration was increasingly yielding to a code of silence that greatly restricted the latitude of statesmen to fashion any new settlement. Foremost among these constitutional unionists was Henry Clay, the great popularizer of the aging compromise tradition. Clay's popularity stemmed at least in part from his reputation as a great compromiser; voters saw in him those qualities they identified with the compromise tradition. Because Clay's understanding of compromise stemmed from that interaction of temperament, ethics, and experience that the civics writers talked so much about, his conception of the polity, the Union, and the Constitution deserves closer attention before we can understand the settlement of 1850, Clay's and the antebellum world's last compromise.

4 Compromise and Statesmanship

Henry Clay's Union

Truth and justice, sound policy and wisdom, always abide in the middle ground.
—Henry Clay

"When business of whatever nature, is to be transacted in a deliberative assembly, or in private life," Henry Clay lectured John Randolph during a sharp debate in 1824, "courtesy, forbearance, and moderation, are best calculated to bring it to a successful conclusion."[1] Two years later Randolph's exquisitely sculptured insults and taunts from the Senate floor led Clay to forget his advice as the two men paced off with pistols on the Virginia side of the Potomac. Poor marksmanship and faulty weapons left this long and bitter personal feud to fester. But years later, as he passed through the capital while Clay was busy urging Congress to enact his compromise tariff, Randolph, ill and near death, asked to be taken into the Senate "to hear that voice once again." Reconciliation followed. "There was no explanation, no intervention," Clay later recalled of their final meeting. "Observing him in the Senate one night, feeble, and looking as if he were not long for this world; and being myself engaged in a work of Peace, with corresponding feelings, I shook hands with him. The salutation was cordial on both sides." Political conciliation won fame and risked censure, but it also could help bring old enemies together across the gulf widened by partisan bickering and ideological warfare. Similar scenes would occur in the aftermath of other grand compromises, too.[2]

To Henry Clay, conciliating enemies was a form of conquering them. It was a political necessity for the leader of a minority party dependent on defections from the other side, and it was a way to reconcile his own passion for politics with his desire to play the role of moderate statesman. Thus, remonstrating his temperamental son Henry, he noted that civility does not signify a retreat from principle: "to all men we should be civil, but there is no incompatibility between the practice of the greatest urbanity and the most ste[a]dfast adherence to our principles." The great irony of the Kentuckian's career was that the more he attempted to project the image of civil, sober moderation in the tradition of early republican statesmanship, the more distant became the ultimate objective of peace and union under his leadership.[3]

It is easy to blame Clay for this failure. His well-known obsession with winning the presidency has become the standard explanation for his frequent political blunders and apparent blindness to changing currents in popular thinking. And how else can we explain his fondness for "the middle ground," where evasive compromises covered his contradictory policy shifts with the halo of patriotic sentiment that he passed off as serious political thought? Clay "thirsted for the Presidency, secretly, persistently, all his life long," George Dangerfield tells us in a memorable portrait of the Kentuckian, "and like Tantalus he thirsted in agony and in vain." A long line of Clay-watchers have agreed.[4]

Yet it is misleading to place Clay's compromises at the service of a lifelong lust for the presidency. Clay's presidential ambitions did not stir until he had at least twenty years of public service to his credit. And whatever the extent of those ambitions, Clay's business address for over forty years was the legislature, a workplace that did much to shape his thinking and his tactics and where he spent just as much time trying to limit the presidency as he did trying to win it.[5]

Daniel Walker Howe has already begun the long-overdue challenge to the traditional depiction of Clay as a narrow partisan. Pointing out that Clay has been overestimated as a politician and underestimated as a statesman, he argues that Clay's frequent political blunders could hardly qualify him as a consummate politician. To Clay, compromise protected cherished principles and nourished a starving ambition for fame, both of which merged in his conception of statesmanship and duty. In a study of the Whig party, Thomas Brown has shown that Clay's popularity cannot simply be attributed to a sparkling personality, a mastery of parliamentary maneuver, a melodious voice, or an adeptness in the art of cloakroom negotiations. The vast majority of Clay's supporters never heard him speak or felt the supple touch of his parliamentary gifts. To them, Brown argues, Clay's appeal was as a symbol of union and peace—of compromise and statesmanship and consensual politics in the old-fashioned way. Clay sought to tap this sentiment in forging intersectional consensus on divisive issues, only to fail, Brown continues, because his political thought apotheosized an organic, consolidated union as the transcendent objective of political action. His compromises sacrificed the ultimate end of union—liberty—to the Union itself.[6]

Although Clay would probably bristle at Howe's declaration that he was a "brilliant ideologist," it is instructive to take Clay's political ideas seriously, to see him as a civic educator with definite ideas about the way the Constitution worked. Experience, if not penetrating intellect, qualified him as a trenchant observer of constitutional processes. In his half-century of public service, Clay practiced law before the Supreme Court and exhorted hardscrabble jurors on the Kentucky circuit, served in the Kentucky legislature and filled the Speaker's chair in the House of Representatives longer than anyone else in the nineteenth century, fought and lost three presidential campaigns and about as many nomination battles, and helped build an anti-Jacksonian opposition and led it through three and a half terms in the Senate.

Furthermore, Clay's role as policymaker, which included long service on every major Senate standing committee from finance to manufactures to foreign affairs, exposed him to the great problem of squaring public policy with the Constitution. In an era that measured policy against the text of the Constitution, experienced politicians like Clay got their constitutional education in office, not in the classroom or in the comfort of the study. These men were not armchair constitutionalists. And few of them practiced the art of constitutional politics with such persistence, zeal, and ability as Henry Clay.

If we let Clay explain compromise, instead of using compromise to explain Clay, his contribution to American political thought becomes more intelligible. And we can clarify the association between Clay and the compromise tradition by putting compromise in its proper position in Clay's political outlook. Clay acted within a tradition that he did not create; he was a popularizer, not a philosopher. All of his justifications for compromise voiced conventional perceptions of what compromise had come to mean in mainstream American politics. As constitutional theory, Clay's ideas paled before the cerebral productions of Daniel Webster or

John C. Calhoun. But when viewed as appeals to a popular understanding of the Constitution and the Union, they also reveal far more than the man's inner tensions and ulterior motives. They underscore Clay's belief that true compromise in the tradition of the founders was possible only in a conciliatory atmosphere shaped by reasoned discourse and civility.

Certainly Clay sensed that compromise as a general proposition risked accusations of timid temporizing, narrow expediency, and an abandonment of principle. No one was more sensitive to the subtle nuances of the term than the man accused of having made a "corrupt bargain" to gain high office in 1824.[7] And compromise was not Clay's guiding philosophy; he refused on many occasions to compromise, even though urged by his friends who cited his well-known association with the tactic. Clay understood that the dynamics of party strife hardened hearts against compromise and conciliation. In fact, Clay's experience as a sectional compromiser would teach him, and the country, about the way such grand compromises imposed limits on party strife, as the founders had hoped. And Clay also understood that in the American context, the term *compromise* evoked images of the framers, the Constitution, and a responsible government that sought conciliation before confrontation, and compromise before civil war.

Of course, Clay was trying to protect, not launch or remake, a constitutional union. His objectives were preeminently conservative, for his actions aimed at maintaining the existing Union, not at creating a new one. "I desire to see in continued safety and prosperity *this* Union, and no other Union," he told the Senate in 1838. "I go for the Union as it is, one and indivisible, without diminution." Perhaps the ultimate fate of the Union would depend on some prospective blending of economic interests fostered by Clay's comprehensive economic program, but in Clay's eyes the existing Union was to be the proper focus of policy, and its immediate fate depended on the citizens' mutual affections, which, properly managed by a beneficent government and wise statesmanship, restrained through sacrifice the passions of party and section. "Our system is one of compromises," an observer heard Clay tell the House during the Missouri crisis, "and in the spirit of harmony come together, in the spirit of brothers compromise any and every jarring sentiment or interest which may arise in the progress of the country. There is security in this; there is peace; and fraternal union." Here, succinctly stated, were Clay's reasons for compromise: peace, stability, and "the Union as it is."[8]

As we have seen, Clay helped negotiate important sectional pacts in 1821 and 1833 as legislative agreements binding in honor if not strictly in law. He exploited his personal magnetism and the public's desire for tranquillity and stability in legislation to impose mutual sacrifices upon sectional interests. This use of compromise did not emerge from focused study of the Constitution and its traditions; he was not known for rarefied argumentation or prodigious research into issues, although the barrenness of his intellect has been greatly exaggerated. The roots of Clay's thinking about compromise rested on an understanding of the Union, the Constitution, and the nature of American politics as filtered through his experience as a statesman, legislator, and candidate. This experience taught Clay a good deal about the sources of conflict in the American polity; and it is from such observations about conflict and its many forms (especially parties and personalities) that attitudes about conflict resolution spring.

In fact, Clay's views on these subjects were already firm before the Jacksonian onslaught dashed his hopes of reaching the pinnacle of national leadership. The last half of his long public career became an elaborate defense of Henry Clay's Union as it had evolved in an earlier age when statesmanship aimed at conserving a civic ideal and a constitutional heritage. Clay's views of principle, parties, and policy—the constitutional union; National Republicanism, Whiggery, and the Democracy; slavery and political economy—all illuminate the simple fact that, as William H. Seward remarked in his eulogy to Clay, "conservatism was the interest of the nation, and the responsibility of its rulers, during the period in which he flourished."[9]

"IF ANYONE DESIRE to know the leading and paramount object of my public life," Henry Clay told the electorate in his first Alabama letter of July 1, 1844, "the preservation of this Union will furnish him the key."[10] This typical pledge of fidelity to the Union invites closer inspection, for Clay's unionism was the most consistent theme of his public life and guided his understanding of the Constitution and of the policies needed to preserve it. Unfortunately, this is a very difficult task because

Clay was not famous as a penetrating thinker on the roots of the political order, a weakness that he readily confessed and that his contemporaries and biographers uniformly observed.[11]

Clay's political beliefs did contain apparent contradictions that resist a comprehensive explanation. On the one hand, his avid patriotism, nationalist political economy, and strong opposition to secessionism suggest that he was championing a rigid, nationalist conception of the Union, one that, unlike the Democrats' more confederationist interpretation, looked forward to the materialistic nationalism of the Republican party of the Gilded Age and that anticipated the "positive liberal" state of the twentieth century. Thus, his compromises seemed to reflect the broker-statesmanship that marked the policies and leadership styles of great presidents from Jackson to Franklin Roosevelt.[12]

On the other hand, Clay's support for the "reserved rights of the states" in the slavery controversy (especially during the conflicts over slavery in Missouri, Arkansas, and Florida) implies that Clay was a closet southerner in western guise, a strict constructionist who agreed with John C. Calhoun on the ends, but not the means, of protecting slavery and states' rights.[13] And it was Clay's strict constructionist arguments in 1811 that helped to defeat the recharter of the Bank of the United States (which later became an important part of Clay's American System).

Clay's apparent inconsistency has left some historians so perplexed about the Kentuckian's real views of the Constitution and the Union as to lead one to claim that Clay "moved from broad to narrow to various in-between interpretations of it with the ease of changing his vest."[14] Some of this confusion about Clay stems from modern conceptions of states' rights and nationalism as opposite poles, when in fact Clay often reconciled the two through his constitutional unionism, which, like Madison's famous statement in Federalist no. 39, comprehended the Constitution as neither wholly national nor wholly federal. Clay saw absolutely no inconsistency, for instance, in vigorously supporting, in March 1820, Missouri's exclusive jurisdiction over slavery and championing a protective tariff about a month later. He thought that this was intelligent constitutionalism and smart politics; it reflected his conservative belief in the limits of both political controversy and the reach of the Constitution while it kept him squarely in the political center, where he most liked to be. Most important, it mirrored his essentially Madisonian conception of the Constitution's division of sovereignty between the states and the federal government.[15]

Clay's political thought distinguished between the "Union" and the "nation." He believed that the nation preexisted the Constitution and the Union—indeed, the three were in sequential, but not interchangeable, relation to one another. The nation, he argued, consisted of a vast and diverse people with "great and powerful principles of cohesion": a common origin, language, law, love of liberty, and history. But these centripetal forces did not create binding mutual affections or national fraternity; they were a latent force for political union, but not openly so. There were stronger, centrifugal forces at work, especially the unalterable conditions of climate, geography, and deeply rooted social and economic institutions that tended to rivet people's perceptions of their welfare close to home and to frustrate efforts at union. This tendency toward separation was especially clear under the Articles of Confederation, the first real attempt at a perpetual union, whose "alarming weakness" and "debility" Clay once cited as more fearsome than a consolidated union.[16]

The Constitutional Convention, Clay believed, sought to consolidate the Union into a peaceful, working confederacy of states, interests, and citizens. In 1818, for instance, after quoting George Washington's cover letter about the Philadelphia Convention's compromises, Clay argued, "Union, . . . peace external and internal, and commerce, but most particularly union and peace were the great objects of the framers of this Constitution, and should be kept steadily in view in the interpretation of any clause of it." The Union, therefore, was not the nation but was, he told Edward Everett in 1824, "precisely what the Constitution" made it, "neither more nor less." He added, "We must look to that instrument for its terms, powers, &c. which wd. carry us back to the original question." The Union was simply the national government, limited and defined by a compact, the Constitution. "The nation may alter that constitution, . . . but until altered it is the grant and the limit of the government. The *government* cannot go out of the Constitution, and appeal to our existence as a Nation for a source of power."[17]

The primacy of peace and union was at the center of Clay's thinking about politics, compromise, and the Constitution. Clay's unionism dictated compromise, but not necessarily the objective of elevating an undefined union over the principles it was supposed to subserve. Promoting the domestic tranquillity was a duty prescribed in the Constitution's preamble and was the starting point of union-saving efforts. Clay sought not just to avert civil war through stopgap compromise but also to prevent it through union-strengthening policies, a distinctive, singular mission for his generation. The problem for Clay was not whether the Union should be preserved, but whether it should be preserved through peaceful conciliation achieved by negotiation and preventive policy or through confrontation and coercion.

Henry Clay's Union was not an absolute, indissoluble consolidation of states and citizens that would brook no opposition. The nation was indivisible, but the Union could be broken up at any moment—peacefully by the states' consent as well as violently through civil war. Although Clay vigorously opposed secession as both illegal and lethal to the Union, he sadly acknowledged the possibility of disunion.[18] As an opponent of "all new lights in politics, if not in religion," Clay had deeply conservative instincts about politics and equally disturbing fears for the Union's survival. The Union existed at the sufferance of peaceful constitutional majorities—by a common consent that no *single* state, class of states, or individual citizen could legally deny. Clay believed that this consensus was "the most valuable element of union, mutual kindness, the feelings of sympathy, the fraternal bonds," which united the nation. This fragile yet hopeful mutuality underlay the Union and dictated the course of statesmen and politicians. The great enemy of "mutual affections" was fanaticism, especially of the partisan or sectional variety, both of which were prone to ideological excesses.[19]

Clay's conception of the Union as a fragile confederacy of states, interests, and citizens informed his constitutionalism, which relied much more on James Madison than on Thomas Jefferson or John Marshall. Like Madison's, Clay's constitutionalism evolved toward a looser and more elitist framework as a result of the War of 1812, eventually surpassing Madison's cautious reliance on the amending process as the prerequisite to any ambitious program of national economic legislation. There was a personal element to this; Clay's legislative style and his general approach to national policy matured during Madison's turn at the helm, from 1809–17. The two men and their families became lifelong friends after Clay first met

Madison in 1807, and for years thereafter Clay frequently sought Madison's advice and support on public measures and constitutional issues ranging from the tariff to the veto power. He even copied Madison's ideas in subsequent letters to friends and political supporters.[20]

House Speaker Clay and President Madison disagreed more on the scope than on the process of determining the constitutionality of national economic legislation. Madison preferred a constitutional amendment to authorize internal improvements and vetoed the Bonus Bill of 1817 as a legislative usurpation of state powers, but he did not rule out a judicial or congressional settlement directing "an intermediate course" between the extremes of states' rights and consolidation. Clay was shocked by Madison's veto and preferred a congressional resolution authorizing the program, but he did not rule out a constitutional amendment.[21]

Despite the president's reluctance to fully endorse Clay's broad reading of the Constitution, Madison did appreciate the Kentuckian's attempts to reconcile interests through compromise. Madison's own unionism became more sentimental and ardent near the close of his life. His final "Advice to My Country," written in October 1834, urged Americans to cherish and perpetuate the "Union of the States." A few days after Madison's death in 1836, George Tucker recounted to Clay how the former president's admiration for the Kentuckian's compromises had stirred Madison's hope that Clay might successfully "fall upon some plan of compromising" the slavery issue and that "then all parties . . . might unite & make him President." Clay could receive no higher compliment or command from a more respected source.[22]

Clay, like Madison and other moderate Republicans, viewed the procedure of constitutional interpretation in broad, dynamic terms, as a function of the system's process of collecting and sifting the sense of the people over time through the states, through the three branches of the federal government, and especially through the give-and-take of public debate in Congress. Practice would make precedent, he believed, supplementing the interpretations received through the instrument's "cotemporaneous expositions" and its evolving case law and those "fixed by an uninterrupted course of Congressional legislation."[23]

The "cotemporaneous exposition" that Clay most admired was Madison's Virginia Resolves of 1798, which Clay frequently extolled as the finest piece of constitutional exegesis that he had ever read or would read.[24] Although the Resolves claimed for the states a right to review and protest unconstitutional federal laws and therefore are known chiefly for their enunciation of a compact theory of the Constitution, they did not firmly locate the full power of constitutional review. Nor did they support the radical position, outlined in Jefferson's Kentucky Resolutions, that a state might go beyond mere protest and might "nullify" an unconstitutional federal law within its borders. As constitutional scholars have noted, the Resolves still accepted the theory of divided sovereignty but did not outline a clear method of reconciling collisions between states and the federal government.[25]

Clay, who accepted Marshall's rulings on judicial review and federal supremacy, denounced as "a modern interpretation" the Old Republicans' claim that the Resolves sanctioned strict constructionism.[26] Broad construction was a natural result of human imperfection, he argued. The written word alone, he pointed out in 1818, was an insufficient safeguard against ambiguities of language and meaning. Reliable interpretation of the Constitution rested on broader foundations than simple reference to its wording or to the pronouncements of a few individuals.[27] Nor did Clay share Madison's apprehensions over the Marshall Court's support for broad construction because he believed that the rest of the system contained sufficient safeguards against abuse.

Given this problem of ambiguity, how were constitutional collisions to be avoided? The judiciary, Clay thought, provided the "Federal means to effectuate the constitutional resolves of the Federal will," but because it was remote from the people, slow to operate, and of limited jurisdiction, this branch's interpretations needed to be supplemented elsewhere. If the Supreme Court was the last resort in expounding the instrument prior to a final appeal to the amending process, Congress was still the first (but not the *only*) resort—paramount to the executive and the embodiment of the collective sense of the people.[28]

Policy "fixed" constitutional principle into law; continuous congressional enactments over time created a "species of faith" in the law that was akin to constitutional principle itself. In Congress, the real interests of the nation were consulted, debated, and reconciled by statesmen acting with moderation, prudence, and the same nonpartisan detachment as the framers themselves.[29] This view stressed the constitutional significance of long-term, comprehensive policy, distinguishing it from mere administrative enactments, like patronage or the organization of executive departments, which were more justifiable targets of party ambition. Here Clay was blurring the distinction between fundamental constitutional law, and legislative statute law. And Madison would oppose such a course; but Clay was also using Madisonian ideas, for even Madison realized that the passage of time affirms precedent, assures stability, and offers opportunity for refinements to meet the dissent of changing minorities.[30]

Clay's experience as a legislator taught him that Congress plays the paramount role in settling conflicts and heading off future trouble. The proper strategy, he maintained, was conciliation: when constitutional collisions loomed, "moderation and good sense" had to "come into the councils of government." The harmony of the system could be preserved only through forbearance, liberality, practical good sense, and mutual concession, all qualities of the good citizen and the good ruler. A sound discretion—restrained by the legislator's oath to the Constitution, by "a regard for our fair fame," and by the knowledge that the representative was subject to his own laws—would simultaneously temper debate, strengthen the Constitution, and protect citizens from abuse.[31]

Constitutional interpretation by Congress was not, however, a simple, impartial, or abstract process. Clay believed that the framers' objects (peace and Union) must guide any constructions of their work and that current circumstances and uniform practice must help to define what policies can serve this purpose. Experience confirmed Clay's and Madison's belief that the country's diverse interests, states, and regions would constantly have to be reconciled in order to protect the Union against extremes of consolidation and disunion. Although the triumph of Jefferson in 1800 had ended the danger of a "consolidated" union under the tyranny of Federalism, the War of 1812 demonstrated that a new danger of dissolution from within still existed. New England's flirtation with secession; the incompetence, petty strife, and disorganization that had plagued the war effort; and the open contempt by the British that Clay had witnessed during the peace negotiations illustrated the effects of what he later called the "water-gruel regimen" that a strict constructionist policy had imposed on the nation's ability to meet a crisis. Although Clay joined in the general celebration that the war's conclusion had successfully demonstrated the country's national character abroad, he still worried about internal strife, especially of the sectional variety.[32]

The war ended the national debate over the stability of republics, but it did not foreclose the question of the Union's origins and future security. Apparently the diverse sections and economic interests of the country did not automatically harmonize; they had to be promoted, fostered, and reconciled in order to secure the Union. The experience forced Clay to conclude that the framers' effort to promote a more perfect union through compromise had marked not only the beginning of the nation's trials but also the path of duty for succeeding generations. "The true friend to his country," he lectured Federalist critics of the war in 1813, "knowing that our constitution was the work of compromise, in which interests apparently conflicting were attempted to be reconciled, aims to extinguish or allay prejudices."[33]

In sum, Clay's Constitution was both national and federal, shaped, but not determined, by the evolution of events and policies as interpreted by disinterested statesmen who surveyed "the whole fabric of the state; to accommodate it to the new circumstances" in which it was placed. If Clay lacked Madison's awesome intellect, he more than made up the deficit with his ambitious effort to realize Madison's more cautious constitutionalism through the enactment of permanent, union-promoting policies that stressed the conciliation of conflicting interests and sections. The "son" had learned his civics lesson well from the Father of the Constitution.[34]

Clay entered the postwar period determined to act on President Madison's suggestion in 1815 that the nation consider a more vigorous commitment to economic development as a way to secure its hard-won independence from foreign commercial domination.[35] Agreeing with Madison and men like Hezekiah Niles and the increasingly influential Philadelphia school of political economists, Clay believed that the encouragement of domestic manufacturing would loosen the country's ties to a domineering Old World. But he further shifted the emphasis of nationalist economics to focus on domestic security against internal divisions, highlighting the preservation of the Union against sectional imbalances.[36]

Actually Clay never mastered the arcane language and logic of nationalist political economics. His many attempts to convince southerners that a protective tariff would neither raise their costs of production nor lower the price of cotton denied the realities most planters confronted each time they tried to balance the plantation ledger. And the tariff became a convenient target for farmers and small businessmen who sought a comprehensive explanation for the depressions of 1819 and 1837. Clay's tariff speeches bristled with mind-numbing statistics on population, wealth, and the country's fiscal condition but rarely displayed any deep understanding of the significance or application of the figures. Yet Clay's appeals to patriotic, mutual sacrifice for the public good, to the idea that, as he frequently remarked, the tariff was "a matter of mutual concession" and that "the cause of the union required heavy sacrifices," carried the conviction that only "Harry of the West" could convey.[37]

It was only natural for a legislator who believed that "all society is an affair of mutual concession" to design an "American System" as a package of benefits to counteract sectionalism with a stable policy of economic conciliation. Noting in 1824 how Americans acted like "jealous rivals" when fighting over glutted foreign markets, Clay predicted that the protective tariff would "transform these competitors into friends and mutual customers; and, by the reciprocal exchanges of their respective productions, . . . place the confederacy upon the most solid of all foundations, the basis of common interest." A moderate tariff would prevent sectional strife by co-opting sectional demands for either extreme protection or complete free trade.[38]

Roads and canals would revert to the states once they were completed, and federal involvement and maintenance would end. Clay argued, "[Future users] will say, I owe this facility, this convenience, to the providence and sagacity of Congress." A national bank would end the excessive currency imbalances between the West and the East, thereby fostering a stable system of money and credit.[39] The effect of the entire program was embodied in the idea of a home market, where Americans could produce, transport, and market their own goods at stable prices buoyed by a system of uniform credit and currency.

The American System's pocketbook patriotism focused more on protection than production. Its objectives were immediate; it sought to yoke self-interest to the national interest by making people grateful to a paternal government for the blessings of growth and the glow of prosperity, to fix *now* the eyes of an easily distracted people onto the Union. Clay's policy did not envision a government with a blank check to mold economic institutions, create new products, and eliminate undesirable ones or to create the good society by wielding the coercive powers we usually expect government regulators to exercise.

His defense of the American System consistently stressed protection and stability—for existing interests and the existing Union—through the calming distribution of benefits, not the disturbing imposition of penalties. Pointing out the importance of a "moderate" tariff as the cornerstone of a stable policy, Clay reminded an audience in Lexington in 1824 "that the business of government is defense and protection;—that it does not produce nor create."[40] Although Clay applauded Marshall's decision supporting the constitutionality of the national bank and the supremacy of federal over state laws, he interpreted the commerce clause as promotive only, for the power to regulate implies continuance, not prohibition—"it is conservative, not destructive."[41]

In sum, the American System was to be an economic counterpart to the legal skeleton of the Constitution: a political scaffold for a rising economy, within which the vital, generally untrammeled energies of an enterprising people could be unleashed upon a rich and empty continent. Interest and affection would mutually reinforce "this Union," whose current "connexion is merely political." In 1825, when Clay began his fateful alliance with the Adams administration, the implementation of this policy seemed assured.[42]

A policy of such constitutional significance as Clay attributed to the American System could endure, Clay believed, only if it remained free of party manipulation. He frequently expressed his desire to remove the tariff, internal improvements, and other elements of the system from party warfare, hoping to preserve a stable policy resting on the deliberate sense of the people over time. Of course, his opponents and some of his friends would frown on elevating mere policy to the exalted plane of constitutional principle. But Clay's desire to do this suggested his own shrewd understanding of the Constitution's significance in American political culture, for like Madison, he believed that constitutional issues could be properly deliberated on only when debated as far from partisan rancor and sectional passion as possible.[43]

CLAY'S UNION-SAVING PRINCIPLES pose a difficult problem. If he believed that mutual affections were the cement of the Union, how could he reconcile his desire for civility with the persistent conflict generated by political parties? The very civic ideals he championed warned against party conflict, yet Clay's historical reputation is chiefly that of a great party leader, one whose personality, tactics, program, and career all were deeply intertwined with the fate of the National Republicans and their successors, the Whigs. To save the Union from internal divisions, Clay resorted to party action; to support a policy designed to promote the domestic tranquillity by muting sectional tensions, Clay participated in the creation of a mass party system that carried political agitation into every corner of the Republic.

Considering the traditional image of Clay as a cunning partisan, it seems he would have been comfortable in a Jacksonian party system that harnessed personal ambition to mass politics. Most accounts of Clay's experience as a party leader assume that he made a smooth transition from the deferential politics of the Jeffersonian period to the mass politics of Jacksonian days. Certainly there is a wealth of evidence to support the suspicion that Clay—ambitious, scheming, and well-placed at the center of national politics—had motive and opportunity to pioneer and master a party system that was evolving considerably in the direction of the mass politics we know today.

In his analysis of Clay's multiple public personality, Merrill Peterson has distilled Clay's personae into four types—"the Prince, the Gamester, the Dictator, and the Actor"—not one of which conjures up his reputation as a nonpartisan "great pacificator." When Henry Clay, Jr., considered a career in politics, Clay's advice to him stressed involvement with the people, not detachment. "Cultivate your popularity, maintain a cheerful and friendly intercourse with our fellow citizens, and be in a position to avail yourself of favorable circumstances, just as well as if you were formally announced as a candidate."[44]

Apparently Clay practiced what he preached. He kept up a mammoth correspondence with political operatives around the country and issued a steady stream of controversial public letters on everything from dueling to Mormonism. He had a hand in the organization, leadership, platform, and candidacies of the Whig party and was acknowledged as its chief for almost twenty years. An accomplished sloganeer, Clay used his many policy declarations, public letters, and speeches to rally his supporters across the country and hold them firmly to the Whig standard while his genius for parliamentary theatrics and cloakroom diplomacy forged a strong anti-Jackson coalition in Congress through the 1830s and into the 1840s.[45]

This picture of Clay seems to match the larger contours of the mass democratic political culture of the late 1830s and the 1840s as it has been described by a number of historians. This system achieved Clay's objectives of peace and union by containing and structuring political conflict, offering alternatives to sectional demands, and hitching the powerful cultural urges and economic interests of a footloose electorate to the comprehensive, nationalizing objectives of the party platform. This "partisan imperative," the historian Joel Silbey has written, outweighed the anti-party attitudes of social reformers and ideologues and created a "partisan golden age—a model of a responsible, and responsive party system."[46]

But mass democratic politics did not appear without real controversy among thoughtful Americans.[47] True, the old debate about parties and factions in a republic was now over; Americans no longer argued after the War of 1812 about the necessity or inevitability of parties. But the recognition of this simple reality coincided with a rising concern about the nature of the Union. Parties in *this* Republic, in *this* Union, each claiming to be coextensive with the Union and the exclusive safeguard of its interests, might not structure or contain conflict but might raise it to more frightening levels of emotion and violence. Indeed, it is arguable that even as Americans came to accept the fact that both parties were actuated by patriotic motives and comprised well-intentioned people, the *principles* of the two parties were still antagonistic, a conflict all the more dangerous in an era that did not see principles as compromisable.

Clay's experience with two "party systems" taught him enough about the morphology of parties to realize that party conflict was a mixed blessing at best and an outright danger to the nation's health at worst. He did not enter the Jacksonian era unfettered from old republican notions about parties in a republic. Clay would have been amazed to hear the Jacksonian party system described as "responsible." His belief that the Union's survival depended on the cultivation of mutual affections originated before the age of mass party politics, and the dynamics of two-party combat never convinced him that such conflict preserved the Union.

Instead, bitter experience and many defeats reinforced his Jeffersonian outlook on parties: as the natural products of free institutions, they needed the strong, guiding hand of experienced national leadership to restrain their natural momentum toward dominating all public life. "I am afraid that the desire to put down parties, which you express," Clay told the Reverend William Ellery Channing in 1837, "has more of humanity than practicability in it. They can only, I apprehend, be extinguished, by extinguishing their cause, free Government, a free press, and freedom of opinion. The effort of the wise and the good should be rather directed to moderate their asperity."[48] In Clay's mind, a party's legitimacy depended on the extent to which it aided the operations of reason in politics. Clay tried to treat parties as effective civic educators, but only insofar as they might yield to the strong direction of independent, reasoning statesmen who could "moderate their asperity."

It is important to remember that although Clay was a very successful politician and party leader, he never won the coveted prize at the end of the presidential campaign trail. That failure, despite his strenuous efforts, can be attributed not only to Clay's miscalculations but also to his attempts to square an outdated conception of the way parties should work with a more modern party system that was rapidly changing the conventions and customs that had lubricated the system in older days.

The backdrop for Clay's understanding of compromise, then, was not a prescient politician's conception of interest-group politics, "responsible" parties, or the positive liberal state. His ideas were too limited in scope and too immediate in their objectives to anticipate such a future. Instead, Clay used compromise in the context of a constitutional tradition that had germinated in the early Republic, when the memory of the conciliatory Washington had still been fresh. This constitutional tradition was translated through the party battles of the Jeffersonian era, only to be challenged by a new style of mass politics that required rapid accommodation and a sure sense of the trend of public opinion.

Clay himself accepted parties as inevitable and worked within the system as he understood it.[49] But his initial response to the rise of mass parties was based on his experience with the earlier party system that he had manipulated successfully in his drive for national prominence. A close examination of Clay's career as a party leader, presidential candidate, and shaper of political issues reveals how Clay's observations about sectional and party conflict defined the meaning and place of compromise in Henry Clay's Union. And such an examination further reveals the close connections between compromise, statesmanship, and the conditions of the civic life as Clay observed them.

Clay's first experience with party combat was in Kentucky, were unrestrained partisanship often became violent. After moving to Kentucky from Virginia in 1797, Clay rapidly established himself among the Jeffersonian hard-liners in the state legislature. There his impetuous behavior and gift for parliamentary legerdemain brought him into open conflict with the state's Federalist faction and eventually led to a duel with its leader, Humphrey Marshall. Clay also pursued his campaign against Federalism in Washington, where, after two brief terms in the Senate (1806–7, 1810–11), he won the House Speakership and energized that office as a counterweight to the executive branch. Clay excelled in the factional politics of the Republican party's congressional caucus, which was the center of a party organization that fanned out into the country.

The nation's terrible trial in the War of 1812 greatly influenced Clay's view of parties, as it did his views of national policy. The Federalists' refusal to close ranks in support of the war seemed a fulfillment of the framers' premonitions about the dangers of party strife. Tainted with treason, infected with sectional rancor, and led by grumping harpies who tried to undermine a staggering war effort, the Federalists eventually went to the party grave that Clay believed they richly deserved. If the Jeffersonian revolution of 1800 had successfully checked what Clay called "the career of a mad administration," the disappearance of the Federalists completed the work. The Federalists were dangerous because their sectional bias suggested the formation of a geographical party, the "worst of parties" in this Union. And the attempt to revitalize Federalism through an alliance with antislavery advocates during the Missouri crisis seemed just as alarming and was one of the reasons why the Republicans, with much effort and lingering bitterness, held together enough to close the controversy with the Missouri Compromise.[50]

This experience did not convince Clay that competing parties would disappear with the Federalists, but it did indicate to him that parties would represent warring, incompatible principles between which there was little moral equivalence. Clay's analysis of the party system then and later did not describe both parties as coalitions of diverse economic and social interests; if it had, Clay would have been much more open to compromise with his opponents. Like the civics writers of his day, Clay thought of a party system as an arena for combat between opposing principles. His opponents, well-intentioned but obviously bereft of common sense, were temporarily attached to unsound leaders and dangerous ideas. They would need conversion.

Clay did not believe that party spirit had been extinguished by the postwar "Era of Good Feelings" or that "the factions by which the country" was divided had been "reduced to their primitive elements, and that this whole society" was "united by brotherly love and friendship." Men were still men, he said in 1818, and had not abandoned old principles. One side, he claimed, still cherished liberty, self-government, and equal rights, confided in human nature, relied "much upon moral power," and resorted "to force as an auxiliary only to the operations of reason." The other, "distrustful of human nature," appreciated "less the influence of reason and of good dispositions," and appealed to physical force.[51] The war of 1798 would never end.

It is well to remember, then, that Clay fashioned his program and honed his ambition for the presidency in the factional world of Jeffersonian politics before 1824. The initial success of the American System combined with his own popularity to convince him that he was a natural successor to the presidency. Grooming himself for the position during James Monroe's second term, he tried to act the disinterested statesman by distancing himself from the president on foreign affairs while privately announcing his "fixed determination" to "make no bargains" to obtain the presidency. "I never have nor can intrigue with any person or party on this subject," he stated. He refused to campaign openly through election tours or the purchase of an editor, which he thought was wrong and demeaning.[52] Having used the Speakership to strengthen the House's backbone against the executive, Clay ably built a congressional following that he felt certain by 1824 would support him both in the Republican caucus and in an election thrown into the House.

Clay's disappointing fourth-place finish that year was a clear signal that the political universe was changing and that he had not properly mended political fences around the country, especially in New York, whose byzantine factionalism would repeatedly frustrate Clay for many years to come. The new president, John Quincy Adams, was not amenable to the new political style. But Adams's opponents in the South and the West, claiming that the House election had cheated Andrew Jackson of a deserved victory, immediately began to organize for 1828 by innovating political techniques that directly challenged the style and content of the politics that Clay and Adams had followed in their climb to prominence.

In 1825, Clay accepted Adams's offer of secretary of state and thereby positioned himself for the succession, as Madison, Monroe, and Adams had done before. But he suddenly faced the bruising accusations of thus executing a "corrupt bargain," with all its implications of sordid partisan maneuver and backstage bribery, accusations that struck directly at his public image both as a candidate and as a statesman. Having shaped a program of economic legislation to strengthen the Union, Clay now confronted a Jacksonian declaration of war against his conception of the Union and the Constitution. While implementing Adams's benign patronage policy, Clay discovered that Jackson's supporters were eagerly exploiting it to undermine the administration's support in such crucial states as Pennsylvania and New York. Apparently there were two parties in the country by 1826, and one of them was not playing by the old rules.

Clay's response to the situation reflected the powerful influence of existing civic conventions and customs, which had yet to accommodate to the idea that a two-party system generates stability and continuity in government. To Clay, Jacksonian ideas were wrong and the Jacksonians were wrong. He refused to accord the Democrats the slightest measure of sincerity or consistency of principle, just as he found their crude methods distasteful and disturbing. To him, style and substance merged in the Jacksonians' unscrupulousness. It was but a short step from such thinking to the conclusion that the Jacksonians were deluding the good people of the country by appealing to their passions rather than their reason. From the beginning, Clay called the Democrats a personal faction, a "mongrel opposition" gathered around a military hero who would trample the Constitution. "You do not know the outrageous character of the spirit of Jacksonism," he wrote to a friend in New York. "It will stop at nothing to carry the day."[53]

Such a party could never win a fair election; the Jacksonians captured the

House of Representatives in 1827 through "misrepresentation" and fraud and amid scenes that belonged "rather to a military campaign . . . than to a civil election." Warned by 1827 that Martin Van Buren was forging a coalition of free and slave states that would "forbid a local division ruinous to our peace," Clay scoffed that such an alliance would never bridge the Democrats' internal division over the tariff, for there were too many protectionists temporarily gathered under the Democratic standard.[54]

Fifty-one years old on the eve of the 1828 presidential election, satisfied that he had successfully launched the American System over the past sixteen years, Clay contemplated permanent retirement from public life. But the Democrats' challenge dictated a renewed political effort, and for the next twenty years, Clay fought a rearguard action in defense of his program and reputation. The overall defensiveness of his goals should not be underestimated, for behind it lay an essentially conservative understanding of politics, one that largely dictated his strategy, the issues he selected (and rejected), and the style of campaigning he pursued. Indeed, Clay rarely chose new battlegrounds for this struggle against the Democrats but acted first on earlier, lasting impressions of parties, issues, and statesmanship that with some significant exceptions yielded the initiative to his foes and set the stage for his defeat.

Jackson's victory over Adams in 1828, after a campaign of mutual slanders and vicious rumors, shocked Clay. He simply could not understand how any rational person would support an inexperienced, vengeful, military hero for president. "There are seasons when passion and delusion take possession of the public mind," he wrote soon after the election. "This has been one."[55] His conviction that Jackson's triumph was due to Van Buren's new political machine, to the defamation of Clay's character, and to the corruption of the election process helped to dictate the strategy and tactics of the opposition. By mid-1829, Clay had decided to add statesmanship and party abuses of government to the defense of the American System as the primary issues between the parties. This choice of issues, the unique type of party that it required, and the curious campaign style that evolved from it indicate that unlike his opponents or even some of his party colleagues, Clay probed but did not sap the political minefields of the Age of Jackson. Mass organization and the martial style of party politics conflicted with existing notions of statesmanship, moderation, and independence of mind, values that Clay tried to articulate in his appeals for votes. The contrast between these themes, which were skeptical if not critical of parties, and the reality of party politics was too great for Clay's enemies and allies to ignore.

Clay's first goal was to defend his program and reputation, especially since Adams's defeat had left him the undisputed leader of the opposition to Jackson. One of Clay's supporters suggested that the new party would "comprehend *all* honest & patriotic citizens," presumably leaving the dishonest and disloyal ones to Jackson. This party would rally under a conservative platform of broad principles, which Clay announced as "the Union; the Constitution; the preser[v]ation of the American System; and the subordination of the Military to civil rule."[56] Although the American System still bulked large in Clay's thinking, his initial tactic was to target the spoils system and Jackson's personality while avoiding a "rash opposition" in Congress so that the Democrats' internal "dissolvent," the tariff, could effectively expose Jackson's inconsistent principles and prove the new majority's inability to enact a program. He would copy Jacksonian organizational innovations, "learning from [his] enemies" and "opposing concert to concert," while repudiating Jackson's version of party statesmanship.[57]

The result was the curious hybrid that became the Whig party, which prided itself on retaining the statesmanship of an older age while it marched across the country touting hard cider and coonskins. Clay tried to lead this party the way he would lead the country if given the chance. After all, a party representing the virtue, the intelligence, and a sampling of the country's diverse economic interests needed disinterested statesmen at the helm. Clay repeatedly urged his followers to practice the politics of conciliation with each other and toward potential converts, for this would produce union, harmony, and victory over a foe known for his vindictiveness and selfishness. Conciliation also comported well with contemporary expectations of what parties were supposed to do. By seeking to gather both the faithful and the wayward, Clay appealed to the moderation and independent-mindedness of the average voter. Defectors to his party presumably had considered the issues and made their choice.

Clay opened his counterattack against Jackson by charging the Old Hero with trying to unite partyism with the power of the executive branch to establish an "elective monarchy" exerting a corrupt influence on Congress, the press, and public opinion. He first raised this issue in a long speech at Fowler's Garden on his return to Lexington from Washington in mid-1829, and he used it (with a few variations) against his opponents for the next twenty years.[58] Clay's denunciation of "King Andrew" echoed Madison's sharp criticisms of Federalist monarchism back in 1798, as did the many variations on this theme one finds in the Whig press. Clay argued that Jackson was using the powers of the executive to "minister to his passions" as a king might, bestowing rewards and inflicting punishments among the press and members of Congress in order to bend them to his will. Artfully combining old images of consolidation, monarchism, and corruption, Clay appealed to the conservative sentiments of his audience, reminding them that the current revolution in politics was injecting emotion and political agitation into previously quiet spheres of public life.

Thus, Jackson's spoils system had created a personal party—a faction—that lured the people away from popular, settled policies and into a patronage system that could "convert the nation into one perpetual theatre for political gladiators." Clay predicted that "there would be one universal scramble for public offices" as each turbulent election blended with the next in an unending cycle of disappointed ambitions and inflamed passions. With "Congress corrupted, and the press corrupted, general corruption would ensue, until the substance of free government having disappeared, some Praetorian band would arise, and, with the general concurrence of a distracted people, put an end to useless forms."

Jackson's party government stemmed from Old Hickory's lack of self-control, Clay continued. Party policy originated with Jackson's emotions, which the cunning band of adventurers in his court manipulated through flattery and deception. Clay contrasted the spectacle of Jackson's rowdy inauguration day with the calm moderation and dignity of Jefferson's back in 1801. Obviously this was no ordinary rotation of parties in the conciliatory tradition of Jefferson but was a full-fledged revolution in party government as Clay had understood it. Clay advised Jackson to "forget the prejudices and passions" of the campaign, "practice dignified moderation and forbearance," and "dedicate the short residue of his life to the God who had so long blessed and spared him, and to the country which had so greatly honored him."

Clay's conception of parties and the presidency clashed with Jackson's, making this a natural starting point for the counteroffensive. The election of a president, Clay told a British visitor to Washington, was one of the American political system's "most unpleasant aspects," displaying "all the worst passions." The presidency was "the weak part" of the Constitution, Clay told the Marquis de Lafayette. "On [this] the enemies of our system chiefly build their hopes."[59] Given these observations, it is understandable that to Clay the issues of statesmanship, party government, and patronage, and eventually the substantive questions of the American System, revolved around Jackson's use of his office, his powers, and his party—his provocative and stern vetoes, his tremendous influence in Congress, and his controversial cabinet appointments and removals.[60]

It is important to realize that these were familiar issues to Clay. The "elective monarchy" issue echoed the great conflict of 1798; Clay even toyed with the idea of pinning the Federalist label on his opponents, but Adams dissuaded him with the simple reminder that former Federalists could be found in both camps. He decided to heed the advice of friends and relatives and resume his familiar role in Congress as the champion of an embattled tradition of congressional government and disinterested statesmanship. From his redoubt in the Senate, to which he returned in 1831, Clay could sally forth to refute the unending "corrupt bargain" charge by contrasting his own statesmanlike image with that of the party warrior in the White House and to lure the "deluded" followers of Jackson away from their "infuriated attachment" to the Old Hero and back to "common sense."[61]

Clay's indictment of Jackson conveniently focused the slowly gathering opposition's shopping list of grievances and became the germ of the Whigs' theory of congressional government, their major contribution to antebellum constitutionalism. Whigs expected the president to ratify congressional policy and to interpose the veto only as the last necessity. Presidents must further defer to Congress on major appointments and on the preparation of important fiscal measures, responding promptly to all requests for information and obtaining the Senate's advice and consent on appointments *and* removals from high office. Eventually every Democratic policy, from the tariff to the Mexican War, plus every component of the Whig coalition could be defined and comprehended within this image of

King Andrew and his Democratic retinue.[62] If, as historians have concluded, the second party system congealed around the emergence of national contests for the presidency, it is hardly surprising to find that this development itself was a source of deep controversy between the parties. "A real crisis in our Republic has arrived," Clay declared in accepting the National Republican nomination in 1832, "and the question which it involves is, whether the government shall be administered according to the principles of purity and moderation which governed all the Administrations prior to the present, or upon a system of corruption and proscription" extending from the White House through Congress and the press and into "the great body of the people."[63]

Clay's initial efforts to stop Jackson displayed a remarkable complacency about the state of public opinion and his own position as an oppositionist and presidential aspirant. He was convinced that the Democrats would collapse because of their own internal disagreements about the tariff and that the American System, in place for so long that it now constituted the "fixed" policy of the government, was too popular for Jackson to dismantle. Sooner or later, if given "the correct information," the deluded followers of the president would desert to Clay. To this end, Clay assumed that temperate, simple, and well-written campaign literature distributed by a national network of committees would be sufficient to combat the emotional outpourings of Jackson's editorial henchmen.[64]

Reaching out to the other side was what Clay expected parties and their leaders to do—especially when they were in the minority. Such an outlook depended heavily on the permeability of political parties; the competition for votes in the attempt to build workable majorities forced parties to seek converts. And once in power, the party was obliged to judge its measures by the principles announced in the campaign. If successful, the party would "remove" issues from further partisan conflict. This was the ultimate end of the politics of conciliation.

Clay's attitude about electioneering offers a striking example of how conciliation clashed with the realities of new political styles. In 1832, Clay's attempt to offer himself as the alternative to Jackson's brand of partisan leadership created endless problems, for it revealed the gulf between his carefully cultivated images as party candidate and as elder statesman. Should he seek votes or remain aloof from campaigning? As Clement

Eaton has pointed out, Clay's "Olympian conception" of the role of the statesman ruled out continuous electioneering for the presidency. In keeping with the current custom, Clay tried to remain aloof from open electioneering while advertising his availability for office. He repeatedly told importunate supporters that he would remain "perfectly neutral" in the presidential question while holding out the possibility of controlling movements that sought to use his name. In fine, he would always be at the call of a majority, but he would not seek to manufacture its decisions.[65] This mixture of involvement and detachment had the advantage of leaving to Clay's discretion the timing and some of the management of his efforts. But it hampered effective and efficient campaigning by leaving him free to speak out when he probably should not and by forcing him to rely on the limited political intelligence of an informal network of correspondents around the country.

In negotiating the unpredictable and dangerous presidential campaign trail from 1832 on, Clay lacked a clear party road-map mainly because he refused to submit entirely to the party discipline that such a plan would impose. Instead, Clay's increased involvement with popular politics led him time and again to misconstrue the scope and size of his following. He frequently concluded that both his seniority in the party and the popular enthusiasm for him were more important than mere "availability," which by the mid-1840s was becoming the party's primary criterion for a nomination. In the end, Clay's experience as a presidential candidate was a long agony of embarrassments, frustrations, and personal and financial sacrifices that dimmed his optimism and soured him on the uses of parties.[66]

The prospect of a long campaign with its suffocating crowd scenes and predictable train of charges against his integrity daunted a man of Clay's advanced age and accomplishments. Before 1832, Clay stuck to the well-worn paths of campaign custom and limited his public appearances to events close to home, workplace, and spots covered along the route to Washington or to his wintering place in New Orleans. His speeches on these occasions were addressed to "moderate men of both parties," and indeed nothing appealed more to his vanity than to head a bipartisan public dinner where he could make his usual pitch for converts from Jacksonism. In 1832, as the candidate for the National Republicans, Clay did no electioneering, made no political tours, and entered the campaign only after his return to the Senate less than a year before the canvass. He concentrated his energies on the tariff, the Bank of the United States, and nullification controversies then raging in Congress, while his loose network of party managers tried to mount a nationwide campaign.[67]

The drubbing that Clay suffered from Andrew Jackson in 1832 was in some ways balanced by the Kentuckian's compromise victory in Congress just a few months later. For the Compromise of 1833 retrieved Clay's reputation as an intersectional diplomat, and more important, it featured what Clay believed was the ultimate purpose of a political program: defections from the enemy camp. Former Jacksonians, mostly southerners, left the Democracy in 1833 and 1834 to help form the emerging Whig opposition; their ranks grew as the Democratic administrations of Jackson and Van Buren expanded on the Old Hero's plan to break down the Bank of the United States and forge ahead with severe monetary and fiscal reforms. This demonstrated the permeability of political parties and the flexibility of voter alignments, both of which were crucial to keeping a party system attuned to the rational give-and-take of public discourse.

Clay's strategy of relying on the popularity of the American System, his position as head of a party that was suspicious of party politics, and his tactic of making Jackson's party government a major issue gained him neither the presidency nor the continuation of the American System. With the significant exception of the compromise tariff of 1833, Jackson confounded Clay on practically every issue through the 1830s. The Old Hero soundly whipped him in 1832 and began to dismantle the American System. Instead of picking new issues to confront the Democrats, Clay relied on the old ones and devised stopgap measures (like the plan to distribute the proceeds of land sales) to shore them up. By the mid-1830s, he had conceded that internal improvements, the Bank of the United States, and, until 1842, the tariff had all been effectively compromised or shifted to the state level and "ought not to agitate the country." But he still had the "elective monarchy" charge, which helped focus the anti-Jackson coalition and, more important, completely encapsulated all of Clay's fears about the new politics.[68]

Clay's skirmishes with the Democrats reinforced his fears of disorder. He became convinced that Jackson's rule portended evil for the Union. "After 44 years of existence under the present Constitution what single principle is fixed?" he asked a close friend during the nullification turmoil in 1833. "The Bank? No. Internal improvements? No. The Tariff? No. Who is to interpret the Constitution? No. We are as much afloat at sea as the day when the Constitution went into operation. There is nothing certain but that the *will* of Andw. Jackson is to govern; and that will fluctuates with the change of every pen which gives expression to it."[69]

A year later he predicted to Van Buren that continued Democratic victories would lead Clay "to feel that [the] experiment of free government had failed; that [Van Buren] would introduce a system of intrigue and corruption that would enable him to designate his successor; and that, after a few years of lingering and fretful existance [*sic*]," the country would "end in a dissolution of the Union or in despotism." Van Buren chuckled, remarking that Clay "entertained morbid feelings." Clay recalled, "I replied, with good nature, that what I said I deliberately and sincerely believed." Burdened by family and financial woes, Clay became more despondent with each failure. He even wondered whether the "religious fanaticism" that had divided England during its civil wars was similar to the "fanaticism towards Genl. Jackson," who had inaugurated a reign of "Blackguards, Bankrupts and Scoundrels, Profligacy and Corruption."[70]

The presidency temporarily lost its allure. Clay had entertained thoughts of running in 1836 against Jackson's hand-picked successor, Martin Van Buren, surmising that both sections would reward him for the Compromise of 1833. But in 1834 his friends had already dissuaded him from such miscalculations, pointing to his 1832 defeat and to Jackson's durable popularity in both sections. Clay deferred to this judgment but deplored its ultimate effect: the Whigs, already divided over economic and sectional questions, opted for multiple regional candidates in 1836. The most successful of these, William Henry Harrison of Ohio, inspired little enthusiasm from Clay. In particular, Harrison's popularity as a military hero disturbed Clay, for it proved that in politics, as in war, the loser copies the tactics of the winner.[71]

Clay's hopes for a Whig victory began to revive soon after Van Buren's inauguration in 1837, however. The economy slid into a deep depression that focused public attention on the administration's stringent monetary policy and shifted the initiative to advocates of federal action to promote recovery. As the Whigs' elder statesman and champion of the American

System, Clay was a leading contender for the 1840 nomination. But the emergence of the slavery issue in the late 1830s confounded his efforts and revealed how new political styles were widening the gap between the requirements of mass political action and the image of disinterested statesmanship that Clay kept trying to foster.

Sectional attitudes about slavery had been hardening since the beginning of the decade. Abolitionists were encouraged by Great Britain's abolition of slavery in the West Indies in 1833 and found in the activist atmosphere of the new mass politics an opportunity to press their cause more openly. Although the abolition movement's tactics initially stressed agitation outside the party system, any clear-eyed observer could see the direction its efforts were taking. By 1835, abolitionists were inundating Congress with petitions for the abolition of slavery in the District of Columbia, any new territories, and the military while threatening to withhold their votes from any slaveholding candidate.

Southerners too became more militant in the aftermath of Nat Turner's slave rebellion in Virginia in 1831, and in response to the growth of abolitionism, they began to strengthen state laws against manumission and to clamp down on the movements of free blacks. In company with sympathetic northern Democrats, southerners demanded action to silence abolition agitation, and they succeeded in getting Congress to suppress antislavery and abolition memorials and petitions from 1836 to 1844. In 1837, John C. Calhoun of South Carolina introduced resolutions to bind the Senate against antislavery agitation and in favor of his theory that the Constitution obligated all the states to protect and promote their respective domestic institutions. Clay thought that Calhoun's action was a partisan maneuver to wreck the Kentuckian's presidential prospects and that it played into the abolitionists' hands. He introduced his own set of counter-resolutions and began to criticize sectional militants more stridently as the election approached, culminating with a well-publicized Senate speech against abolitionists and southern radicals in February 1839.[72]

Although Clay had spoken out on slavery before, his renewed efforts in the late 1830s again revealed his conservative views of race, politics, and the Constitution. The cornerstone of Clay's thinking about slavery was race, not economics. He accepted the conventional belief that slavery had been forced on southerners by the English, that it had been necessary to retain the institution in order to control an inferior and barbarous race, and that slavery hurt both blacks and whites. Slavery was a burden on the South, Clay believed, and only attracted the condemnation of an enlightened and liberal world. The institution also had "an unfavorable tendency on the Union" as a sore point between the sections.[73]

Slavery was a dying institution, Clay thought, so the country should prepare for that eventuality. He anticipated that the influx of cheap foreign labor and the nation's expansion into the West would undermine the slave's value relative to the price of produce and land and would force slaveowners to manumit or face ruin. For the present, slavery's evils could be mitigated only by masters restrained by Christian benevolence and public scrutiny. He favored state regulation of slave traders to check their abuses and supported gradual, compensated emancipation in states with a minority of blacks.

But the thought of a large population of free blacks in the United States made Clay uncomfortable. Throughout his life, Clay ardently backed colonization not as an antislavery program but to prevent the inevitable struggle between the races once slavery's restraints had been removed. In this context, Clay favored federal action on slavery in the same spirit as his economic program. The government should admit the legitimacy of the institution, placate whites by separating the races, and quietly encourage former slaveholders to substitute new forms of labor and production.[74]

But Clay carefully drew tight boundaries around the idea of federal action on slavery. His analysis of slavery's social basis prescribed his ultimate objectives and limited his methods, which were firmly tied to his constitutional unionism. He regarded slavery as part of the compromises of the Constitution, which, he thought, permitted no interference with it whatsoever where it already existed, except in those areas under direct federal jurisdiction, like the District of Columbia and the territories. And even where the government was empowered to act, it should do so only with the utmost respect for the feelings of slaveholders. "Public opinion alone can bring about the abolition of slavery, and public opinion is on the march," he remarked in 1833. "We should wait in patience for its operation without attempting measures that might throw it back." Slavery was a legitimate subject of public discussion only if both sides practiced "mutual forbearance." Under these conditions, he concluded, slavery and the Union were compatible, just as the eventual abolition of the institution was compatible with the Union.[75]

Even as the inevitable laws of population and economics slowly eroded the institution, sectional conflict was bound to arise, and Clay thought that it was the statesman's duty to mute dissension. He believed that the best safeguard against sectional agitation over slavery was the American System, which he treated as an economic extension of the constitutional compact. Government-promoted prosperity would create a bond of interest between the slaveholder and the nonslaveholder while fixing the attention of both on the maintenance of an orderly federal system. Meanwhile, moderate and conservative plans, like colonization funded by land receipts (which he asked President Monroe, in vain, to support), and state-sponsored programs of gradual emancipation on the Pennsylvania model could proceed.

The slavery debate in the 1830s manifested little patience with such palliatives, however. What bothered Clay and other conservatives was the overtly political cast of the rising abolition movement in the North and the shrill, resentful reaction in the South. Clay thought that sectional militants distorted the Constitution in their attempt to strike at each other through the political system. He rejected Calhoun's theory that southern rights must be permanently institutionalized, because Clay regarded slavery as outmoded and the South's minority position as irreversible. More important, Clay thought that the cycle of mutual recriminations was in fact riveting the institution ever more firmly in the South. As a slaveholder, Clay sympathized with the planter's outrage at abolitionist accusations of immorality and brutality, and he feared that a Calhoun could build his presidential ambitions on just such a mixture of anger and resentment. On the other hand, Clay demanded that northerners restrain their antislavery sentiments, since they had a smaller stake in the matter. As long as southerners remained good customers in a home market, he thought, abolitionists had no practical reason to enter politics and should rely purely on moral suasion.[76]

Clay understood the difference between a mere dislike of slavery and the desire to abolish it, but he regarded both beliefs as dangerous when politicized. Politics, he thought, intensifies emotions and leads men away from persuasion to force. Moral sentiment, be it the misguided "philanthropy" that drove the abolitionist forces or the understandable outrage of northerners at the South's privileged political influence, should not dominate politics or determine party lines.[77]

In keeping with his outlook on the dangers and limits of parties, Clay sought to prevent slavery from becoming a party issue, and that meant resisting the overtures of abolitionists both within and outside his party. Clay had frequent contact with Whig abolitionists like Joshua Giddings, but he ignored their suggestions that he reach out to abolitionist constituencies. And he politely but firmly rejected similar overtures from James G. Birney and Lewis Tappan in 1834, 1837, and 1838.[78] Clay's conception of how parties develop issues and implement policy excluded the possibility that Birney and other political abolitionists were separating from the radical, antiparty supporters of William Lloyd Garrison, were moving into the mainstream of Jacksonian political culture, and were potential junior partners in a national coalition. Clay did not take their split with Garrison as a sign of growing moderation; instead, he recoiled at the growth of political abolitionism, fearing it even more than Garrison's radicalism.[79]

Clay regarded any attempt by the major parties to mollify sectional soreheads as pandering to sectional ambitions. His chilly reception to abolitionist overtures disgusted Birney and his abolitionist friends, who concluded that Clay had thrown in with the slave interest to save his political skin. And Clay resented the abolitionists' ungentlemanly appeal to his vanity and ambition, rejecting their suggestions that he buy northern support for his presidential aspirations by freeing his slaves and backing immediate emancipation in Kentucky.

The rise of an organized, vocal abolition movement challenged Clay's notions about civility in public discourse and intensified his apprehension that the passions aroused by party conflict would in turn encourage sectional feelings as party politicians reached out for new issues. The irruption of abolitionism and southern radicalism in the mid-1830s coincided with the triumph of Jackson and the defeat of the Union-promoting American System; it is little wonder that Clay perceived a connection. The spirit of Jackson—factious, fanatical, selfish, unprincipled, and emotional—encouraged political abolitionists, whom Clay denounced for sharing the "same loose and licentious spirit" of Jacksonian "Agrarianism" that attacked "the foundations of all property and all good faith in the Community." The Democrats, he thought, were willing to stir up sectional warfare because it hurt the Whigs. Clay noticed that his party was more vulnerable to "one idea" third-party movements, and even though he never figured out why, he did notice how the Democrats exploited the weakness.[80]

Throughout the late 1830s, Clay's former flexibility on slavery began to wane, and his innate conservatism hardened. Since 1828, he thought, the rise of the Jacksonians and of sectional tensions had signaled a declension of the American political order. The Democrats' domination of politics had set loose sectional feelings and disturbed the social order. "New and alarming principles, dangerous practices, great abuses, and extensive corruption have been introduced into the general administration, during the last few years," he charged in 1839. Listing the Democrats' abuses of the electoral process, Clay predicted that the disease would spread as the Whigs would be "tempted to appeal to the same arts. And the corruption of the whole mass [would] quickly follow. Then, farewell to Liberty."[81]

This grim analysis of public affairs prompted him to redouble his efforts to capture the presidency and redeem the country. Unfortunately, Clay's unbounded confidence that he was the real choice of the Whigs after the 1836 debacle lured him into complacency until it was too late. In 1838, as his Whig rivals worked to undermine his cause in the Middle Atlantic states, Clay refused invitations to visit New York. His campaign was going well, he told his New York manager. "There is more danger of my impairing than improving it by the display of eagerness." In July 1839, concerned that his long-distance efforts were collapsing, Clay reversed his stated policy of avoiding election tours and traveled through upstate New York, the heart of reformist and antislavery constituencies that were increasingly crucial to the capture of the state. Throughout the journey he urged his followers to conciliate any converts from Jacksonism and to practice the necessary mutual forbearance that would unite them behind a winning candidate.[82]

But Clay's tardiness hurt his image, already tarnished by his recent outspoken attack against abolitionism, and prevented him from reinforcing conservative opinion in the North. Whig organizers in New York and New England, sensitive to the influence of antislavery sentiment, opposed Clay's nomination and built a powerful coalition among his rivals to beat him. The nod went to William Henry Harrison, much to Clay's dismay. He made three public appearances during the ensuing "log cabin" campaign (including a raucous trip to Nashville for a slashing harangue against Jackson), but otherwise he remained quiet, to avoid becoming "an itinerant Lecturer or Stump orator to advance the Cause of a successful competitor."[83]

The Jeffersonian image of statesmanship that Clay tried to stamp on the Whig party caused further trouble when the Whigs won a thumping victory under Harrison in 1840. Harrison had committed himself to enacting the Whig program of executive restraint and economic legislation, but the organizational techniques that the Whigs had copied from their opponents and had used to win the election imposed their own set of imperatives on the party's leaders. Constituencies had to be served, pledges kept, and patronage parceled out in order to hold the coalition together.

Clay realized this but misunderstood its implications for his role in the new government. He had determined to act the role of Senate majority leader in the Jeffersonian tradition—dominating committee assignments and the daily agenda during a special session in 1841. Clay had long believed that the legislative majority was obligated to devise and enact a comprehensive program in which the minority should acquiesce unless its principles were violated.[84] He wrote up a party program and pressed it on the already harried president, along with his own list of recommendations concerning the cabinet and patronage. Harrison bristled at the substance and tone of Clay's initiatives and told him to back off.[85]

Harrison's death soon after his inauguration elevated the untried states' righter John Tyler to the presidency. Clay renewed his aggressive efforts at enacting a program and clashed with the headstrong president. The subsequent conflict between Clay's congressional party and John Tyler's executive clique wrecked Clay's only effort at Whig party government. Tyler's vetoes and his eventual apostasy from Whiggery outraged Clay, who never forgave him and urged the party to stand fast in defense of congressional prerogatives even at the expense of its program.[86]

Historians have echoed contemporary Whig leaders' intense criticism of Clay's uncompromising and "dictatorial" behavior at this time, seeing in it the temper of disappointed ambition. Certainly his domineering personality and barbed parries in debate alienated some of his supporters. But the situation was unprecedented for a man of Clay's political antecedents; given the party's stated preference for congressional initiative in policy making, Clay's action is at least understandable. President Jefferson did not use his office to confront his party in Congress. He cultivated congressional support through casual dinner parties and informal contacts between his cabinet and committee members on Capitol Hill, and he isolated the party's dissenters by letting the party caucus work its will.

Yet Jackson, and now Tyler, seemed to use the office to confront Congress. As a member of the formal opposition to Jackson, Clay had felt the same sting of party animosity that his Republicans had directed against Federalists; and as an opponent to Tyler, Clay felt betrayed by a leader who used his office to repudiate both Congress and his party. "What can I do?" Clay asked a friend. "In former epochs, the object to be accomplished was to reconcile conflicting opinions *in Congress*. If that were now the case, I should not be without hope. But it is far different. Now the object is to reconcile conflicting opinions between Congress and the President, between a faithful Congress and a faithless President."[87]

The collapse of Whig governance by 1842 intensified Clay's drive to capture the White House. This goal also exposed the tensions created by his conservative approach to Jacksonian politics. In 1844, after two years' rest from the struggle with Tyler, Clay emerged again, this time as the undisputed nominee of his party. He threw himself into this campaign, including a long southern tour in 1844 that took him through the sultry, steaming black belt over dusty, bumpy roads that actually left him frightened for his life. At every stop he roared himself hoarse to stifling crowds and winced at a sniping opposition press full of the usual accusations. "A man has to give up his own self-respect or every hour give offence to some pedagogue that stands over him with uplifted rod," one of Clay's friends grumbled about the new campaign style. This was a far cry from the safe and casual rhythms of a senatorial election by the state legislature.[88]

The tour confirmed Clay's long-standing discomfort with extensive campaigning just as it separated him from the Whig high command in Washington at a critical time. Determined to be his own campaign manager, free of irritating commands from the usual crowd of handlers in presidential campaigns, Clay harrumphed that he would "not surrender [his] independence, or submit to be guided by anybody." Convinced that the South was not eager to support the Democrats' demand for the annexation of Texas, Clay wrote a public letter from Raleigh near the end of an exhausting, noisy, and hurried day of celebrations that gave him no time to check his facts, polish his prose, or consult closely with politicians outside the South. Certain that northerners opposed annexation and that southerners were indifferent about it, Clay argued in his Raleigh letter that annexation must depend on the status of relations with Mexico, the climate of opinion in the United States, and the financial burden it might impose. None of these justified annexation in 1844, he claimed. "What the United States most need are union, peace, and patience," he declared, in a typical statement of his political priorities.[89]

Clay's mounting anger that poor communications with the party in Washington had left him in the dark about growing support in the Senate for annexation led him to conclude that the party wheelhorses were out of touch with popular sentiment. Furthermore, Clay reasoned that putting off the annexation of Texas would keep the "old issues" of elective monarchy and the American System squarely in the public eye while suppressing new and divisive ones that would stir up trouble across the country. This was a classic Clay calculation that a display of restraint would attract the moderate men of all parties to his standard. So he sent the letter off to Washington and asked his friends at the Capitol to publish it immediately in the party's national organ, the *National Intelligencer*. When John J. Crittenden and other Whig leaders balked, Clay ordered them to publish it.[90]

The letter caused such a stir that Clay decided to issue one explanation after another throughout the summer and fall. He would have been better off had he let the matter drop, for his stand on the issue was not as equivocal as some had claimed. His later letters did not alter his initial position but added only that he would be happy to see Texas in the Union if his earlier conditions could be met. Even worse, his mailbox filled with demands that he clarify his views on other issues too, especially nativism, another new issue that he wished to sidestep but that was causing ceaseless trouble for the Whigs in Philadelphia and New York. Clay became more diplomatic after this, obeying his friend Thomas Ewing's advice that he leave nativism alone and let his friends "confide in [his] conservative opinions."[91]

The narrow loss to James K. Polk was hard for the temperamental Clay to take. He believed that the Democrats had deluded a majority of the electorate and that "one-idea" third-party movements had siphoned off crucial votes and weakened his cause. Clay grew despondent. "I entertain many serious apprehensions," he despaired in early 1845. "There is a tendency to disorder, to unsettle every thing, to violence and to war, that is truly alarming. . . . My fear is that every thing will be sacrificed to the absorbing spirit of party."[92]

The annexation of Texas and the consequent war with Mexico confirmed Clay's fears. When his favorite son died at the Battle of Buena Vista, Clay's despair and anger redoubled. In a speech in Lexington in 1847, he tried to rally Whigs to his standard once again, denouncing the war as an unrestrained abuse of executive power. But Clay deplored this new issue's intrusion into politics because of its effects on popular emotions. The cycle of party dynamics could push the Whigs into trumpeting military heroes, as their opponents had done so successfully, whereas the Democrats' policy of dismantling protection and debasing statesmanship would no longer be such an "open palpable issue which all can understand," as John Davis of Massachusetts put it to Clay, so as "to excite public alarm without Coon skins, hard cider, log cabins, or even a song or a hurrah."[93]

Zachary Taylor's nomination by the Whigs in 1848 seemed a depressing fulfillment of Clay's premonitions. He had convinced himself that he was again the party's natural choice, especially after an enthusiastic reception to his visit to New York City in the summer of 1847. Throughout 1848 he permitted his New York supporters to push his name for the nomination, even as many former allies were working for Taylor. Still thinking in the old categories, Clay predicted that the selection of another military hero would sink the party to the level of its opponents. And Taylor's announcement that he would be a "no party" president only further confirmed Clay's predictions of disaster, for a party without principles and headed by a military hero was Clay's exact definition of the Democrats he so deeply despised: a personal party unrestrained by a distinctive program. Little did he understand that many of his friends opposed his nomination for the very same reason he opposed Taylor: it would sink the party to the level of a faction tied to the fortunes of a single ambitious man.[94]

Taylor's nomination capped sixteen years of frustration for Clay. Whiggery had come full circle to be absorbed by a party system that sacrificed principle to popularity; the party was no longer distinguished by unique, principled statesmanship. As a Whig editor explained to Clay in August 1848, the old philosophical difference between Whigs and Democrats "*was*, that the former dealt with man *as he should be*, while the latter appealed to him *as he is*." Whigs "endeavored to educate him up to nobler ends," whereas Democrats tried "to drag him down to base uses—the one addressing the reason and the conscience, the other inflaming the wild passions." Now the parties were mirror images: similar organizations, similar leaders, similar base objectives. The choice between the naive Zachary Taylor and the cynical Lewis Cass in 1848 was, Clay wrote, "between the frying pan and the fire."[95]

Clay's opinions of the Democratic leaders never changed throughout his long struggle with them. Although he might respect a few individuals, he found it impossible to accept their claim to the people's support. Naturally, such thinking led him to blame his defeats on the unfortunate divisions of his own party and the military discipline of his opponents, both of which prevented his leadership from drawing converts back to the fold. Unlike the placid Van Buren, whom he genuinely liked, Clay intertwined his emotions with his profession and lacked the crucial detachment that could transform a coalition into a party that might outlive him. More important, Clay never appreciated the stabilizing effects of party conflict the way Van Buren did. Although both men built powerful political parties and could properly lay claim to being the prime architects of a mass party system, they did not share the same optimism about the cleansing, democratizing effects of two-party competition.

Clay, then, never fully graduated from the school of mass politics. His belief that the new style of political action endangered reasoned political discourse led him to yield the initiative to the Democrats so that they could take the blame for debasing republican politics. The expansion of the electorate, the increased power and influence of a cheap press, and the importance of patronage as a source of party funds were all crucial to party success in the Jacksonian world, but Clay's desire to play the statesman and his fundamental distrust of democratic politics braked his accommodation to these techniques until after he had isolated himself from the party leadership and from new constituencies that pressed in from the

North. Deep down, Clay, like all conservatives, believed that there must be limits to political controversy. His was not so much a politics of consensus as it was a politics of limits and moderation, which saw private self-restraint and public, mutual sacrifice as the real sentinels of domestic peace, order, and liberty.[96]

In this sense, grand compromise assumed an important role in Clay's outlook on politics, parties, and the Constitution. Great compromises represented a break from party conflict, a breathing space that gave wide latitude for independent statesmen to break down rigid party and sectional loyalties and return the people to their senses. On those rare yet important occasions, Clay and his peers could restage the old ritual of conciliation as a fresh contrast to the frantic chaos of democratic politics and sectional rancor.

Clay would get his chance again in 1850. By then, the seventy-three-year-old Clay had managed to survive the devolution of his leadership with one great asset—"that admirable judgment and tact" for which he was "so much celebrated, of compelling men to think alike in spite of former prejudices and opinions."[97] Twenty years of party warfare had left its scars, but it had not banked the fires of Clay's devotion to "the Union as it is." The brewing sectional struggle would give him a last opportunity to defend "this Union" in the tradition of the Founding Fathers and in the manner he thought they would approve: through compromise, the remaining window to a rapidly receding past.

5 Last Ritual
The Compromise of 1850

> Sir, where *compromise ends, force begins*, and when *force* begins, *war* begins, and the tocsin of civil war is the death knell of Republicanism.
> —James Shields

Henry Clay's lament that the narrow Democratic victory in 1844 exposed the country to the "absorbing spirit of party" expressed the classic whiggish skepticism of political parties. Had he lost by a large margin, Clay might have found it easier to accept the verdict, as in 1832. But the close vote and the rising importance of sectional issues in the campaign suggested that the country was being divided into dangerously hostile parties tied either to military heroes or to militaristic expansionism. His analysis of the constitutional system limited parties to specific, if important, functions that still left room for independent-minded statesmen to limit the sectional and party excesses that threatened to erode the "mutual affections" supporting the Union. Grand sectional compromises, he believed, applied reason and common sense to deep-rooted conflicts that could not otherwise be resolved in one stroke. The symptomatic relief offered by such compromises was not an evasion of issues or of responsibility but was a direct confrontation with the hard facts of America's unique political circumstances.

The sectional conflict of 1846–50 gave Clay another opportunity to implement his vision of how the system was supposed to operate. The old ritual of comprehensive sectional compromise encased in a package of mutual concessions, which extended from the Constitutional Convention to the present day, was the classic formula for dampening sectional and party spirit. Certainly the events leading up to and culminating in the Compromise of 1850 closely fit the Federalist template of 1787 that Clay and his supporters had used with such tremendous effect in 1820 and 1833.

The pattern of sectional conflict from the late 1830s up to 1850 uncovered sectional interpretations of the Constitution's jurisdiction over slavery in the new territories, in the District of Columbia, and in interstate relations that challenged the moderate constitutional unionism of the political center. Invigorated by an increasingly activist political culture, sectional militants forced moderates in both parties to grapple on a national level with issues they had hoped either to contain within their coalitions or to repel altogether. By hitching their constitutional ideas to uncompromisable moral imperatives, sectional leaders such as John C. Calhoun and William H. Seward helped to deprive old compromise formulas, such as the Missouri Compromise line, of the traditional power of intersectional magnetism. To be sure, each side might proclaim its faith to the Missouri formula, but not so much as a union-saving device as a stalking-horse for a sectional agenda. By narrowing the options available to moderates, the resulting sectional conflict forced the major parties in the late 1840s to resort to more abstract, ambiguous plans that failed to obtain the concurrence of both sides and advertised the apparent inadequacy of the political system to reconcile principles and interests through compromise.

Here was the opportunity to replay the drama of 1787. Indeed, old habits died hard; by the end of the 1840s, compromise had become a ritual, a "shibboleth" as Max Farrand has put it, and the politicians who negotiated and passed the Compromise of 1850 knew it. "After a few more speeches, we shall begin to feel comfortable," the Baltimore *Sun*'s Washington correspondent predicted in late February 1850 as the sectional argument raged in Congress, "and then we shall compromise; first back to back, then shoulder to shoulder, and at last face to face, with a cordial shake of the hand, as becomes two great sections of a country guided by the *prestige* of future world-dominion." Seven months later the passage of the Texas, New Mexico, and Utah provisions of the Compromise of 1850 prompted him to proclaim that Congress had "re-enacted the federal compact— . . . re-affirmed the Constitution—re-animated the hopes of every patriot—and sustained the faith of millions in the capacity of man for self-government."[1]

In the Senate debates of 1849–50 one finds all the old themes of the compromise tradition as it was expressed in the civic ideals of the old Madisonian Union. Here were the premonitions about sectional parties, the fears of ideological rigidity and party passion, the hope that reason would finally purge the atmosphere of emotion and violence and permit moderate men of comprehensive, national views to bridge the sectional gulf. Here was the call for compromise that preserved the "Union as it is," the federal Union bolstered by national sentiment and protected against the dangers of sectional and party strife. And here echoed the old assumption that legislative compromises reflected Congress's important constitutional function as the arena of conciliation, where the mutual pledges of restraint in 1787, 1820, and 1833 were renewed and reinvigorated by men of sober moderation and honor.

But the Compromise of 1850 as it was implemented by Stephen Douglas and Millard Fillmore turned out to be a transitional event because it could neither pass Congress nor foster strong enough support in the country without the powerful influence of party loyalties. These men were particularly concerned about maintaining party unity; to them, any settlement that healed their intraparty split thereby healed the Union. Fillmore and his conservative Whigs saw the Compromise as an opportunity to tranquilize the party's annoying antislavery faction that had blocked the settlement. It is not surprising that after a brief tussle with the decaying Whig party for succession to the compromise throne, the Democrats fastened on the territorial provisions of the settlement and put them to use as a party program to keep their southern and northern wings aligned. A sectional compromise designed to remove an issue from party politics, to serve as a break from partisan rancor, became a hostage to the fortunes of a single party.

Thus two conceptions of how the party system operated were at work in 1850. One tried to limit the harmful effects of party passion by removing sectional questions from the party system through a comprehensive, balanced settlement reminiscent of the political science of the founding generation. The other tried to protect a party's national base by containing sectional questions *within* the party, whether Whig or Democrat. Party coalitions that necessarily incorporated sectional factions could not simply exile increasingly important constituencies: they had to mollify them. The distinction between these approaches to sectional conflict revealed the underlying transformation of popular political attitudes and customs that had been evolving throughout the 1840s. And it indicated how the imperatives of party loyalty and survival could dictate a different use of the compromise tradition after 1850.

Both outlooks shared important views that permitted them to cooperate in fashioning a settlement. They accepted the traditional constitutional unionist belief that slavery and freedom were at least temporarily compatible within the "Union as it is," even though they tolerated differing opinions about how slavery and freedom might be adjusted through time. And they both scorned the rival pro- and antislavery constitutionalisms of southern and northern militants as fanatical, one-idea abstractions that blocked a realistic treatment of sectional issues.

The paralysis of the political system by 1849 forced a temporary marriage of old and new styles of conflict resolution, an alliance that would be embodied in the Compromise of 1850. The politics of conciliation, so important to the older generation of Henry Clay and Daniel Webster, was an important element in the scope, grand strategy, and design of the package. The politics of pragmatic interest-group compromise, characteristic of the new generation of Stephen Douglas and Millard Fillmore, was the crucial element in the tactical maneuvering and eventual passage of the Compromise. In the aftermath of the settlement, a brief resurgence of the compromise ethic seemed to promise an end to sectional strife. But the seductive ambiguity of "popular sovereignty," incorporated in the territorial provisions of the Compromise, offered the Democratic party a way out of the festering turmoil over the future of slavery in the new West and drew the party and the nation down the increasingly violent path away from further compromise and toward civil war.

THE TRANSFORMATION OF American political culture and the hardening of sectional attitudes during the 1840s altered the meaning of sectional compromise as it had been understood since 1787–88. With the rise of mass politics and the spread of sectional interpretations of the Constitution already apparent in the 1830s, *compromise* began to lose its older emphasis on conciliation, mutuality, and moderation. Instead, both the advocates and the opponents of further sectional compromise began to stress the costs and benefits of a final, irrevocable compromise settlement. By 1850, the convergence of sectionalism and activist politics produced the most serious domestic crisis since the breakdown of the Articles of Confederation. The growing uniformity of the new party system, the rise of political abolitionism and its southern radical opposition, and the intrusion of the slavery issue into Congress via the territorial question strained the constitutional system to the breaking point.

Significantly, the triumph of democratic political culture in the raucous "log-cabin" campaign of 1840 marked the appearance of the nation's first avowedly sectional political organization, the Liberty party, which nominated James G. Birney for president. The formation of the Liberty party had two important implications that require some elaboration. The party revitalized and offered a political platform for the early Republic's antislavery constitutionalism, which would provoke southerners to respond in kind, and it signaled an important decision by determined abolitionists to seek political legitimacy by adopting formal party organization. These two developments would greatly accelerate the sectionalizing of the new party system even as the system was experiencing its initial growing pains.[2]

The Liberty party's platform employed a plausible antislavery constitutional doctrine that would challenge both the moderate, Madisonian compromise tradition and John C. Calhoun's theory of state sovereignty. By the mid-1830s, a number of abolitionists had offered constitutional interpretations that justified stronger federal action against slavery. The history of the Convention and of subsequent congressional legislation, they argued, clearly revealed a determination to end slavery, a determination that had been checked by southern power. Building on the thesis that there was no moral or legal equivalence between freedom and slavery, abolitionists like Theodore Dwight Weld and Salmon P. Chase reworked the traditional antislavery doctrine that slavery—and therefore any compromises with it—controverted both natural and constitutional law. These abolitionists discerned a distinct series of antislavery precedents in the landmark *Somerset* case of 1772 (which pronounced the natural law doctrine), the Declaration of Independence, the Northwest Ordinance, the slave trade ban, the framers' refusal to use the word *slavery* in the Constitution, and the Missouri Compromise restriction, which all defined the limits of the Constitution's sordid compromises on slavery.[3]

In keeping with the antislavery tradition, abolitionists generally agreed that slavery's only legal immunity from federal legislation was within the existing slave states. All other jurisdictions were rightful arenas for federal regulation or prohibition. The innovation lay in the extent to which abolitionists promised to apply federal power. Federal action was not a question of constitutional limitations but of policy to be directed by moral imperatives. Because slavery *should* be extinguished, and because the federal government *could* legislate on slavery anywhere within its jurisdiction, then, they concluded, the government *must* "denationalize" the institution. Meanwhile, in the states, abolitionists used their constitutional theories to support passage of personal liberty and antikidnapping statutes as proper and moral efforts to prevent any complicity with slavery.

To southerners, the most immediate danger from this antislavery constitutionalism was its erosion of the fugitive slave clause, which they regarded as the cornerstone of a national compact on slavery. The traditional interstate comity on the status of blacks began to break down, especially after northern states interpreted an 1842 Supreme Court decision, which restricted jurisdiction over fugitives to Congress, as an opportunity to terminate state and local assistance to slave catchers. Slave states responded by refusing to honor the free status of northern blacks traveling in the South, acting on the traditional southern presumption that race determined legal status. And southerners began to press for a more effective federal fugitive slave law to overrule northern statutes and suppress licit and illicit assistance to fugitive slaves in the free states.[4]

Of course, John C. Calhoun was on the cutting edge of southern retaliation. In his Senate resolutions in both 1837 and 1847, Calhoun argued that as a compact of equal, sovereign states, the Constitution protected anything the states defined as property. Furthermore, he claimed, the sectional compact on slavery obligated every state to *strengthen* the domestic institutions of copartners in the compact, which meant that even the agitation of the question, by undermining interstate cooperation and raising a generation of antislavery voters, violated a solemn pledge of mutual support and defense. Already, he warned in 1837, the alarming arithmetic of each succeeding census was undermining slavery's "great conservative power" as the "balance" of the constitutional system.[5]

Even more ominous for the country was Calhoun's analysis of the impact of abolition politics on the party system. Admitting that the major parties were essentially antiabolition and therefore a force for union, Calhoun noted how northern politicians nonetheless had to court abolition votes. Antipartyism had always been an important component of Calhoun's analysis of civic life, but by the late 1830s the rise of political abolitionism pushed him closer to calling for a new southern party to defend southern rights. Calhoun knew that this would precipitate a major sectional crisis and would be widely perceived as a prelude to secession. Sincerely devoted to the Union as he defined it, Calhoun deplored this possibility. Throughout the late 1830s, he tried in vain to awaken southerners to the magnitude of the danger and to repel further discussion of slavery in Congress.

But at the same time, Calhoun wrote the South's platform for disunion. His call for a southern party and his frequent references to the legality of secession impressed a new generation of southern radicals—men such as Jeremiah Clemens, David Yulee, James Murray Mason, Robert M. T. Hunter, and Jefferson Davis—who saw parties as effective instruments of sectional agitation. They acted on Calhoun's propositions, testing political candidates according to fidelity to the slave system and eventually seeking to replace the national Democratic party with a southern organization.[6]

The hardening of rival interpretations of the Constitution signified a momentous, fateful turn in the direction of American politics. By turning essentially sectional positions into constitutional and moral imperatives, the two outlooks offered the public a choice between competing and mutually exclusive options. Both claimed a historical and intellectual legitimacy by reasoning from the widely accepted principle that the Constitution was a compact. The next step in the development of these sectional positions was obvious: any further compromise, as a compact, must advance a sectional position instead of imposing mutual restraints on the impulse to force one doctrine on a rival. In this manner, the substance of the compromises of the Constitution became hostage to sectional arguments that undermined the conciliatory spirit of those compromises.

To Calhoun and his abolitionist opponents, compromise no longer meant conciliation. It was a contract without the soul of mutuality and was subject to the moral yardstick of universal principle. The ethics of compromise, which justified both mutual concessions as a moderation of passions and the acceptance of a plurality of ends, faced a politics of conscience that deplored compromise as an unacceptable sacrifice of moral principles. To Calhoun, concessions merely masked the retreat of a beleaguered minority and encouraged a rapacious majority in its grasp for national power. "Expediency, concession, compromise! Away with such weakness and folly," he demanded. "Right, justice, plighted faith, and the Constitution: these, and these only, can be relied on to avert conflict." And to the abolitionists, compromise dulled the North's antislavery conscience while protecting slave oligarchs in their unholy plantation citadel.[7]

It was possible for rival constitutional doctrines to coexist without violence only if the political system tempered, modified, and blended them over time. But the rise of mass politics encouraged more immediate gratification of political desires and actually stimulated sectional agitation even as party politicians strove mightily to suppress sectional issues. As parties consolidated their organizations, regularized their convention cycles, imposed more uniformity in elections during the 1840s, and reached out for new issues, they became more vulnerable to and increasingly molded by local pressures (like nativism) and factional disputes in critical states like New York and Pennsylvania. The party system began to lose the flexibility of a loose, decentralized, federal structure at the same time that sectional politicians entered the party conduit to national political power. The intensifying debate about the federal government's jurisdiction over slavery threatened to overwhelm the traditional organizations, so the major parties had little choice but to seek a formula for sectional compromise.[8]

The emergence of political abolitionism and southern radicalism, then, challenged the party system from within. The increasingly democratic political culture of the 1840s celebrated political action as both a duty and a right. It was not surprising that abolitionists, fed up with trying to convert slaveholders from sin, would try to broaden their appeal and seek the adoption of their views through political organization. By turning away from Garrisonian radicalism, by developing a strong and useful constitutional doctrine, and finally by reaching for political power through new as well as traditional party organizations, the abolitionist movement had accepted all but one of the basic requirements of political legitimacy in American politics by the 1840s.[9]

The missing ingredient in both southern radicalism and political abolitionism was constitutional unionism—the belief that union, freedom, and slavery were ultimately compatible through compromise in a system based on divided sovereignty. This fact became obvious at different times and under the impact of different issues. For its part, abolitionism was a sectional position with national ambitions, and any party supporting it automatically risked arousing the traditional, deep-seated fear of geographical parties. In the mid-1830s, this gave southern radicals a slight edge. As defenders of an institution that had flourished within the Union, they could cloak their righteous indignation and radical rhetoric in the mantle of unionist conservatism. The abolitionists loudly and sincerely protested their willingness to tolerate slavery in the existing slave states, but they could not overcome their public image as one-issue fanatics advocating a new union both without slavery and with a huge population of free blacks. So as long as the conflict centered on the status of slavery in those places where it had long existed under the Union, political moderates like Henry Clay and Stephen Douglas could excuse southern anger as an understandable if exaggerated reaction to the disturbing agitation of a sectional question.[10]

During the 1840s, the acquisition of Texas, Oregon, and territories formerly under Mexican jurisdiction had a tremendous effect on the nature of the sectional debate because it stripped away southern unionism's conservative image, revealing a Calhounite doctrine of static sectional equilibrium at odds with the notion of a union partly federal, partly national. The first signs of trouble appeared over Texas's petition for annexation in 1837, which northerners like John Quincy Adams and Joshua Giddings denounced as an attempt to alter the sectional balance and to perpetuate slavery's unjust influence over a growing northern majority. The admission of Texas in 1845 after a long and bitter struggle, the settlement of the Oregon dispute with Britain in 1846, and the acquisition of five hundred thousand square miles of territory from Mexico after the Mexican War offered a new arena for Calhoun to apply his theory that the Constitution protected slave property anywhere within reach of the Fifth Amendment, including territories that were the "common property" of the states and under the administration of their "agent," the federal government. His claim that the Constitution negated Mexico's abolition statute in the Mexican Cession directly threatened the deep economic interest that northerners had developed in the new territories and therefore bespoke a callous disregard for northern interests.

The territorial issue replayed the old quarrel about slavery's constitutional status, but it permitted abolitionists to shift the weight of their arguments away from seeking the end of slavery where it already existed and toward a conservative cry for protection against an aggressive, expanding slavocracy. The Free-Soil movement of the mid to late 1840s reflected this defensiveness. It offered a haven for political abolitionists, but it masked their objectives behind a conservative argument that slavery's expansion threatened a union based on majority rule.

In particular, the Wilmot Proviso, introduced in the House of Representatives in 1846 by the Pennsylvania Democrat David Wilmot and designed to ban slavery from any territory acquired from Mexico, served the dual purpose of fighting off southern dominance of the Democratic party and of reminding northerners what they stood to lose should slavery spread into territories already free by Mexican law. Northern Democrats who worried about southern influence over their party could support free soil as an extension of the Jacksonian faith in majority rule, states' rights, and territorial expansion. And antislavery "conscience" Whigs, already sympathetic to abolitionism's religious and moral appeals, could find in free soil a platform compatible with their long-standing philosophy of an integrated, entrepreneurial economy based on free labor.

Southern radicals in the late 1840s now faced the dilemma of fending off charges of disunionism, for they denied the compatibility of union and free soil. For all of Calhoun's claims of protecting states' rights in the Jeffersonian tradition, he was really defending sectional privilege by demanding specific, irrevocable guarantees of equilibrium between classes of states. Calhoun's Union was not Madison's. His argument that the Constitution ratified a permanent sectional equilibrium, which broad constructionists and abolitionist fanatics had destroyed, dismissed the possibility that the deliberate sense of the political community could change over time.

The danger from the emergence of rival sectional constitutionalisms was that their implementation would be decided not in a Congress elected by a fraction of the adult male population but in a political system encompassing Congress, an activist and emotional party press, and mass political parties that extended their reach into the remotest corners of the country.

THE GROWING STRENGTH of sectional and party alignments within an increasingly centralized and rigid political system made it very difficult to reenact the old ritual of sectional compromise. Previous compromises had been negotiated when the party system had been in disarray and party loyalties fluid enough to permit defections. But in the late 1840s, a decade of party development had produced durable voting patterns that politicians were determined to nourish and expand. The parties' response to the reemergence of the slavery issue through the medium of the territorial question revealed both their common assumptions about compromise and the Constitution and the difference between their way of handling sectional conflict and the surviving compromise ethic of the early Republic.

Surely party leaders wanted to escape the divisiveness of the slavery issue. If they could have pushed the issue back down to the local level, they would have been content. If they could have compromised it and retained their national base, well and good. But the advocates of sectional compromise could not agree on how to manage sectional politics even as the intensifying sectional rift of the mid to late 1840s amplified their fears and demanded immediate action. Old personal rivalries, the imperatives of party unity, deep suspicions of the other party's motives, and a strange mixture of nervous apprehension and complacent confidence that abolitionists and southern radicals were cranky "abstractionists" characterized their attitudes. As we shall see, the first major casualty of the parties' mismanagement of the territorial and slavery issues in the 1840s would be the Missouri Compromise, whose slow demise during the 1840s signified the intensifying pressure that the sectional extremes were placing on the old political center.

Influential party politicians, such men as Thomas Corwin, John M. Clayton, John J. Crittenden, and Alexander Stephens of the Whig party and Stephen Douglas, Lewis Cass, James Buchanan, and William R. King of the Democrats, immediately detected the danger to their national coalitions and sought a formula for intraparty sectional harmony. These men had cut their teeth on the party battles of the Jackson era and had found their respective organizations to be useful vehicles for their rise to national prominence. Having proclaimed their unswerving fidelity to the compromises of the Constitution, party regulars saw in the compromise tradition a centrist continuity that did uphold the Union. To them, legislative compromises could be tailored to the needs of the moment, but more important such compacts were best enforced by parties "coextensive with the Union." Although both parties promoted this viewpoint, they carried it out within the context of intense party competition. Whigs and Democrats maintained that their respective parties offered the best defense of the Union while they accused each other of sectional designs.[11]

Generally, Whigs and Democrats alike supported the vague but familiar constitutional unionist doctrines that preserved the compatibility of freedom, union, and slavery, in direct contrast to the free-soil and common-property doctrines. Both parties officially recognized slavery's immunity in the slave states, but they offered different policy prescriptions for the territorial issue. Their views may be summarized as follows: The compromises of the Constitution formed a national compact that treated slavery as it had existed and not as the framers hoped it eventually would become. These compromises also imposed restraints on any attempt to use the federal government to strengthen or weaken slavery's condition outside of jurisdictions specified in the fugitive slave and slave trade clauses. Furthermore, tradition and common sense seemed to dictate that those most qualified to decide the fate of slavery were slaveholders themselves, for, as Henry Clay had argued, they had the greatest stake in whatever changes might occur in the institution's status.[12]

Just like the abolitionists and southern defenders of slavery, party regulars and moderates traced their constitutional duties to the framers. Outside the states, they believed, Congress should be guided by the institution's current condition and influence, by legislative or judicial precedents, and by the state of public opinion consistent with the preservation of the Union. In effect, this meant congressional inaction either until the Supreme Court ruled on the question of jurisdiction or until deliberate, constitutional majorities fostered a peaceful consensus on what to do. If congressional discussions of slavery endangered the Union by unleashing dangerous passions into politics, and if the Court remained mute, then the government must fall back on the most recent mutual agreement on slavery and, failing that, ultimately on a policy of noninterference. Territory already free by law or nature should be treated as free while territory already allowing slavery should be treated as slave territory.

This position gauged the expediency of action according to the temperature of public discourse. Too much "agitation"—especially by the "fanatics" and "one-idea" men regarded as the villains of civic life—was a sure sign that the public (and therefore Congress) were not ready to make a decision on slavery consistent with the preservation of the Union. In the face of rival, exclusive demands for congressional protection or prohibition of slavery, moderates in both parties argued for compromises that simultaneously imposed mutual restraints on conflicting opinions and applied to new conditions any useful "principle" (such as the Missouri line) derivable from policies generated in quieter times.

The territorial debate evolving from 1844 to 1850 persistently challenged this equivocal constitutionalism and forced the parties into narrower constitutional and policy grounds. It effectively undermined any sense of mutual benefit gained from sectional restraint and replaced it with sectional demands for a new agreement implementing a sectional agenda. From 1844 until 1847, the most familiar alternative to the free-soil and common-property doctrines was the Missouri Compromise line. Its advantage for the parties lay in the implication, if not the mandate, that national territory be divided between freedom and noninterference. Most important, the "principle" of national division had reinforced popular belief that neither side should be allowed to dominate the federal government. In that sense, the Compromise was a policy of sectional restraint that appealed to political parties trying to stop the geographical polarization of American politics. In 1845, the Texas annexation resolution reaffirmed the Compromise line by extending it across the northern border of the new state as a limitation on Texas's claims to territory further north.[13]

The slow demise of the Missouri Compromise formula is an important subtheme of the sectional drama in the late 1840s and 1850s. It deserves some close attention for several reasons. First, the erosion of support for continuing the division of national territories forced the parties to hunt for a new constitutional rationale for compromise, a search that would take them to the idea of popular sovereignty (i.e., local option), an abstract doctrine that, unlike the biform Missouri Compromise, was traceable to the "compromises of the Constitution." Second, the rejection of the Missouri line was a direct precipitant of the congressional deadlock of 1846–49 and was therefore an important sign that the parties, by themselves or in tandem, were incapable of compromising sectional militants. Certainly it is well to remember that the line never really "died" before the final rejection of John J. Crittenden's compromise proposal in 1861; the principle of territorial division would be resurrected time and again over the next decade. But its failure as a national bond freed bits and pieces of the old Compromise—the pledge of free soil north of thirty-six thirty and the implication that the division recognized the continuing influence of a shrinking southern minority—to stand alone as lingering sectional benefits of a national bargain.

The Mexican War and the Wilmot Proviso temporarily foreclosed the extension of the Missouri Compromise line as a viable policy option for the political parties. Whigs were strongly united in opposition to the acquisition of any new territory, but the Democrats' successful coupling of Oregon and Texas as "concessions" to both sections proved more popular. In effect, the parties' first response to the territorial issue had been to offer either something to everyone beyond the Mississippi (the Democrats) or nothing at all (the Whigs). By 1848, the acquisition of territory from Mexico had rendered the Whig "no territory" plank superfluous. When the organization of Oregon Territory came up in Congress in early 1847, antislavery Whigs and Democrats, claiming that territorial aggrandizement had disrupted the constitutional compact and had released them from obligations imposed by the Missouri Compromise, reintroduced the Wilmot Proviso in expanded form, applying it to "any territory on the continent of America" thereafter acquired.[14]

Southerners reverted to their time-honored tactic of holding free territory hostage until slave territory had received guarantees. In resolutions sponsored by Armistead Burt of South Carolina and instigated by Calhoun, southerners agreed to the organization of Oregon as a free territory inasmuch as it lay above the Missouri line, by implication extending that line to the Pacific and "recognizing" slavery south of it. But at the same time, they claimed that the old Missouri Compromise was unconstitutional. Northern votes killed this proposal in the House. Even though the original Missouri line remained intact, the failure to extend the line indicated that the old formula of territorial division no longer carried with it an aura of restraint and mutual concession. Thus, when both antislavery and southern radical forces had basically agreed in early 1847 with a southern congressman's observation that the Missouri Compromise was clearly "no longer of any obligation," they were trying to free themselves of the implied, mutual bond reaffirmed in 1820–21, without precluding a future implementation of that part of the formula favorable to their sectional interests.[15]

The Missouri Compromise thus lost two important attributes that had made it a successful bond between the sections. Without the spell of mutual restraint and the intersectional acquiescence to its constitutionality, the Compromise could not draw the sections together. Northerners accepted the old line and opposed its extension, whereas southerners eventually rejected the old line after demanding its extension. Predictably, the collapse of the Missouri formula precipitated two years of sectional deadlock in Congress.

It took the Democrats longer to abandon the Missouri line than it had taken Congress. Throughout 1847 and early 1848, Democrats debated whether to advocate the Missouri line or to support popular sovereignty. In the summer of 1847, the administration intensified its fruitless campaign for the Missouri line. President James K. Polk toured the northeastern states preaching the gospel of compromise, concord, and Democratic solidarity.[16] Secretary of State James Buchanan, eyeing the 1848 nomination, came out for the Missouri line in August. His "Herkimer Letter" to a group of Pennsylvania Democrats echoed the old compromise argument that northerners did not need to approve slavery "in the abstract" but owed it to the Union, to peace, and to prosperity to "abide by the compromise of the Constitution & leave the question where that instrument . . . left it, to the States wherein slavery" existed. He added, "Our fathers have made this agreement with their brethren of the South: & it is not for the descendants of either party in the present generation to cancel this solemn compact." Extending the Compromise line to the Pacific, he argued, would save the Democratic party, "on the ascendancy of whose principles & measures," he "firmly" believed, depended "the success of our grand experiment in Self Government."[17]

In December 1847, other Democrats came out for popular sovereignty as the party's best hope for sectional harmony. Although many politicians claimed paternity for popular sovereignty, the Michigan Democrat Lewis Cass popularized it and attached it to his presidential ambitions in his Christmas Eve letter to A.O.P. Nicholson. Calling for congressional noninterference with slavery in the territories, Cass based his version of popular sovereignty on an extremely narrow reading of the territorial clause, which conferred congressional power over the "territory and other property" of the United States. Cass claimed that the clause mandated only the enactment of land policies and a rudimentary territorial government, and he argued that the citizens of territories enjoyed the same rights of self-government as did citizens of states, so that the power to decide slavery's fate rested with the pioneers on the prairies, not with Congress. He tried to reassure northerners by predicting that slavery's unsuitability to the new West effectively guaranteed free soil during the formative territorial period. Meanwhile, he castigated agitation of the Proviso as an unnecessary insult to southerners and a source of dangerous divisions within the party.[18]

But Cass and other supporters of popular sovereignty resorted to more than the legalistic hairsplitting and frustrating ambiguities that historians and contemporary critics have analyzed and criticized so thoroughly. He and his supporters treated popular sovereignty as a compromise position and offered the usual historical arguments for compromise in its support. Popular sovereignty seemed like a compromise because it emulated the framers' decision to treat the institution as a local matter and to protect the Constitution's slavery compromises from amendment for twenty years. Popular sovereignty simply tried to keep that old pact alive as it restrained impatient advocates of sectional policies until the territories decided the question. This was not a final settlement; it was a truce, with concessions of sentiment, opinion, and emotion, while the new West made its decision about slavery.[19]

In 1848, Whigs also tried to devise an answer to the territorial problem. In July, amid a round of partisan campaign speeches in Congress, Delaware's Whig Senator John M. Clayton declared, "If this becomes a geographical question . . . I shall act in the spirit of the men who made the Constitution, and compromise the question, if I can." He then managed to get a select committee of conservatives from both sections and parties to approve a compromise proposal. His plan retained free soil in Oregon territory, organized California and New Mexico with a ban on territorial legislation "respecting the prohibition or establishment of African slavery," and permitted a Supreme Court review of any lawsuit challenging the status of slaves carried into the territories.[20]

Defending the committee proposal, Clayton said that "Congress would avoid the decision of this distracting question, leaving it to the silent operation of the Constitution itself." This was a classic Whig position, with its respect for legal, juridical approaches to the problem and its purpose of transferring the rest of the issue out of presidential, party politics and into the hands of the Supreme Court. "We desire to abide by the compromises of the Constitution," Clayton told the Senate. "But neither the one side nor the other of the question forms any part of [the Whig] platform."[21]

The House and the Senate tussled over the plan, deadlocked, and decided to pass the Oregon bill with its antislavery clause intact. Southerners preferred the Missouri line extension but had to content themselves with President Polk's claim, made when he signed the bill, that Oregon was north of the Missouri line and therefore was free territory.[22]

Polk's gesture was futile. The Missouri line was dead as a Democratic party measure. As the 1848 campaign geared up, it became clear that sectional pressures were pushing party leaders toward safer, more abstract grounds. Popular sovereignty, despite its dangers, could get northern votes that the Missouri line could not. The doctrine's seductive ambiguity about the timing of the territory's decision about slavery permitted nervous northern and southern Democrats to remain allied. To give slaveholders enough time to settle in the West, southerners claimed that the people must wait until they applied for statehood before they could act against slavery. Northerners argued that the territorial government could ban or admit it right away. But each side also knew what the other saw in popular sovereignty and preferred, in the interest of party unity, to defer the conflict over timing. In contrast, the Missouri line was too precise an answer to the territorial problem. In 1848, Cass's nomination by the Democrats signaled the victory of popular sovereignty over the Missouri line in the party's councils.

During the late 1840s and especially into the 1848 campaign, Whigs hoped to use economic issues and the party's traditional image of statesmanship to suppress slavery's divisive influence on their coalition. They continued to rail at the "one man power" of Democratic presidents who provoked war with a weak, neighboring republic and who gleefully vetoed Whig economic measures.[23] The *American Whig Review* increasingly emphasized conservative themes that simultaneously deplored slavery and celebrated the party's unique ability to blend a variety of opinions on the institution. Conservatism, Whigs argued, was "the middle term of Politics," since it rested "in the very centre" and could "therefore understand and correct the extremes" of "bigotry" and "radicalism." The *Review* declared in 1849, "The extremes of party feeling in regard to slavery lie outside [the] Conservative Whig Party." For on the Union, all Whigs were "essentially and profoundly conservative." Sentiments about a social contract extending through the generations and affirming a unity of society based on faith, honor, and forbearance became a staple of party rhetoric. "The citizen *must* be a statesman," Whigs intoned, urging northerners to obey "the law of kindness" and "the principle of self-control" by refraining from agitation about slavery.[24]

The Whig party, "a grand national party . . . holding to its original purposes of peace, order, union, and a free and gradual amelioration," was the real guardian of freedom and union, a Whig writer claimed. The party could "embrace within its circle men of all sects, and living under various private institutions, but agreeing in the one idea of republican nationality and union" that stood as "the golden mean" of American politics.[25]

In keeping with these appeals to misty nationality and conservative party statesmanship, Whigs in 1848 turned to Zachary Taylor, a war hero, slaveholder, political novice, and believer in a "no party" presidency. Their vice presidential nominee, Millard Fillmore of New York, displayed all the "safe" qualities of a divided party's national candidate: "careful, discreet, painstaking, and indisposed to give offence or excite commotion."[26] Meanwhile, the party refused to commit itself to a specific territorial policy, instead permitting its sectional wings to advocate their own positions without national party interference. The party went into the 1848 campaign with northern Whigs favoring the Wilmot Proviso, southern Whigs backing the Missouri line, and both wings accusing the Democrats of using expansionism as a party trick to divide the Whigs!

"Conscience" Whigs, antislavery Democrats, and most Liberty men backed Martin Van Buren as the candidate of the Free Soil party in 1848. Although Free-Soilers failed to crack the traditional party organizations, they did succeed both in forcing northern Whigs and Democrats to proclaim their candidates' fidelity to the nonextension of slavery and in depriving the parties of a House majority in the next Congress. The Free-

Soilers obtained only 10 percent of the popular vote, but their doctrines had clearly invaded and greatly influenced the northern wings of both parties. Northern Whig regulars urged antislavery voters to choose Taylor because his antiveto pledge presumably would spare the Wilmot Proviso should it reach his desk. Southerners made the Free-Soil menace a major issue between the two parties. Southern Democrats reminded the electorate of the southern Whigs' party ties to abolitionism, and southern Whigs claimed that the northerner Cass was less reliable on slavery than was Zachary Taylor.[27]

Although sectional feelings were evident in these party appeals, compromise arguments and conservative sentiments already prominent in the party press also carried great weight. Whigs portrayed Taylor as a "national" man of presidential timber grown from hardy Washingtonian stock. Democrats charged that Whigs and Free-Soilers vied "with each other in the present crusade against the South." Cass and his party, a New York Democrat told the Georgia Democrat Howell Cobb, were "the only advocates of a strict adherence to the Constitution and its compromises to be found in the North." Taylor's razor-thin victory prompted Whigs to proclaim the revival of the era of good feelings under the aegis of a party that, in Fillmore's words, occupied "that safe and conservative ground" that left "fanatics and disunionists, North and South, without hope of destroying the fair fabric of our Constitution."[28]

The congressional deadlock over the territories resumed after the election. When the lame-duck Thirtieth Congress reconvened in December, Stephen Douglas again tried unsuccessfully to get three different territorial bills through Congress. Meanwhile, the House reaffirmed the Wilmot Proviso, revived a bill to abolish slavery in the District of Columbia, drafted a bill to organize California as a territory under the Northwest Ordinance, and passed a resolution for the abolition of the District slave trade.

A perilous paralysis loomed in Congress as the new year dawned. The parties could not overcome sectional divisions, and as the year progressed it became clear that sectional blocs could not overcome party loyalties. In January, John C. Calhoun, angered by the House's threatening legislation and a flurry of northern state resolutions supporting the Wilmot Proviso, urged all slave-state representatives to sign a "Southern Address" calling for a southern party to stop northern aggression. Although southern

Whigs and moderate Democrats denounced the address as disunionist and a vehicle for Calhoun's perennial presidential ambitions, a number of southern states heeded Calhoun's call for solidarity. In October, Mississippi summoned the slave states to meet in Nashville the following spring to discuss measures of redress. Widely regarded as a prelude to secession, this proposal came on the heels of southern threats of disunion should California, now in the throes of the gold rush, be admitted without significant guarantees for slavery in the Southwest.[29]

To moderates in both parties, it seemed that all the ingredients for a first-class crisis were converging. The states were binding senators by instruction and trying to circumscribe their negotiating flexibility; coalitions of Free-Soilers and Democrats or Whigs had appeared in several northern states; the South was listening attentively to Calhoun's call for unity and resistance; and the parties were deadlocked in Congress as a northern House and a southern Senate blocked legislation. The old Federalist premonitions about a "universal alarm for the public safety" were on the verge of fulfillment: geographical parties were close at hand.

THE COUNTRY WAS "ripe and ready for a rational compromise," which alone could "satisfy the members of a confederacy of independent states," the New York *Herald*'s Washington correspondent remarked at the opening of the Thirty-first Congress in December 1849.[30] But the recent defeat of Douglas's proposals, of the Clayton Compromise, and of the Missouri line already demonstrated the parties' inability to work out a compromise on the territorial question, and the new Congress continued the party gridlock. The House of Representatives sank into a long, grueling fight over the Speakership, lasting sixty-three ballots over three weeks and preventing Congress from officially commencing the session and conducting the nation's business. Personal animosities split state delegations and further prevented effective caucusing to end the conflict.[31] And after choosing a Speaker, the members fought for another week over the selection of a doorkeeper. Obviously this branch of Congress was not in the mood for a "rational compromise." The vast majority of its members were political novices and one-termers, products of the heady and confident 1840s, unleavened by experience with severe domestic crises.[32]

The House's disappointing performance had other important effects as well. It confirmed the general impression that even a turn of the electoral cycle had failed to refresh the two major parties with leaders strong enough to manage the territorial issue. The old parties were dying, some said, and good riddance to them. The irascible conservative James Gordon Bennett was already pronouncing Whiggery's postmortem from his post at the New York *Herald*. Free soil had killed the Whig party, he noted, whereas the southern reaction to it was killing the old Democracy; Bennett sniffed a realignment in the wind. The conservative press, watching the House descend into chaos, began talking of a great national party of union, composed of "the middle men of both parties," to replace the current factionalized organizations. And as the sectional crisis mounted during the coming months, antiparty sentiments flowed freely from the nation's press and pulpits as unionists lamented how "the permanent interests of this great country depended on a sacrifice of party position by . . . the old democratic and whig line."[33]

The House's eventual organization permitted Congress to receive President Taylor's annual message and consider the sheaf of pending bills on slavery-related matters. During his first year in office, Taylor had aligned himself with antislavery northern Whigs led by William H. Seward and Thurlow Weed of New York and Truman Smith of Connecticut. These men had already channeled patronage to their supporters, cutting out conservative backers of Vice President Fillmore and alienating some southern Whigs. Taylor began to make remarks about preserving the Union against secessionist traitors and permitting the Wilmot Proviso to pass his desk should Congress send it to him.[34]

Taylor also tried to defuse the sectional crisis through indirection. Throughout 1849 he had quietly encouraged California to write a constitution and apply for admission without bothersome delay at the territorial stage. In two messages to Congress, the president urged California's admission as a free state and suggested that Congress accept New Mexico's admission once the area, as a territory, had followed a similar path. Taylor hoped to slip California into the Union without a divisive fight over the Wilmot Proviso, for his plan effectively favored free soil in the West by a kind of accelerated popular sovereignty.

Southern Whigs had accepted similar measures before (perhaps because Californians and New Mexicans would be acting at the *statehood* stage, instead of at the earlier territorial stage), but the rift in the party and the size of the concession to the North left Taylor's plan stillborn among his former southern allies. Southerners were not ready to permit the Senate balance to shift northward without guarantees more solid than congressional avoidance of the Wilmot Proviso. Taylor's plan also ignored the problems of slavery in the District, fugitive slaves, and a gathering quarrel over Texas's claims on the New Mexico border. Territorial plans alone had failed repeatedly over the past three years; the conflict had spilled over into slavery-related issues. Thus, in January, Senator James Murray Mason introduced a harsh fugitive slave bill that quickly became the centerpiece of southern demands in the controversy. Taylor's plan, then, did not hold out to southern Whigs the kind of concessions they expected from a Whig president.[35]

"It is the danger to the Union that gives this slavery agitation its importance, and makes a compromise a matter of first necessity," James Gordon Bennett pointed out a week before Taylor's first message. Other conservatives agreed, pointing out the ease with which disunion was discussed in the halls of Congress, a circumstance that itself presaged the end of the old Union. "The dissolution must precede these things if it ever does take place," Kentucky Representative Charles Morehead wrote to his friend John J. Crittenden. "The fear I entertain is of the establishment of mere sectional parties, and the commencement of a system of retaliatory local or State legislation." The only way to arrange a settlement, Bennett argued, was to change the issue from slavery to union. No one was better equipped to do this than that "class of statesmen now in Congress," who had "grown gray in the service of the nation and . . . grown tired in the service of party," Bennett explained later. "The livery of whiggery and democracy which they have so long worn, has grown shabby by time, and before they lay their heads in the grace, they would wish to signalize their history in some grand national service."[36] Bennett was referring to Daniel Webster, John C. Calhoun, Henry Clay, and Thomas Hart Benton, the nation's elder statesmen who were gathering in Washington for the session. Having seen the Republic through many dark days, these men of the second generation had devoted their political lives to the maintenance of the Union.

Of this group, only Calhoun was no longer a unionist of the first fire. He had been sounding the alarm for the Union for the previous twelve years;

he had already concluded that the old Union, wholly federal and not at all national, had been subverted by northern aggression against the compact of 1787. Benton, the Missouri solon and Jacksonian stalwart, had crossed swords with Calhoun in the previous session, denouncing the Southern Address and accusing radicals of kicking up a storm over nothing important. Like Webster and Clay, he believed that Congress was fully empowered to ban slavery in the territories, and he supported Taylor's plan, but Benton spent most of the session quarreling with Clay about tactics and with southern hotheads about their single-mindedness on slavery. Webster had free soil sympathies but was also on record opposing abolitionism as disunionist. Furthermore, Webster was not convinced of the seriousness of the situation until the session had gotten fairly well under way and he had sat through secessionist tirades over the Wilmot Proviso and a free California.[37]

Clay had been officially retired for the past eight years, but in January 1849 he had accepted the Kentucky legislature's call to the Senate. It would have been impossible to find a single major politician in Washington who genuinely welcomed Clay's return to national politics. Fellow statesmen feared him, hated him, pitied him, or dismissed him as a sore loser with old scores to settle, especially with Zachary Taylor. Yet there is little evidence that Clay came to Washington out of any motive other than to help settle the territorial controversy and thereby add another compromise to his crown.[38] Instead, Clay remained in Lexington through a dreadful cholera outbreak that summer, briefly vacationed in New York and Newport, and after returning home, made his way to Washington just before the session was to open. In feeble health (already suffering from symptoms of the congestive heart failure that would kill him two years hence), detested by the administration, and generally out of touch with party affairs, Clay was not a man hankering for office. Although he sized up the situation immediately on his arrival and began working to foster a conciliatory atmosphere, much of his planning was impromptu and worked with materials at hand. Clay tried to cultivate friendly relations with the president, but Taylor was openly cool and privately hostile while the cabinet in general wished that he would go back home. Rebuffed, the Kentuckian concentrated his efforts in his old stomping ground on Capitol Hill.[39]

Actually, Clay's compromise proposal required little planning or secrecy. His views on the territorial question, slavery in the District of Columbia, and fugitive slaves were a matter of public record. His published comment in Baltimore en route to Washington—that his views "on these questions" were "altogether conservative"—hardly suggested novel ideas in the offing. He sought Webster's endorsement and undoubtedly spoke with influential senators, but his plan was merely a mixture of old ideas stitched together and, in the classic tradition, introduced as a set of resolutions to cultivate the sense of the Senate.

Clay made his move on January 29 and followed up on February 5 and 6 with a two-day speech in defense of his proposals and of sectional compromise.[40] The new element of Clay's plan was its scope and design; it comprehended all the "questions arising out of slavery" and currently before the country. Clay addressed four issues in four pairs of resolutions: the first and last pairs respectively were concessions to the North and the South; the middle two pairs linked sectional concessions. This was why Clay asked the Senate to consider them all "as a system."[41]

Clay's proposals—their scope, design, and substance—and the strategy their author tried to implement deserve close examination, for the resolutions were an excellent example of the old constitutional unionism at work. Each pair, to some extent, reflected Clay's firm belief that both the compound nature of the Constitution and the web of formal and informal historical compromises on slavery imposed legal and practical limits on the exercise of federal power over the institution. The breadth of the proposals suggested the importance of comprehensive, balanced settlements that removed the symptoms of disunion from the vortex of party and congressional strife. Clay's strategy, as we shall see, relied on the old politics of conciliation, which valued good faith and civility as the true safeguards of smooth debate and eventual passage.

Clay's first two resolutions addressed the territorial question.[42] The Kentuckian urged that California be admitted and New Mexico and Utah organized all without "the adoption of any restriction or condition on the subject of slavery" by Congress. Both resolutions assumed that congressional inaction on slavery would leave the Mexican Cession free soil because the laws of Mexico, of California, and of economics excluded it. In this case, inaction favored the North, as in Taylor's plan, unless slaveholders moved into the territories or into California and made the areas into slave country. But slaveholders would not take their chattels into the new West, Clay maintained, because cheap labor in California underpriced slave labor. Northerners could forbear agitating the Wilmot Proviso, Clay thought, "for the sake of peace, and in a spirit of mutual forbearance to other members of the Union." In return, they would get something "worth more than a thousand Wilmot Provisos"—a free California and probably a free New Mexico.

But was there a constitutional imperative either to prohibit or to protect slavery in the territories? No, Clay answered. How could a constitution of a nation half-slave and half-free automatically exclude slavery or freedom from the territories? Congress's power to introduce or prohibit slavery in territories acquired by conquest or by treaty had been "fixed and settled" for some fifty years past, he explained, and had not been "seriously disturbed until recently." But the existence of a power does not require its exercise. Instead, this was an issue on which reasonable men might differ without furnishing just cause for breaking up the Union. The answer, Clay thought, was congressional inaction, for it permitted differing opinions to coexist without imposing one or the other on the territories.

Clay was not proposing popular sovereignty. He did not share Cass's narrow view of the territorial clause, and he did not want to injure Congress's constitutional power to make such a decision in the future. Instead, Clay was calling for prudent restraints on the urge to legislate one section's vision of the future at the other's expense. In his view, the real danger lay in Congress, where closely matched forces were paralyzing the legislative process. In effect, Clay accepted popular sovereignty, but only as corollary to federal inaction and as nonbinding on future Congresses. In his mind, the constitutionality of the Wilmot Proviso was unshakable.

Perhaps this was why the Great Compromiser rejected the Missouri line as a possible solution. Extending the line would automatically admit slavery south of it, Clay reasoned, because any congressional action would vacate Mexico's abolition statute and permit slaveholders to enter. He would never vote to make free territory slave, he said, yet he conceded that neither would he oppose extension of the line. But he noted of extension, "It is contrary to my own judgment and to my own conscience." Better, he thought, "to keep the whole of these matters untouched by any legislation of Congress upon the subject of slavery, leaving it open and undecided." This matter was best left to the Supreme Court.[43]

The second pair of resolutions dealt with the Texas question. Militant southerners were demanding the full allotment of Texas's huge claims on its western border so as to enforce the compact in the Texas annexation resolution that anticipated the formation of at least four new slave states in the Southwest. Northerners opposed this as an unwarranted addition of slave states to the Union. Clay proposed that Texas recede from some of its demands in return for federal assumption of the state's large preannexation debt. Clay hoped that bribing Texas would calm southern hotheads, that limiting the state's expansion would answer northern demands, and that offering federal money to lubricate the deal would attract powerful Texas bondholders from both sections to the standard of compromise. It was a calculated attempt to "buy peace," as Webster later called it.[44]

Clay's third pair of resolutions faced the problem of slavery in the District of Columbia. Clay proposed that the slave trade be abolished in the District but that slavery be left intact unless Maryland consented to abolition and slaveowners received "just compensation." Both resolutions assumed the constitutionality of federal power over slavery in the District but asked "the parties to forbear urging their respective opinions the one to the exclusion of the other." This was in line with Clay's long-standing belief that slavery's status in the District was subject to the terms of the original cession from Virginia and Maryland, a compact "made when all was peace, harmony, and concord—when brotherly affections, fraternal feelings, prevailed throughout this whole Union." No one then had anticipated the agitation of this issue, which now threatened obligations that were not, in Clay's opinion, "less sacred or less binding than if they had been inserted in the constitutional instrument itself." So here was another historic sectional compromise of constitutional force, technically reversible but only on pain of dishonor and the erosion of civility in government.[45]

The final pair of resolutions dealt with interstate relations on slavery.[46] Here Clay backed the South to the hilt, calling for a more effective fugitive slave law and a congressional resolution affirming the unconstitutionality of congressional power to prohibit or obstruct the interstate slave trade. Clay denounced the North's personal liberty laws both as unconstitutional impediments to the rendition of fugitive slaves and as an unwarranted interpretation of the Supreme Court's rulings on the subject. Speaking from recent experience with an escaped slave, Clay thought it "a mark of no good brotherhood, of no kindness, of no courtesy," that a slaveholder could no longer safely sojourn with his slaves in most northern states.

As for the interstate slave trade, Clay equated this resolution with his second Missouri Compromise: a congressional declaration of "an incontested principle of Constitutional law." In the present case, northerners would be conceding their constitutional opinion and limiting the scope of future action on slavery for the sake of sectional harmony. In tandem with the first pair of free-soil resolutions, these prosouthern proposals were designed to circumscribe the future course of debate over slavery by reaffirming the constitutional compact that left slavery undisturbed in the states but otherwise subject to federal law consistent with the preservation of the Union.

None of these ideas were new. Clay rightly assumed that creative statesmanship in this crisis required a new form for old ideas by expanding the range of possible concessions. Douglas, Clayton, and President Taylor had already tried and failed to build support for innovative but substantively narrow territorial measures because the intensity of the sectional quarrel had spilled over into other slavery-related issues. It was also clear that the deadlock between the two houses, symbolic of deepening sectional distrust, would prevent separate consideration of slavery-related bills.[47] Under these conditions, Clay hoped to change votes by changing what Congress was voting on. He knew that aside from a small group of moderates and undecided senators, most of the members had come to Washington encumbered both by opinions honed and hardened from four years of congressional wrangling and by state legislative resolutions spurning compromise. Parties had worsened the situation, he thought, by preventing politicians from acting like statesmen. Indeed, he launched his defense of the plan with a vehement denunciation of "passion, passion; party, party—and intemperance" as the great stumbling blocks to compromise.[48]

Clay's contribution to the Compromise of 1850, then, was neither his parliamentary skill (for despite some minor successes his parliamentary tactics ultimately failed) nor his ability to sway doubters (for he probably changed few, if any, votes). Rather, it was his dramatic transformation of the issue to the question of union or disunion. The new focus permitted him to assemble in awesome array the patriotic images of statesmanship, union, and compromise, images that had collectively constituted the compromise tradition since 1787. By shifting the debate onto the ground of union or disunion and away from the desirability or morality of slavery, Clay expected to unite moderates on a platform that reminded citizens of what they stood to lose should Free-Soilers or fire-eaters triumph. In fine, Clay was outlining a conservative vision of the past in opposition to incompatible, revolutionary, sectional visions of the future. Thus, he lambasted southern radical notions that a sectional equilibrium had ever existed. Both sections had at different times dominated the government, but especially southerners, whose constitutional protections had always been sufficient to prevent complaint. No one could seriously contemplate legislating a diminishing minority's privileged status into the nation's fundamental law, he asserted. Concurring majorities could be cultivated only through the flexible and safer process of congressional debate and legislation, not through constitutional amendments. And abolitionists who demanded the immediate denationalization of slavery were breaking the historic interstate comity symbolized in the District of Columbia cession, the fugitive slave clause, and the years of judicial reciprocity on the treatment of blacks in interstate transit.[49]

Strong support for Clay came from Webster. On March 7, Webster gave a packed Senate chamber a learned history lesson in antislavery constitutionalism that nonetheless broke with Free-Soil demands for the imposition of the Wilmot Proviso. Reiterating his powerful antiextension arguments of 1845, 1847, and 1848, Webster chided northern Democrats for stimulating annexationist sentiment back in the 1840s and thereby passing up the opportunity to avert this crisis. Now the country had to clean up their mess. Claiming that the laws of nature barred slavery from the new West, Webster urged northerners to be patient and conciliatory with a South that clearly had no future in the West and legitimate grievances in the East. Webster's speech alienated antislavery Whigs and further attached the powerful support of northern mercantile interests to the cause of compromise.[50]

The opponents of compromise were active and powerful. Jefferson

Davis of Mississippi denounced Clay's plan and demanded the Missouri line at the very least. On March 4, Calhoun made his valedictory to the Senate, reviewing his arguments that the North had broken the sectional compact and that cries of "Union!" were useless palliatives. Secession was inevitable without solid constitutional guarantees for southern rights, he said. Southern militants balked at Calhoun's blunt predictions and constitutional demands, but they accepted his analysis of the issues. Throughout the spring and summer, Jeremiah Clemens of Alabama, David Yulee and Marcus Morton of Florida, Solon Borland of Arkansas, Pierre Soulé of Louisiana, James Murray Mason and R.M.T. Hunter of Virginia, and Clay's old friend John M. Berrien of Georgia took stern ground against Clay. Compromise, they argued, meant surrender to a domineering North that scoffed at the compromises of the Constitution. "If we are to go on compromising away provision after provision of the Constitution," Clemens declared, "it is better that it should be abrogated at once."[51]

Free-Soilers and antislavery northerners rallied behind New York Senator William Henry Seward. On March 11, Seward denounced all legislative compromises as vicious and immoral, demanded California's immediate, unencumbered entry into the Union, opposed any new fugitive slave law, called for the abolition of slavery in the District, and confidently predicted that slavery's inevitable demise was near at hand. Joining him were Free-Soilers John P. Hale of New Hampshire and Salmon P. Chase of Ohio and several antislavery Whigs from Rhode Island, Connecticut, and Vermont. Later in the summer, Seward expanded on his position and excoriated compromisers who appealed to national sentiments while ignoring in fact "everything of paramount and ultimate importance, in regard to the perfection and permanence of the institutions of the country." He stated, "I believe that concession today only increases the evils and embarrassments of to-morrow." Calhoun couldn't have said it better.[52]

With these opening broadsides by moderates and militants, the debate over Clay's proposals shifted to parliamentary strategy. The tactical dynamics of the debate temporarily forged a powerful coalition of extremes against a divided center. Moderates could not agree on whether the proposals should be considered separately or as a single bill. The course and outcome of this disagreement revealed the extent to which the old compromise tradition was yielding to the party culture of a new political era. The two leaders of the moderate camp—Clay and Douglas—pursued different and occasionally conflicting strategies that reflected their different political worlds. Clay's strategy generally set the course for debate until late July, when his opponents succeeded in knocking his plan to pieces on the Senate floor. Douglas's strategy then swung into action, eventually achieving victory for the compromisers with the passage of separate bills by September. In fine, Clay's attempt to replay the old, sentimental ritual of sectional compromise succeeded in cultivating enough popular support to permit Douglas and his allies to press the issue to a successful conclusion. A close look at their tactics confirms David Herbert Donald's observation that the eventual Compromise of 1850 was "designed by men of one generation and adopted by those of another."[53]

Clay's strategy was evident not only in the design of his proposals but also in the tactics he pursued to get their substance enacted. A master of atmospherics, Clay took every opportunity to shame militants, praise the Union, and challenge senators to transcend party and sectional divisions and act like statesmen. At the start of the session, he moved that Congress buy the remaining copy of Washington's Farewell Address, accompanying his proposal with a burst of unionist oratory. He urged his followers across the country to organize union meetings, and at his few public appearances during the session, Clay spread the word of peace, bipartisanship, and union. When southern radicals injected slavery into routine legislative matters, Clay rebuked them for their willingness to foment disorder and violate Senate decorum. During the long debate stretching well into a very hot summer, Clay kept maneuvering for rhetorical advantage, portraying his opponents as rigid, dogmatic abstractionists who could not see above regional interests while praising compromisers as patriotic unionists. As sincerely as his opponents might proclaim fidelity to the Union, they could not overcome the firm link between union and compromise that Clay personified.[54]

Supporters of compromise from around the country, including many former enemies of Clay's and Webster's, echoed the style, tone, and sentiment of Clay's patriotic rhetoric. This brief bipartisanship had been characteristic of the old compromise ritual in 1820 and 1833.[55] Much of this unionist rhetoric embellished the old themes of sectional compromise and constitutional unionism with patriotic, partisan, and religious images. At

Castle Garden in New York City, local and national politicians appealed to a huge crowd with cries for peace and union, accusing the North of obstructing the enforcement of the fugitive slave clause, "one of the compromises of the Constitution that brought us together." Joseph L. White vowed, "We will compromise—we will continue to compromise; for the principle of Union is far above all other principles."[56] A Tammany Democrat told an anti-Proviso meeting in New York that the great "contract" of 1787 prevented Congress from compelling freemen to hold slaves and slaveholders to free their bondsmen. "The Union belongs to us all," William Fell Giles told a crowd of Baltimore unionists. "It originated in the sanctities of compromise and sacrifice, and no one party has the right to dissolve it without the consent of the whole." In the Constitution, another speaker claimed, the sections agreed "to share . . . in one grand destiny, and the original compact which bound them together, was viewed as a marriage contract—to be regarded with solemnity. The North took the South, 'for better or for worse,'" only to break its vows by meddling with slavery.[57]

Even the framework of the Compromise—its temporary incorporation into an "omnibus" measure uniting several bills—reflected older conceptions of legislative procedure that stemmed from the politics of conciliation. In this case, southerners demanded the combining of territorial bills into one to force simultaneous concessions from the North. Clay reluctantly yielded to their arguments that packaging the bills would promote his initial objective of seeking a comprehensive solution. Operating on the conclusion that the House-Senate deadlock would prevent the passage of separate *bills*, Clay's initial resolutions had still tried to link separate *issues* in order to forge a strong enough coalition of moderates to obtain passage. This was intended to awaken the Senate to the widening reach and deepening danger of the slavery issue without committing members to any one proposal. Clay hoped the tactic would pry members loose from their sectional and party attachments, alert them to the Union's peril, and pave the way for compromise. This was the old politics of conciliation, for if the Senate became more conciliatory in spirit, he expected that "good faith" and mutual trust would tie conflicting opinions and laws together, so that the passage of one sectional measure would imply a promise to pass a subsequent concession to the other side.[58]

The decision to submit Clay's resolutions (along with a plan offered by John Bell of Tennessee) to a Select Committee of Thirteen also smacked of the old constitutional ritual, especially of 1787 and 1820–21. The committee deliberated unhampered by senatorial instruction, but it was commonly known that its members would unite Clay's resolutions (also embodied in separate bills) into a single bill. Clay chaired the committee, joined by a judicious mixture of radicals and moderates from both parties and sections. This was a familiar ritual rich in historical and patriotic associations, which made it even more appealing to compromisers in 1850. Select committees of the states had defused the Missouri crisis, had developed Clayton's compromise, and had been crucial to the genesis of the great compromise in the Constitutional Convention back in 1787. The committee's purpose, in the tradition of select committees, was not to create new legislation but to develop a rationale for the measures entrusted to its care and, in this case, "to embody a moral influence in favor of some plan of settlement."[59]

Clay wrote the committee report during a lull in Senate action during early May. It combined, into one omnibus measure, territorial bills for New Mexico and Utah, a statehood bill for California, and propositions to settle the Texas question. Significantly, Clay had again reluctantly yielded to southern demands that the territorial sections not refer to the validity of Mexican law, and he had inserted language preventing the new territorial governments from legislating "in respect to African slavery." Mason's fugitive slave bill emerged separately (amended to include jury trial in the fugitive's home state), as did a bill to eliminate the slave trade in the District of Columbia. Clay's resolution on the interstate slave trade was dropped altogether.[60]

Clay's defense of his report throughout May, June, and July repeatedly stressed the themes that had shaped his long public career: peace and union through compromise. Uniting the territorial, Texas, and California bills would prevent either section from dominating the other, he argued, for both sides would be reconciled to the greater good of peace, "for the sake of that harmony so desirable in such a confederacy as this."[61] The omnibus tried to satisfy both sides by eliminating free-soil language offensive to the South while retaining free soil in fact in California and the Mexican Cession. But radicals remained unsoothed, Clay noted. Northerners demanded the Wilmot Proviso, and southerners were still threatening to block legislation without specific repudiation of free soil. Both sides were therefore arguing over abstractions and matters of form regardless of consequences to the Union. Was this patriotic? he asked. Did it promote peace?[62]

Alluding to the mounting evidence of unionist sentiment around the country, Clay challenged militants to heed the nation's cooling passions, relinquish extreme opinions, and unite on a single plan that reaffirmed the country's unity.[63] He lectured the opposition to act like statesmen in the tradition of the framers and to comprehend all the nation's interests, opinions, and prejudices instead of attaching themselves "to a single position, and viewing from that point everything, and seeking to bring everything to the standard" of their "own peculiar opinions, . . . own bed of Procrustes."[64] In keeping with his belief that certain issues were best kept out of the emotional strife of popular politics, Clay warned that if this Congress failed its duty to the voters, the members would return home embittered, "with a heated press, with heated men" awaiting them. Agitators would continue to exploit party divisions, he predicted, so that the next session would face insurmountable obstacles to reasoned debate.[65]

Slavery was the cause of the trouble, Clay believed, but it was an untouchable cause. Sectionalists demanded too much of a Congress as yet unready to cope with such monumental questions. As a conservative journalist had put it back in mid-March, "The very object of any compromise is, to put an end to the agitation, and to 'save the ship,' not, as Mr. Webster eloquently remarked, to select a 'fragment on which to float from the wreck.'"[66] Symptomatic relief that stopped agitation dangerous to fraternal union was the only way to preserve a union that was partly federal, partly national, and that required compromise to keep it perpetual. But this was not a prescription for static sectional balance. Like past sectional compromises, this one had a dynamic element in it; it assumed that the *underlying* issue would eventually be settled even as the present danger was averted. Clay assumed that the West was going to be free, so that the politically unresolvable issue of slavery would be left to settle itself while the immediate danger of disunion could be met directly. The ultimate outcome was as predictable as the sunrise: slavery, safe within the Union, would wither and die within the Union.[67]

Such arguments infuriated southerners. Better to face the Wilmot Proviso, Pierre Soulé stormed, than to grapple with a bill that meant all things to all men and therefore had no consistent meaning at all. "Aggressions, in the garb of *aggressions*, can be confronted and resisted; but aggressions, in the garb of *concessions*, that look you *fair* but mean you *foul*, gilding the bolus which masks the hemlock, is the worst form that the worst wrong can assume," he charged. Northern militants agreed.[68]

Throughout June, anticompromise senators loaded the omnibus with amendments to hone its ambiguous language to a sharp sectional edge. Soulé succeeded in amending the territorial sections to include the southern version of popular sovereignty: any states formed out of the territories would be admitted to the Union with or without slavery as their constitutions prescribed at the time of their admission. Clay supported the amendment, breezily denominating it another "abstraction" not binding future Congresses and barely worth "the pinch of snuff . . . in [his] fingers" because the territories would never have to deal with slaves anyway. But Soulé's triumph was Clay's defeat, for Soulé called this clause a "compromise" that was "to all intents and purposes, a compact" that would be "binding *in future*."[69] George Badger, a Whig from North Carolina, agreed with Soulé, arguing that the South's security now lay in such a compromise, which would bind future Congresses composed of "high-minded honorable men" acting on "that sense of honor and integrity on which" people relied "in most of the transactions of life."[70] Here was the core of the "principle" of popular sovereignty, which Douglas would later appropriate to overturn the Missouri Compromise in the Nebraska country.[71]

The fate of Clay's omnibus hung precariously throughout June and July as the Senate debated Texas, fugitive slaves, slavery in the District, and the territories. The administration remained sullen and in late June and early July bestirred itself enough to rally a few pro-Taylor senators in defense of the president's original plan. "Mr. Clay's compromises had never done any good," Taylor growled to a North Carolina Whig in late June, vowing to push his own plan.[72] Despite opposition from the executive, from old foes like Benton, and from sectional militants, Clay remained undaunted—after all, these were his traditional opponents, and he had lived and worked under such conditions for most of his career.

On July 9 fate intervened on the side of the compromisers when Taylor died after a bout with fever contracted over the Fourth of July holiday. Vice President Fillmore ascended to the presidency, threw the administration's weight behind the omnibus, turned out Taylor's cabinet, and used the patronage to buy support for the compromise. Unlike Taylor, Fillmore was eager to restore Whig unity through a comprehensive settlement. Fillmore's actions, coming on the heels of the Nashville Convention's meek endorsement of the Missouri line in mid-June, strengthened Clay's hopes for victory.[73]

In late July, Clay made his last, greatest effort in the Senate, defending the omnibus in a speech that naturally stressed the historical and ethical traditions of compromise since the founding of the nation. Clay worked all the old themes before a rapt gallery. Compromise is natural to all social relations, he observed, for it rests on civility, tolerance, respect, and good citizenship. Remember the Constitutional Convention, he urged, and recall the great crises of 1820 and 1833. Radicals scoffed then at the Union, he said, while patriots hewed to their vision of the Founding Fathers and risked their lives, fortunes, and sacred honor on behalf of compromise. "The bells rang, and every demonstration of joy throughout the whole land" followed those compromises.[74]

Mutual recriminations, Clay argued, destroyed the harmony of the old Union by unleashing into public discourse dangerous passions that alienated "mutual affections." References to "lords of the loom" and "lords of the lash" might be fitting for "the barrooms of crossroads taverns" but not for the Senate, where such language poisoned sectional fraternity. Men forgot their humility and fallibility when they demanded universal obedience to some newfangled constitutional principle. In such an atmosphere, he wondered, could men ever exercise their reason, compare their opinions, and achieve practical ends? Could any settlement emerge from an environment bereft of civility, moderation, and rational discussion?

Abolitionists and southern radicals were like the Federalists of old, Clay charged as he moved onto familiar ground. Only by the wildest and most fanatical interpretations of the general welfare clause could anyone justify an inalienable right to carry slaves into California or the new West, he told southerners. And the abolitionists, he declaimed, used the Constitution to implement fanciful theories that struck at the foundations of property and order. The victory of these forces would "be a triumph of ultraism and impracticability—a triumph of a most extraordinary conjunction of extremes; a victory won by abolitionism; a victory achieved by free-soilism; the victory of discord and agitation over peace and tranquility."

It was a bravura performance—three and a half hours of unionist oratory. But Clay's old magic, his appeal to conservative sentiment and the old constitutional unionism, could no longer carry the day. As an observer had noted back in February, these days Clay's eloquence no longer drew sustenance from the "*entourage* of partisan followers that [had] once listened to every word which fell from his lips." The numbers just were not there to pass his bill.[75] On July 31, conservatives unwittingly crashed the omnibus into a wall of radical opposition. To the undisguised glee of anticompromise senators, an attempt by the procompromise James Pearce of Maryland to excise a minor clause briefly divided the bill. Opponents gathered the votes to prevent its reconstruction, undoing half a year's hard work. Clay, his strategy defeated and his ineffectiveness evident to all around him, left town to recover his spirits and health in the salty breezes and cool waters of Newport.

With Clay's strategy in ruins, Stephen Douglas, always an opponent of the omnibus strategy, took control of the legislative forces for compromise. Douglas represented a substantial bloc of northern Democrats who urgently desired compromise but were hampered by legislative instructions to support the Wilmot Proviso.[76] Senators James Shields of Illinois, Lewis Cass and Alpheus Felch of Michigan, James Whitcomb and Jesse Bright of Indiana, and A. C. Dodge and George W. Jones of Iowa had been searching for a way to back Clay. Cass and Shields had given eloquent speeches on behalf of the principle of compromise; Dodge and Bright had denounced abolitionist agitators and had raised the cry against geographical parties. But these men would have had trouble voting for an omnibus bill that did not apply the Wilmot Proviso. They had hoped to vote for a separate California bill as a sop to antislavery constituents back home and therefore as a prelude to further compromise with their party allies in the South.

To Douglas, party ties and economic interests were the alpha and omega of politics. He admired Clay's courage and eloquence but regretted his tactics. Back in February, the Illinois senator had devised his own compromise, which, like his previous proposals, had focused solely on the territorial question. It called for the admission of California balanced by the admission of a new slave state created out of Texas, territorial status for New Mexico and Utah, and compensation to Texas for ceding most of its claims to New Mexico. On the territorial issue, Douglas's popular sovereignty views were by now well established. Granting that Congress possessed the power to act, Douglas argued that it was nevertheless dangerous and inexpedient to do so. "If you prohibit; if you establish; if you recognize; if you control; if you touch the question of slavery, your bill cannot, in my opinion, pass this body," he declared in early June.[77]

But, to Douglas's dismay, Clay's resolutions and the omnibus strategy shoved aside the Illinois senator's proposals and tactics. During the long debate, Douglas had threatened to bring up separate bills, only to face Clay's counterthreat to amend them into another omnibus. Douglas believed that the omnibus tactic had backfired by combining the opponents of compromise while dividing the supporters of each component of the bill. Furthermore, Clay's strategy ignored the House of Representatives, where Douglas's henchmen were busy making real bargains over railroads and Texas bonds, deals that would smooth the passage of any bills coming over from the Senate. Now, with Clay gone and Fillmore cracking the patronage whip, Douglas implemented his plan for separate measures, shepherding bills through the Senate for the organization of Utah and New Mexico territories, the admission of California as a free state, a fugitive slave law minus its jury-trial provision, the settlement of the Texas boundary question, and the abolition of the District's slave trade. In the House, his party managers united the Texas and the New Mexico bills into a "little omnibus" and rammed the entire package through by mid-September.

One key to Douglas's success, aside from his remarkable parliamentary persistence and wizardry, was his recognition that separate bills could pass only by sectional majorities with the aid of a small swing bloc of moderates—especially his northern Democrats. Southerners were free to oppose the California and the slave trade bills, whereas northerners could oppose the territorial bills and the fugitive slave bill. Cross-sectional majorities for these measures appeared only once in the House and the Senate, on the New Mexico bill in the latter and on the little omnibus in the former. The swing bloc was dominated by Democrats; of the sixty-one congressmen who voted for at least four and opposed none of the Compromise measures, thirty-eight were northern Democrats, eleven were southern Whigs, and the rest were evenly divided between northern Whigs and southern Democrats. If the Compromise of 1850 proved anything, it was that the Democrats, and not the two parties in tandem or the actions of disinterested statesmen, as Clay had hoped, were now the remaining shield of "the Union as it is."[78]

Douglas and Fillmore understood something about parties, interests, and compromise that Clay did not. The bonds of party affiliation were strong enough, and the rewards of party success great enough, to offer alienated southern Democrats and a few northern Whigs a way to reconcile conscience and partisan associations. Clay had written off as hopeless the views and votes of anticompromisers, concentrating instead on the fence-sitters in the middle. Separate bills, Texas bonds, the power of patronage, and under-the-table bargains of which only a few hints survive today all helped to bring the victory denied to Clay in July.

Although Douglas certainly masterminded the winning parliamentary strategy, he could not have succeeded without Clay. It is important to recall that Douglas's tactic of separate territorial bills had already failed several times before Clay broadened the range of issues with his proposals. If, as Douglas claimed, Clay's tactics and leadership *delayed* success, Douglas never explained how he could have rounded up enough votes for separate measures in the spring, when Clay took the heat of administration opposition and worked out a modus operandi with southern standpatters. Clay's successful transformation of the issue from slavery to union, backed by Webster's weighty and eloquent call for compromise, put enough pressure on the opposition to give Douglas his opportunity.

THE SUBSEQUENT HISTORY of the Compromise of 1850 is as clouded and controversial as the original debates over it.[79] Judging by the immediate wave of relief and celebration around the country, many contemporaries quickly pronounced the Compromise a final, irrevocable settlement of the day's outstanding issues. The major parties each claimed credit for its passage, and President Fillmore declared in his annual message that these laws, in effect, closed for good the controversy over slavery.

Radicals immediately challenged this verdict and refused to be bound by those measures they had opposed from the start. The new fugitive slave law became the source of deep anxiety in the North, for its harsh and inequitable provisions encouraged the deportation of blacks into the South on the flimsiest evidence. Abolitionists declared the law unconstitutional and void, vowing to repeal it at the earliest possible opportunity. And many southerners saw little comfort in Congress's avoidance of the Wilmot Proviso, which still left the territorial question vulnerable to northern majorities. Southern conservatives fastened on the fugitive slave law as the primary test of northern fidelity to the Compromise, but they also warned that any attempt to move against slavery where it already existed would also be cause for disunion.

Furthermore, the slavery issue itself would not go away, for the temporary suppression of the territorial issue merely redirected sectional agitation back to the root problem of slavery's morality. Over the next three years, during the "lull" between the Compromise and the revival of the territorial controversy in the Kansas-Nebraska Act, sectional tensions continued to tug at Congress, especially with the publication of *Uncle Tom's Cabin* in 1851–52 and the growing agitation in the North against enforcement of the fugitive slave law.

These events, plus the sectional pattern of voting on the Compromise, have convinced most recent historians that the Compromise of 1850 was not a compromise because neither side accepted any of the other's terms. At most, it could be seen as a truce in the ongoing sectional war over slavery. The Compromise failed to develop a strong consensus between the sections because it did not bridge the sectional gap over the nature of the Union it intended to preserve. According to Robert Seager, the fugitive slave controversy rendered the Compromise "stillborn," a complete failure as a settlement of the sectional crisis.[80]

If so many Americans rejected the measures, why were so many politicians eager to claim credit for being great compromisers? In fact, given the continuation of the sectional controversy, why did the name *compromise* even become permanently attached to a series of bills that so many historians claim was not a compromise at all? Why is there so little reference in contemporary sources to the Compromise as a truce instead of a compromise? The answer is that the Compromise of 1850 represented the culmination of a compromise tradition that many people regarded as a highly successful way to manage sectional conflict. Very few people predicted that a civil war would render nugatory any claims of "finality" for the Compromise of 1850. Past experience showed that major sectional compromises had "removed" divisive issues from Congress and the party system, to be followed by a period of relative national peace and prosperity.

And this compromise *did* "remove" some issues as sources of disunion. The slave trade in the District of Columbia ended with little fuss. The threat of civil war over Texas evaporated in the speculators' rush to make a killing on Texas bonds. Mormonism replaced slavery as the bone of contention in Utah. The question of slavery in Utah and New Mexico no longer troubled the nation; no more slaves entered these territories, and New Mexico's slave code of 1859 was a response to the *Dred Scott* decision, which superseded the territorial legislation of 1850. California entered the Union and placed two more Democratic votes in the Senate. The fugitive slave act stirred the North's conscience but not enough to come anywhere near repeal, and by the late 1850s, even moderate Republicans were grudgingly willing to enforce it. In effect, the Compromise of 1850 tugged the reluctant sections a bit closer together.

Another reason the pact was denominated a compromise had nothing to do with its provisions or with principles that might be inferred from it. After four years of increasingly dangerous congressional deadlock, the passage of *any* bill touching on slavery would demonstrate that both sides had renewed their faith in the constitutional processes that undergirded the very existence of the government. By ending the deadlock, militants permitted the government to operate again. There was always an anti-compromise majority in Congress, but enough of these congressmen abstained on principal elements of the package to let it go through. That exercise of restraint by the abstainers adds their names to the list of moderate Democrats who constituted the swing votes behind the passage of the Compromise. This was how many people thought the government was supposed to work: the moderation of passions would fortify and facilitate fundamental constitutional processes. A striking theme of pro-compromise argumentation in 1850 was the nagging fear that American constitutional processes had slipped into a coma, and conservatives, like an anxious family at the sickbed of an unconscious child, scrutinized the face of American politics for any sign of life.[81] At the heart of compromise sentiment in 1850 was the recognition that a crisis of the Union was a crisis of constitutional processes.

Furthermore, the Compromise of 1850 succeeded, if only briefly, in harnessing the power of party politics to an old tradition that had been skeptical of parties. The *parties* called it a compromise, not a truce. The importance of this development cannot be overstressed, for future political parties would try to appropriate the old rhetoric of compromise for their own ends. Democrats, as we shall see, tried to tout themselves as the true party of national union and compromise in their bid to impose party unity and to defeat both the Whigs and later the Republicans. Whigs seized on the Compromise, tried to impose it as a party standard, and succeeded only in exacerbating the corrosive elements already working to undermine their fragile coalition. Republicans would adopt the idea of a compromise as a "solemn pledge" in seeking support from northerners angry over Congress's decision in 1854 to abandon the Missouri Compromise. These were hardly the actions of politicians who viewed the Compromise of 1850 as a truce. They thought that the settlement generally had worked, whether for good or evil.

Some striking evidence of this may be found in the post-Compromise actions of formerly anticompromise politicians. Many congressmen either voted their consciences or suspended judgment for the present, hoping to feel the public pulse later on. Southern Democrats Henry S. Foote, Jeremiah Clemens, William R. King, and Solomon Downs all abstained or voted against the California and District slave trade bills but came out for the Compromise once they returned home. To these men, Douglas had provided a way to accommodate sectional and party pressures, for they saw the Democracy as the only party of union and viewed northern Democrats as allies willing to sacrifice for the South. Robert Toombs voted against the California bill, but not for sectional reasons; he joined other Georgia conservatives in supporting the Compromise. Some senators, like John Bell of Tennessee, did not consider their votes a measure of their willingness to compromise, either. And on the crucial Texas issue, which some historians exclude from their roll-call tallies, cross-sectional majorities did appear in both houses.[82]

Others, faced with defeat on one or another measure, merely minimized their losses and cheerfully gave up to the other side what they considered a minor concession. David Outlaw of North Carolina opposed the District slave trade bill but consoled himself that it would not prevent slave traders from moving their commerce to the Virginia end of the Potomac Bridge. But many northerners saw the bill as a real concession by the South, a view Outlaw was perfectly willing to let them hold.[83]

Of several internal contradictions in the compromise tradition, one—the parties' willingness to exploit the Compromise of 1850—would help to make the Compromise a transitional event. Older sectional compromises were fashioned in an atmosphere that permitted them to survive in the public consciousness only at a relatively high level of abstraction. Viewed as general compacts of restraint on sectional questions, the Compromises of 1820–21 and 1833 were not subsequently imposed by the parties as a test of intersectional faith. The Compromise of 1850 was not so fortunate: the parties incorporated it into their platforms, even though its provisions included a controversial fugitive slave law that undermined support for the rest of the package and kept the slavery issue alive.

Furthermore, the parties' use and abuse of the compromise tradition revealed the fatal irony bound up with the concept of "finality." Compromises are rarely final. They invariably leave a residue of dissatisfaction, which can eventually lead to further conflict and more compromise. But contemporaries failed to see compromise as a prelude instead of an end to controversy. Even though the fugitive slave law's more odious and inequitable provisions could have been softened by further compromise and negotiation, procompromise northerners sided with the South on the issue and shut off this outlet for sectional pressures. Both parties officially tried to make the act a law-and-order issue and therefore a test of intersectional trust.[84]

This degraded the Compromise just as it bound the pact, through "finality," to the fate of the regime's legitimacy. The old formula for sectional compromise had forged a chain of association among statesmanship, compromise, and the federal Union. *Statesmen* could be held accountable for sectional pacts. The Union could outlive the downfall or death of a Henry Clay, but by 1850 the Union could not survive the downfall of any major party as long as the slavery question remained a source of sectional hostility. The Compromise of 1850 would not destroy the two major parties; but "finality," by cutting off opportunities for future negotiation, confined the parties to positions that weakened their national appeal and damaged the legitimacy of the government.

In the end, the Compromise of 1850, in the tradition of previous compromises, was a *legislative* act, for which no single "author" could take responsibility and which was designed to prevent slavery from becoming a party issue.[85] And like previous compromises, from the great compromise through the Missouri and the tariff compromises, it was a package of concessions that was passed by different voting blocs but that collectively was understood as a comprehensive settlement.

The Achilles' heel of constitutional unionism was its assumption that future crises of the Union would be settled under circumstances approximating those of 1787, when a "universal alarm for the public safety, or an absolute extinction of liberty,"[86] in the words of "Publius," would mute partisanship and pave the way for mutual concessions. The Compromise of 1850 was the work largely of a generation that accepted these assumptions even as it helped to create a party system that undermined the old republican view of politics. The political crisis of the 1850s would test a new generation's confidence that parties could save the Union rather than destroy it.

6 The Template Breaks 1854–1861

> Who, after this [the Kansas-Nebraska Act], will ever trust in a national compromise?
> —Abraham Lincoln

The erosion of sectional trust is the great theme of antebellum politics. At the center of the drama was the question of compromise, for the legitimacy of a political system based on consent cannot survive its failure to reconcile differences between majorities and minorities. Indeed, the rich, voluminous literature on the breakdown of democratic processes in the 1850s treats the ability to compromise as a register of institutional health. Specifically, there is an exclusive focus on compromise as a strategy whose intrinsic significance lay in the linear relationship between the parties' motivations (sordid, patriotic, or simply self-interested) and the consequences of compromise (institutional collapse, peace, or war). The fact that peace efforts failed in 1861 has tended further to circumscribe the kinds of questions we ask about compromise. Preoccupied with the strategy's failure, historians rarely have asked why so many Americans expected it to succeed.[1]

As we have seen in the foregoing chapters, Americans did attach a special significance to compromise, especially to grand compromise in the tradition of the founding generation. Although Americans would see the failure to compromise as a sign of trouble, they did not necessarily associate the problem with the same set of conditions that modern observers have noted. The consensus among experts on this period is that the dynamics of party combat across a loose, federal political system enabled the parties to compromise on dangerous sectional questions at the national level while exploiting sectional tensions at the local level. Therefore, sectionalism and partisanship, if localized, were not necessarily dangerous to the country. Once sectional questions entered national debate through the medium of the territorial issue in the 1840s, the parties saw it as imperative to push the conflict, through compromise, back down to the local level, where they could control it. The Compromise of 1850 culminated four years of such efforts, but by suppressing the territorial question, it helped accelerate the breakdown of two-party competition as both parties' support for the Compromise blurred their differences and angered their restive sectional wings.[2]

This scenario rests on historical hindsight, not the Federalists' foresight. We know the outcome of the political crisis of the 1850s and can point to the collapse of parties as a major precipitant to civil war. But this does not mean that the revival of national two-party competition was among the contemporaries' antidotes to the disease. In fact, recent research indicates that the failure of compromise in the 1850s was accompanied with a rising unease about the effects of parties and the corruption of politics.[3]

The Whig/Democratic exploitation of the compromise issue in the aftermath of the Compromise of 1850 demonstrated to many Americans how parties could *undermine* compromise rather than promote it. And the Democrats' particular abuse of the issue suggested to some that perhaps the way out of the sectional morass was through a return to older notions of civility, self-restraint, and the muting of partisanship. Nor did Republicans act as if their exclusively sectional base spelled the end of the old Union. They made no genuine attempts to court southern votes and build a national organization.

The template of 1787, which prescribed a nonpartisan politics of conciliation as the best antidote to sectional conflict, cracked in 1854, when Stephen Douglas's Kansas-Nebraska Act used the principle of one compromise to overturn part of another, arousing a fury in the North. It is significant that the "Appeal of the Independent Democrats," the angry manifesto of the future Republican coalition, referred to the act as a "gross violation of a sacred pledge." Judging by the frequency of its references to the Missouri Compromise as "sacred," "inviolable," and a "solemn compact," it appears that the Appeal aimed not only at its authors' traditional antislavery constituency in the North but also at the conservative sentiments about compromise that the abolitionist movement had been struggling for years to overcome. Breaking a compromise constituted betrayal in the eyes of many northerners. Douglas broke the compromise tradition and split wide open the older consensus on compromise. In the ensuing sectional controversy, he and his supporters built on earlier claims that the Missouri Compromise was "mere legislation," revocable at the will of succeeding Congresses, as they broadened the scope of the compromises of the Constitution in order to narrow the range of options to a single policy, that of popular sovereignty.[4]

Small wonder that Douglas's maneuver fulfilled his prediction of "a hell of a storm."[5] The political realignment that followed the act left the Democrats as the only organized expression of the old constitutional unionism. Their increasingly bitter attacks on their opponents as fanatics and disunionists retained something of the old categories of whiggish civics, but this hardly held out hope for another sectional compromise negotiated above the party fray.

HAVING ENACTED a compromise in 1850, Americans proceeded to abuse it in ways that demonstrated their intense faith in sectional compromises as a quasi-constitutional method of enacting timeless "principles" into law. The primary agent of this belief in the 1850s was the Democratic party, which seized the mantle of compromise, yoked it to popular sovereignty, and sought to impose it in 1854 as a consistent extension of a "principle" established in the territorial legislation of 1850. In fact, a kind of ideological realignment stimulated by the crisis of 1850 occurred in the wake of the Compromise, to the Democrats' advantage. Conservatives in both sections leaped old partisan barriers in a rare display of bipartisan mutual congratulation. Many conservative Whigs now saw the Democrats as the only party of union, especially because only the Democrats had large procompromise elements in both sections. Henry Clay spoke favorably of such a realignment but, given his declining health, did not call for a new party or express a desire to head a new ticket.[6]

Aside from Georgia, where a "Constitutional Union" ticket briefly competed with a states' rights faction through 1851, this talk of a national Union party, although revealing of politicians' uneasiness about the state of the party system, did not result in a change of labels. But it did offer the Democrats a powerful issue for the 1850s, for they openly exploited their role in enacting the Compromise of 1850 and claimed that only the Democracy truly held the sections together against disunionist radicals in the North and the South.

Although the Whigs sought to use compromise in a similar fashion, their internal divisions ran too deep to make it work. Pro- and anticompromise factions appeared in crucial northern states. Antislavery Whigs lost their faith in the party after its national leaders, especially Daniel Webster and Millard Fillmore, pronounced the Compromise an irrevocable party doctrine. Undermined by a tide of nativist reaction against the party's attempt to court immigrant votes, Whiggery lost more support when the 1852 nominating convention coupled a procompromise platform with a candidate (Winfield Scott) associated with anticompromise northerners. Southern Whigs who remembered Zachary Taylor's apostasy must have found this a very unsatisfactory decision.

By 1852, then, the parties' official consensus on the Compromise was benefiting mostly the Democrats. Inevitably, compromise as a technique became compromise as a party doctrine, associated completely with the Democrats' demand for silence on slavery where it existed and noninterference with it in the territories. Democratic editors emphasized a rigid, dogmatic ideology of laissez-faire and confederationist constitutionalism, claiming that national expansion and strict construction would prevent local issues from dividing the country. Their narrow view of the Constitution, often analogized as a business partnership founded in contract, left no room for negotiation on constitutional questions. The "reserved rights of the states," they claimed, was a doctrine "so plain that it might be framed into an algebraic equation and demonstrated mathematically."[7]

Such a constitution had little need of independent statesmen to defend it when a party coextensive with the Union and determined to preserve the sovereignty of states stood ready to the task. Old compromises for the sake of union were no longer reliable, for they insured "only a lingering death." "For the time will come when the burdens accumulated by conciliation 'will break the camel's back.'" In fact, Democratic party pronouncements during the 1850s increasingly adopted neo-Calhounite views of concurring majorities and the need for a sectional veto power. Powerfully revealing the growth of southern influence in the party, Democratic propagandists in effect argued for the removal of entire packages of issues from congressional jurisdiction, including the tariff, internal improvements, slavery, and the territorial question, all of which were now classified as issues "involving constitutional principles [that] would be best settled, not by a compromise in congress, but in the mode pointed out by the Constitution itself"—by three-fourths of the states.[8]

On the other hand, to the Democrats, national expansion offered hope for sectional peace. The bonds of union were stronger than ever, Douglas asserted soon after the Compromise passed. "We are united from shore to shore; and while the mighty West remained as the connecting link between the North and the South, there could be no disunion."[9] Of course, it was the Democratic party that had added the "mighty West" to the Union, had settled the crisis over slavery in the Southwest, and now planned to superintend the area's rapid settlement. In the short run, this tactic worked. The Democrats romped to victory over a disintegrating Whig party in 1852, with the procompromise Franklin Pierce at the head of the ticket and solid Democratic majorities in both houses to back the party's program.

When the routine problem of establishing territorial organization for the remaining lands of the West arose in 1853, Douglas moved to handle it in routine manner, counting on his party to support him. His initial bill for the organization of Nebraska Territory left intact the Missouri Compromise's restriction on slavery. But southerners called in the bond exacted by Pierre Soulé in 1850, threatening to withhold their support for Douglas's Nebraska bill unless the Missouri restriction was removed entirely. Believing that rapid settlement of the West under the aegis of a united Democratic party was more important than a compact that had lost its intersectional magnetism back in 1848, Douglas caved in to southern pressure. His Kansas-Nebraska Act removed the restriction on slavery and substituted the language of the territorial legislation of 1850.

In his defense, Douglas claimed that compromise in 1850 had produced a new territorial consensus that repudiated the Missouri Compromise. In a bit of historical legerdemain, Douglas claimed that the North's opposition to the Missouri line's extension into new territories constituted a rejection of the line where it already existed, paving the way for the insertion of the popular sovereignty "principle" in the Compromise of 1850. Naturally, the Missouri Compromise deteriorated even further in Democratic and southern calculations, given this argument. Popular sovereignty therefore had to inherit the legacy of the Missouri Compromise: its ambiguities and obvious appeal to Democrats in particular and to homeless conservative Whigs in general would, in the eyes of its advocates, overcome sectional antagonisms that the Missouri line could no longer fence in.

The bitterness of the Democracy's attack on the Missouri Compromise suggests the depth of underlying residual support for the line (and helps explain its resurgent popularity among conservatives during the secession crisis). Democratic campaign literature—along with speeches by major party officials and articles in the party organ, the *United States Review*—repeatedly sought to devalue the Missouri line's historic position as an intersectional agreement to restrain the agitation of slavery. The line was a "cancerous excrescence," an "unauthorized assumption of power by Congress and therefore it was void in its inception," Democrats argued. As a "mere clause of an act of Congress," under, not above, the Constitution, it carried no moral authority, President Pierce argued.[10]

Popular sovereignty became the Democrats' national compromise, an intraparty agreement to banish the slavery issue to the prairies in the interest of the expanding Union. Douglas thought that once applied, popular sovereignty would "destroy all sectional parties and sectional agitation." Predictably, the passage of the act confirmed in Democratic councils that only the Democrats remained as the party of union and peace.[11]

This tactic failed utterly. It did not bring peace, or reaffirm the Union, or tolerate conflicting opinions. It led directly to the formation of a sectional Republican party, which made a strong issue out of Douglas's violation of an old, sacred pledge. Democrats who complacently suggested that if the battle between freedom and slavery must be fought somewhere, let it happen in the territories, got their wish as Kansas became a bloody battleground between free- and slave-state forces for the next two years.[12]

For the next six years, the Democrats fought their rearguard action against the sectionalization of the party system, accusing Republicans of disunionism while they themselves fell further under southern control. To such men as the Democratic historian and propagandist Nahum Capen, it was inconceivable that any old-line Whig, who by 1856 should have been "almost in sympathy with the National Democrat," might associate with such factious organizations as the nativist Know-Nothings or the Republicans. The latter group, he charged, was simply a "political amalgamation" of loose factions distinguished by their absurd abstractions and devotion to "*isms*." Indeed, the Republicans had misappropriated and abused a title associated with Thomas Jefferson, who would have condemned their free-soil doctrines, and had pledged themselves to "sectionalism, to disunion, to treason." They were, in short, the sectional faction that Washington had warned against in his Farewell Address.[13]

The conservative Whigs who temporarily remained aloof from the Republican party might have agreed with Capen's analysis, but not with his party's handling of sectional matters. Historians have focused on the realignment that followed the Kansas-Nebraska Act, properly judging Douglas's move a blunder of major proportions. But they have missed the other significance of this move: it alienated conservatives open to Democratic unionism, and it thereby delayed the movement of conservative Whigs into Democratic ranks. Throughout the 1850s and the secession winter of 1860–61, Democrats courted these old-line Whigs, holding out the temptation of a national Union party to fight off disunionists in the North and the South.[14]

But popular sovereignty as a party doctrine would not suffice as a national symbol of mutual affections in the tradition of intersectional comity. Many Clay and Webster Whigs, drawn to the Democrats after 1850, found it extremely difficult to support Douglas and the Democrats' brand of conservative unionism. Edward Everett, John J. Crittenden, and John Bell, future candidates of the procompromise Constitutional Union party of 1860, opposed the Kansas-Nebraska Act, regarding it as a gratuitous slap at the North and a surefire way to reopen old wounds by provoking abolitionists into intensifying their efforts to build an antislavery party.

Crittenden, the Clay protégé, announced his support for the principle of the act but disapproved the substitution of popular sovereignty for the Missouri Compromise without a substantial northern agreement to do so. "The Missouri Compromise has long been considered as a sort of landmark in our political progress," Crittenden told his fellow Kentuckian Archibald Dixon (who was instrumental in persuading Douglas to insert repeal in his bill).

> It does not appear to me that it has ever been superseded or abrogated; and I think it is to be apprehended that its repeal, without sincere concurrence of the North, will be productive of serious agita-

> tions and disturbances. That concurrence will relieve the subject from difficulty, as the parties to compromise have an undoubted right to set it aside at their pleasure. By such a course it seems to me the North would lose nothing, and would but afford another evidence of her wisdom and her patriotism. This, however, is a subject for her own consideration.[15]

Caught between northern and southern radicals, and uncertain and suspicious of the Democrats' increasingly cynical accusations of disunionism against even moderate dissenters, the old-line unionists drifted in suspended animation throughout the 1850s. Their lack of organization was evident in 1856, when unionists split their votes between two conservatives, Fillmore and James Buchanan. Their "sentimental regression," in George Forgie's apt phrase, soaked their aging oratory in nostalgic tears of yearning for the Union of Washington, Madison, and the Founding Fathers who had sacrificed local and party attachments to the public good.[16]

In 1860, these conservatives, after a brief dalliance with nativism, formed a Constitutional Union party, nominated Bell and Everett for president and vice president, and wrote a simple platform calling on Americans to stand by the Constitution and the Union. The platform drew snickers in both sections, but to the conservatives, constitutional unionism simply meant preserving a union that was partly federal, partly national. A curious mixture of homeless Whigs and Madisonian conservatives, this party would share the political center with the national Democrats supporting Stephen Douglas; together, these two groups would make the last stand for the old constitutional union.[17]

John J. Crittenden, in outlining his support for the party, pointed directly to sectionalism and partyism as the twin dangers to further union. Although he praised Douglas's devotion to the Union, Crittenden nonetheless preferred Bell because, unlike Douglas, he was not "engaged in the hottest of the present party warfare" and therefore "would come into office without those fierce excitements through which Mr. Douglas, under existing circumstances," could "alone reach it."[18]

The failure of the Constitutional Union party in 1860, the election of Abraham Lincoln, and the secession of the Lower South pushed Crittenden and his fellow conservatives into a desperate attempt at compromise. During that secession winter of 1860–61, Crittenden made a last appeal for a divided nation to compromise and reunite in the spirit of the framers. His speeches reiterated the themes of past sectional compromises, articulating the common heritage of a constitutional union as the centerpoint of true compromise.[19] His proposals were similar to Clay's original package in 1850, but they also reflected the hardening and narrowing of a political center battered by "bleeding Kansas," *Dred Scott*, and Harpers Ferry. He called for the repeal of personal liberty laws and for efficient, strict enforcement of the fugitive slave law and the laws against the African slave trade. More important than these demands were his major proposals, submitted as "unamendable" amendments to the Constitution. These included the extension of the Missouri line to the Pacific with iron-clad guarantees of slavery south and freedom north of it. He also wanted a firm constitutional commitment to noninterference with slavery within and among the states and authority for federal compensation to slaveowners whose fugitives were liberated by force. Here was the ultimate "finality," a permanent compact resurrecting the sectional equilibrium of 1787 and denying the Madisonian belief in deliberate, changing majorities as the foundation of a conservative constitutional order.[20]

A flurry of other compromise proposals emerged from the ranks of conservatives in the Republican party and the Upper South. Their common denominator also was the revival of the Missouri line, which the seceders rejected as wholly inadequate.[21] And all of these proposals assumed what the compromisers had resisted admitting since 1787: that classes of states carried more weight in the constitutional calculus than did individual states, for the compromise proposals of 1860 and 1861 ratified a sectional pact and would have transformed an equivocal union of states and of citizens into an uneasy amalgam of dual, divergent civilizations.

This was hardly what conservatives preferred in 1860; they felt pushed into it by party and sectional pressures, and they tried to organize a conservative party to stop the sectional polarization of politics. Old partisan animosities made such a coalition difficult, despite Douglas's titanic efforts to achieve some kind of fusion in the North during the campaign. But as Daniel Crofts has shown, as the Gulf states left the Union and began preparing for war during the secession winter of 1860–61, the abortive conservative realignment of the early 1850s revived in the Upper South when a firm coalition of conservative Whigs, Americans (former Know-Nothings), and Douglas Democrats resisted the first wave of secession fever and made desperate efforts to build a loose, working alliance with the incoming Republican administration.[22]

The significance of this attempted coalition lay partly in its assumption that new party lines might be drawn on the basis of union or disunion. With the Confederacy already forming and with strong secessionist elements in the Upper South states, viable two-party competition based on this issue could not have restored the party equilibrium of the second party system, which had rested on a firm belief in the essential legitimacy of the constitutional union. Furthermore, the anticoercionist constitutionalism of many conditional unionists—southern unionists who premised their unionism on protection for slaveholders—revealed a terrible weakness of antebellum constitutional unionism: its belief that the government could not maintain the Union by force, a belief reflected in both President James Buchanan's timid response to secession and the southern unionists' argument that only a conciliatory policy could restore the Union.

Like the civics writers of the 1830s and 1840s, constitutional unionists were divided over how to handle the problem of how a government based on consent could force a state to remain against its consent. This was an artifact of the constitutional unionist emphasis on the need for large majorities in political decisions, for the system in 1860 faced large minorities surrounding a helpless center. In the end, the most remarkable characteristic of centrists in 1860 was not their numbers but the deep divisions and inner contradictions that prevented them from acting in unison.

It is easy to be harsh with the compromisers of 1860. Kenneth Stampp and Harold Hyman, for instance, have hurled Churchillian thunderbolts at the "appeasers" of 1860, who, in Hyman's words, believed that "any peace was better than any war."[23] In this view, the compromisers' willingness to continue a union of freedom and slavery, to concede even more of the few freedoms remaining to free blacks, and to appease a militant South's extortionate demands for slavery's expansion into the territories belied their protestations of concern for the Union. Yet the anticoercionist majority in 1860 (if one reads the combined Bell and Douglas votes as an indication of anticoercion sentiment) operated at least in part on the belief that any peace was preferable to *civil* war, which they regarded with a special horror uncharacteristic of a people who had eagerly invaded Mexico in 1846 and who waged total war against the native Indian population.

Little wonder that Crittenden's compromise, like the Constitutional Union party, went down in defeat. The secession winter produced not only a strong reaction in both sections against any further compromise but also an outpouring of abuse against past compromises and compromisers. The old rhetoric of compromise had lost its appeal to a significant number of Americans; the tie between union and compromise had been broken.[24] New, deliberate majorities were forming with new, different notions of the "Union as it is." During the Civil War, "the Union as it was" became the rallying cry of opposition Democrats, who equated this notion with white supremacy, states' rights, and negotiation rather than confrontation with the South.[25]

And after the war, Democrats revived the slogan in their struggle to control the government's southern policy and to permit home rule in the South. Another grand compromise, which symbolically closed the Reconstruction period in 1876–77, recalled in some ways the compromise tradition of prewar days. But this compromise and the Democrats' war cry of "the Union as it was" said less of the old constitutional unionism than it did of the new politics of race and resource development that drove the party system after the Civil War. For the Civil War ended the old Union and the politics of conciliation. In the 1850s, the compromise tradition—which had been planted in the act of constitution making, had been cultivated in the lush garden of early national political culture, had flowered in the sectional pacts that punctuated the antebellum decades, and had withered under the pressure of new political styles, organizations, and issues—could no longer thrive on its ambiguities about slavery, federalism, and nationhood. In 1861, James Madison's Union was dead, and Abraham Lincoln's was being born.

Notes

ABBREVIATIONS

AC *Annals of Congress*. Cited as Congress:session, date, page number.

CG *Congressional Globe*. Same citation format as *Annals of Congress*.

DHRC *Documentary History of the Ratification of the Constitution*. Edited by Merrill Jensen et al. Vols. published nonsequentially. Madison, 1976–90. Where applicable, "mfm." refers to the microform supplements to individual volumes of this series.

HC *The Papers of Henry Clay*. Edited by James F. Hopkins et al. 9 vols. to date. Lexington, Ky., 1959–88.

MHS Massachusetts Historical Society, Boston.

MPP *A Compilation of the Messages and Papers of the Presidents, 1789–1897*. Compiled by James D. Richardson. 10 vols. Washington, D.C., 1988.

NWR *Niles' Weekly Register*.

PHC Typescripts of letters, documents, and other materials arranged chronologically in the files of the Papers of Henry Clay Project, University of Kentucky, Lexington.

RD *Register of Debates*. Same citation format as *Annals of Congress*.

SHC Southern Historical Collection, University of North Carolina, Chapel Hill.

PREFACE

1. Epigraph quoted in Friedman, *Revolt of the Conservative Democrats*, p. 102.
2. Curti, *Growth of American Thought*, p. 638.

INTRODUCTION

1. CG 31:1, Apr. 4, 1850, p. 647.
2. On determining the meaning of an idea, see Bouwsma, "History of Ideas to History of Meaning," p. 283.

3. For more on "public moralists," whose "myths, languages, and arguments can be shown to serve at least some Americans as Americans," see Hollinger, "American Intellectual History," p. 313.
4. Mill quoted in Formisano, *Transformation of Political Culture*, p. 4. Of the many works on the problem of American character and culture in the early Republic, Welter, *Mind of America*, pp. 3–77, offers the best summary of existing concerns about past, present, and future.
5. "Compromise not only allows an explanation, but demands one," writes Seltser in *Political Compromise*, p. 29.
6. For some varying approaches to the term, see McCarthy, *Current Dictionary of American Politics*, p. 31, and idem, "Compromise and Politics," p. 19; *Encyclopaedia Britannica*, 11th ed., p. 813; Plano and Greenberg, *American Political Dictionary*, p. 5 (which discusses *conciliation* and *consensus*); Seltser, *Political Compromise*, pp. 3–54.
7. The distinction between principles and interests runs throughout Pennock and Chapman, *Compromise*; see esp. Benditt, "Compromising Interests and Principles."
8. The rhetoric of conciliation and compromise in the period under study has been surveyed extensively but without sufficient attention to political culture. A good starting point is Auer, *Antislavery and Disunion, 1858–1861*.
9. See Carens, "Compromises in Politics," pp. 126–28, 132–36, and Seltser, *Political Compromise*, p. 35.
10. For variations, see Smith and Zurcher, *New Dictionary of American Politics*, p. 82, on the Anglo-Saxon concept of *compromis*, and Webster, *A Compendious Dictionary*, p. 59, which defines the noun as "an agreement, a bargain," the verb as "to compound, adjust, make up," and the past participle as "settled, adjusted, made up."
11. *Oxford English Dictionary*, pp. 746–47; Webster, *A Compendious Dictionary*, p. 59. For a good example of *compromit* in usage, see Henry Clay to Peter B. Porter, Washington, Feb. 3, 1823, *HC* 3:365; Clay to William H. Richardson et al., Ashland, May 30, 1825, ibid. 4:404; Committee Report on the Missouri Resolution, Feb. 10, 1821, ibid. 3:26–29.
12. George Armstrong Kelly, "Mediation versus Compromise in Hegel," p. 91.
13. Golding, "Nature of Compromise," pp. 5–6, distinguishes for the purpose of analysis the morality of compromise (that is, whether or not to compromise) from the subsidiary but related issue of the morality in compromise (the actual strategy, tactics, and substance of any particular compromise). Others see the two as so closely related that ethical standards apply equally well to both. In practice, prospective compromisers approach the moral dimensions of this distinction in linear fashion, first deciding on the morality of whether or not to compromise and then, if they decide to go ahead, considering the morality of the substance of any proposed bargain.

The certainty of making concessions in either case is what unites the two phases of ethical thinking in a compromise situation.

14. For the first view, see Thomas V. Smith, *Ethics of Compromise*, and the severe criticism of it in Hallowell, "Compromise As a Political Ideal." Morley, *On Compromise*, pp. 4, 217; Konvitz, "John Morley on Liberty and Compromise."
15. Weber, "Politics As a Vocation"; Dahl, *Pluralist Democracy*, p. 53; Seltser, *Political Compromise*, p. 46; Berki, "Distinction between Moderation and Extremism"; Kuflick, "Morality and Compromise," pp. 43–50.
16. A good recent survey of this trend in political thought is Robert Booth Fowler, *Believing Skeptics*, esp. pp. 198–214. For a discussion of the background of pluralist theory and Madisonian constitutionalism, see Bourke, "The Pluralist Reading of James Madison's Tenth *Federalist*." The most comprehensive example of this genre of pluralism, compromise, and the American polity is Dahl, *Pluralist Democracy*.
17. This is the theme, for instance, of Nichols, *Disruption of American Democracy*.
18. See the extensive review of this massive literature in the articles by Joyce Appleby et al. in *American Quarterly* 37, no. 4 (Fall 1985).
19. A good recent attempt to mesh these ideas is Kloppenberg, "Virtues of Liberalism."
20. On integrative solutions, see Follett, "Constructive Conflict," pp. 31, 32, 35; on arbitration, see Golding, "Nature of Compromise," pp. 18–23, and Kuflick, "Morality and Compromise," pp. 53–54. According to Follett, "There is . . . an essential difference between the compromise of arbitration and the compromise of conciliation: in the one case you have an adjudicated compromise; in the other, an internally adjusted compromise, a compromise to which both parties agree, to which both parties have perhaps contributed": Follett, "The Psychology of Conciliation and Arbitration," p. 233.
21. Nelson, "Reason and Compromise."
22. De Jouvenel, *Pure Theory of Politics*, pp. 212 and 189, 207–8. See also the discussion of rational choice and coalition formation in Riker, "Heresthetics of Constitution-Making," p. 15, and idem, "Political Theory and the Art of Heresthetics."
23. A good summary of this school of thought in the history of political ideas is Ball, Farr, and Hanson, *Political Innovation and Conceptual Change*; on the Constitution and language, see Ball and Pocock, *Conceptual Change and the Constitution*, esp. Farr's essay in chapter two, "Conceptual Change and Constitutional Innovation."
24. See Gough, *Social Contract*, pp. 84–104, 229–43.
25. For these developments, see several works by Jack P. Greene: "Growth of

Political Stability," pp. 42–44, 48, and "From the Perspective of Law." Idem, *Peripheries and Center*, pp. 38–41, 45–47, 119–20, discusses the importance of custom in the development of constitutional law and legislative prerogatives of local assemblies, as well as the maturation of political professionalism during the period of salutary neglect in the mid-eighteenth century. Three works—Carr, "Foundations of Social Order," pp. 77, 86, 95–96; Konig, "English Legal Change," p. 17; Zemsky, *Merchants, Farmers, and River Gods*, pp. 16–18, 23–24, 39–74—discuss traditional legislative and judicial customs that found later justification in contract theory and that served as a basis for a tradition of compromise. On consociational polities and colonial institutions, see Kukla, "Order and Chaos in Early America."

26. *Papers of George Mason* 1:289; Commager, *Documents of American History* 1:104, 109. On moderation and the Enlightenment, see May, *Enlightenment in America*, pp. 307–62.
27. The relationship of union, compromise, and interstate relations is explored in Onuf, *Origins of the Federal Republic*. A good contemporary example of Federalist arguments for compromise as the prerequisite to union is George Washington's circular letter to the states, June 18, 1783, in *DHRC* 13:62–70.
28. Davis, *Slavery in the Age of Revolution*, p. 82.
29. For an interesting contemporary observation of this trend in constitutional development, see Daniel D. Barnard, "The Constitution Written and Unwritten," *American Whig Review* 6, no. 1 (July 1849): 399–406.
30. Farr, "Conceptual Change and Constitutional Innovation," pp. 23–27.

CHAPTER 1

1. *CG* 31:1, July 22, 1850, Appendix, p. 1408. Gerry epigraph is from Farrand, *Records* 1:532.
2. Aristotle, *Politics*, book 5, i, sec. 14, 1302a.
3. *DHRC* 13:211–12, which is the source of the quotations in the following three paragraphs. On Morris's authorship of the letter, see Farrand, *Framing of the Constitution*, p. 183.
4. On the diversity of republican theory in early America, see Wharton, *Polity and the Public Good*, and McDonald, *Novus Ordo Seclorum*.
5. A good basic description of the Convention's proceedings is in Farrand, *Framing of the Constitution*, pp. 91–133. Rossiter, *1787*, pp. 185–96, is the best of the celebratory histories. On slavery and representation, see Robinson, *Slavery in the Structure of American Politics*, pp. 168–206. For more detailed discussion, see Rakove, "The Great Compromise," and Nelson,

"Reason and Compromise." On coalitions in the Convention, see Jillson, "Constitution-Making," and Jillson and Anderson, "The Slave Trade Compromise."

6. McDonald, *Novus Ordo Seclorum*, pp. 234–35. On three-fifths, see the exchange between Madison and William Paterson and the remarks of Pierce Butler (Georgia), Gouverneur Morris, and James Wilson in Farrand, *Records* 1: 562–63, 605, 588, 587. The rule as a compromise has been the subject of controversy among historians. See Farrand, "Compromises of the Constitution," pp. 479–80; Lynd, "Compromise of 1787"; Simpson, "Slave Representation"; Davis, *Slavery in the Age of Revolution*, pp. 104, 107, 155 n. 75, and see note 67 below. On the census, see Ohline, "Republicanism and Slavery." On sectionalism and planning for the First Congress, see Robinson, *Slavery in the Structure of American Politics*, pp. 177–206.
7. On the slave trade–commerce compromise, see McDonald, *Formation*, pp. 176–84, 184n, which argues that this bargain was "no compromise at all." See also Jillson and Anderson, "The Slave Trade Compromise"; Davis, *Slavery in the Age of Revolution*, pp. 119–33; Robinson, *Slavery in the Structure of American Politics*, pp. 223–32. On the electoral college, see Slonin, "Electoral College at Philadelphia"; McDonald, *Novus Ordo Seclorum*, pp. 240–53; Riker, "Heresthetics of Constitution-Making"; and Robinson, *Slavery in the Structure of American Politics*, p. 205.
8. See Nelson, "Reason and Compromise."
9. Farrand, *Records* 1:468–69. Madison's remarks are in *Papers of James Madison* 10:88–89. Gerry recalled that mutual concessions had been necessary to constitution making in the several states: Farrand, *Records* 1:515. The ingredients for a compromise had been drifting in and out of the debate since the beginning of the meeting—see ibid. 1:87, 196, 201, 343, 461–62, 488–89, for conciliatory suggestions by John Dickinson, Roger Sherman, and Samuel Johnson.
10. Farrand, *Records* 2:3–11, 15; see also Benjamin Franklin's use of some homespun metaphors in behalf of his compromise proposals, ibid. 1:532, which Nelson refers to as strong examples of instrumental reasoning. On the powerful urge for "fame," see Colbourn, *Fame and the Founding Fathers*, pp. 3–26, and McDonald, *Novus Ordo Seclorum*, pp. 3, 189–91. Ellsworth's remark is in Farrand, *Records* 1:468–69.
11. For Madison's disappointment with the Constitution, see his famous letters to Thomas Jefferson, New York, Sept. 6, Oct. 24, 1787, in *Papers of James Madison* 10:163–64, 205. But see Lance Banning's recent argument that Madison's desire for a strong central government moderated under the weight of the debate: "James Madison and the Dynamics of the Constitutional Convention," and "The Practicable Sphere of a Republic."
12. Gilman to Joseph Gilman, Philadelphia, Sept. 18, 1787, in Farrand, *Records*

3:82. See also Benjamin Franklin to Jane Mecom, Philadelphia, Sept. 20, 1787, in *DHRC* 13:218; George Washington to Marquis de Lafayette, Philadelphia, Sept. 18, 1787, in Letterbook, George Washington Papers, Library of Congress, Washington, D.C.; Washington to Patrick Henry, Benjamin Harrison, and Thomas Nelson, Mount Vernon, Sept. 24, 1787, in *DHRC* 13:224; Pierce Butler to Weedon Butler, New York, Oct. 8, 1787, ibid. 13:352.

13. Alexander Hamilton's famous speech of June 18 favoring an elective monarch modeled after the British Constitution impressed several delegates, but, as William Samuel Johnson later observed, Hamilton "had been praised by everybody [but] . . . supported by none." "The British government cannot be our model," James Wilson declared to the Convention. Both quotations are from Alfred F. Young, "Conservatives, the Constitution, and the 'Spirit of Accommodation,'" p. 117. Federalists were very careful when comparing the British and new American constitutions and usually confined their remarks to criticisms of the former as justifications for the latter's innovations. See, for example, "A Plain Citizen," *Pennsylvania Packet*, Oct. 11, 1787, in *DHRC* 2:602–9. See also "A Freeman," *Newport Herald*, Mar. 20, 1788, and "Americanus VI," New York *Daily Advertiser*, Jan. 12, 1788.
14. New York *Daily Advertiser*, Sept. 24, 1787, in *DHRC* 13:224–26.
15. Wood, *Creation of the American Republic*, follows this format.
16. On congressional debate, see *DHRC* 1:322–53. Federalists managed to block Antifederalist amendments in Congress by proposing the transmittal of the Constitution to the states without an expression of congressional opinion. Washington quotation from Washington to Madison, Mount Vernon, Oct. 10, 1787, in ibid. 8:49; see also Madison to Washington, Sept. 30, 1787, in ibid. 8:26–27. Antifederalists disputed this interpretation of Congress's proceedings, of course. See Richard Henry Lee to George Mason, New York, Oct. 1, 1787, in ibid. 8:28–30, and *Pennsylvania Herald*, Oct. 6, 1787, in ibid. 2:551.
17. "Curtius" essay, New York *Daily Advertiser*, Sept. 29, 1787, in ibid. 13:268–72. See also Philadelphia *Independent Gazetteer*, June 27, 1787, in ibid. 13:147–48; *Pennsylvania Gazette*, Sept. 19, 1787, in ibid. 13:582; "Social Compact," *New Haven Gazette*, Oct. 4, 1787, in ibid. 13:310–12.
18. *United States Chronicle* (Providence, R.I.), Sept. 27, 1787, in ibid. 13:258–59.
19. Speech at Public Meeting in Philadelphia, Oct. 6, 1787, in ibid. 13:341; see also "Federal Constitution," *Pennsylvania Gazette*, Oct. 10, 1787, and *A Farmer of New Jersey: Observations on Government . . .*, Nov. 3, 1787, both in ibid. 13:364, 559, and Miers Fisher to Robert Barclay, Philadelphia, Oct. 20, 1787, in ibid. 2:781–82.
20. Onuf, *Origins of the Federal Republic*, pp. 208–9; Rossiter, *1787*, pp. 279–80.

The Convention's compromises of sectional and interstate conflicts, Onuf argues, were hardly miraculous, for they built on a new, dynamic conception already embodied in the Northwest Ordinance, which had achieved a reconciliation of these conflicts through the organization of western territories under federal jurisdiction.

21. For the speech and its publication history, see *DHRC* 13:212–14. See, for instance, Joseph Barrell to Samuel Blacheley Webb, Boston, Feb. 6, 1788, in *Correspondence and Journal of Samuel Blacheley Webb* 3:92; John Avery to George Thatcher, Boston, Feb. 6, 1788, in Chamberlain Collection, Thatcher Papers, Boston Public Library; Rufus King to James Madison, Feb. 6, 1788, in *Life and Correspondence of Rufus King* 1:319–20; George Washington to Benjamin Lincoln, Mount Vernon, Jan. 31, 1788, in *Writings of George Washington* 29:395–97, 412–13; *New Hampshire Recorder*, June 24, 1788; *Pennsylvania Gazette*, Feb. 20, 1788, in *DHRC* 2:1793; "Conciliator," Philadelphia *Independent Gazetteer*, Feb. 20, 1788, in ibid. 2:1773.
22. On Pennsylvania's minority, see *Pennsylvania Herald*, Sept. 29, Dec. 19, 1787, in *DHRC* 2:123–24, 1383, and "Address of the Six Assemblymen," plus a sampling of private and public comment in ibid. 2:112–26, 1066, 1603, 1389. On Rhode Island, see "Anarchy," *Pennsylvania Mercury*, Jan. 26, 1788, in ibid. 2:1600, and "Correspondent from Rhode Island," *Maryland Gazette*, Apr. 15, 1788.
23. Philadelphia *Independent Gazetteer*, Oct. 2, 1787, in *DHRC* 13:290–92; Onuf, *Origins of the Federal Republic*, p. 201.
24. See "On the love of our country," an "Ode to Washington," *American Museum*, Oct. 8–10, 1787, in *DHRC* 2:559–64; "*On Chusing a Convention in Pennsylvania* for the Purpose of *considering the Federal Constitution*," *Pennsylvania Packet*, Nov. 13, 1787, in ibid. 2:1069. On the importance of civics training, see McDonald, *Novus Ordo Seclorum*, pp. 190–91, and Lienesch, "The Constitutional Tradition." On the Federalist argument that the people had to try the system to see how it would work, see A Flatbush Farmer, *To the Inhabitants of King's County*.
25. On the Antifederalists, see Rutland, *Ordeal of the Constitution*; Boyd, *Politics of Opposition*; Main, *Antifederalists*; Hutson, "Country, Court, and Constitution."
26. "One of the Late Army," Philadelphia *Freeman's Journal*, Nov. 14, 1787, in *DHRC* 2:1095.
27. Compromise was necessary in any government "founded in freedom and compact," a "Federal Farmer" observed, but in this case it meant that haste had defeated wisdom: "Federal Farmer I," in ibid. 14:23–24. See also "Old Whig III," Philadelphia *Independent Gazetteer*, Oct. 20, 1787, in ibid. 13:425; "Brutus, Junior," *New York Journal*, Nov. 8, 1787, in ibid. 14:5; "Address and Dissent of the Minority of . . . Pennsylvania," Dec. 18, 1787, in ibid. 15:15;

"Sommers," *Pittsburgh Gazette*, Mar. 15, 1788, in ibid. 2:2084; John Tyler's remarks in Virginia Convention, June 25, 1788, in Elliot, *Debates in the . . . State Conventions* 3:641.

28. On nonsigners, see [A correspondent], Philadelphia *Independent Gazetteer*, Jan. 25, 1788, in *DHRC* 15:572. Quotation from "An Officer of the Late Continental Army," Philadelphia *Independent Gazetteer*, Nov. 6, 1787, in ibid. 2:214–15; see also "Rusticus," *New York Journal*, May 23, 1788.
29. "Centinel I," Philadelphia *Independent Gazetteer*, Oct. 5, 1787, in *DHRC* 13:329.
30. "Genuine Information III," *Maryland Gazette*, Jan. 4, 1788, in ibid. 15:249–56.
31. "Centinel XI," Philadelphia *Independent Gazetteer*, Jan. 16, 1788, in ibid. 3:387; "Plebeian" [Melancton Smith], *An Address to the People of the State of New York . . .* , in Ford, *Pamphlets on the Constitution*, p. 115; *Pennsylvania Herald*, Dec. 19, 1787, in *DHRC* 15:555. See also "A Republican Federalist," Philadelphia *Freeman's Journal*, Jan. 16, 1788, in ibid. 2:1512–20.
32. See Thomas B. Wait to George Thatcher, Portland, Maine, Jan. 8, 1788, in *DHRC* 15:285; "Letter from Massachusetts," *Connecticut Journal*, Oct. 17, 1787, in ibid. 3:374–76; remarks of Patrick Henry, Virginia Convention, June 7, 12, 1788, in Elliot, *Debates in the . . . State Conventions* 3:313–14, 149, 623; [Mercy Warren], *Observations on the New Constitution, and on the Federal and State Conventions By a Columbian Patriot* (Boston, 1788), in Ford, *Pamphlets on the Constitution*, pp. 6, 9; "A Georgian," *Gazette of the State of Georgia*, Nov. 15, 1787, in *DHRC* 3:238–39; remarks of George Mason, Virginia Convention, June 11, 1788, in Elliot, *Debates in the . . . State Conventions* 3:269–70, 452, and Mason's objections to the Constitution in *Massachusetts Centinel*, Nov. 21–Dec. 19, 1787, in *DHRC* 14:150.
33. Onuf, *Origins of the Federal Republic*, pp. 174, 186–87, 191, 201.
34. "Brutus I," *New York Journal*, Oct. 18, 1787, in *DHRC* 13:412–21. "Cato III," *New York Journal*, Oct. 25, 1787, in ibid. 13:473–77. For a general listing of Antifederalist objections to the Constitution, see Main, *Antifederalists*, pp. 120–58.
35. On concurrent powers, see "Centinel V," Philadelphia *Independent Gazetteer*, Dec. 4, 1787, in *DHRC* 14:345–47; remarks of James Monroe, Virginia Convention, June 10, 1788, in Elliot, *Debates in the . . . State Conventions* 3:219; Main, *Antifederalists*, pp. 135, 154–55. "Cincinnatus V," *New York Journal*, Nov. 29, 1787, in *DHRC* 14:306–7. And see remarks of John Tyler, Virginia Convention, June 25, 1788, in Elliot, *Debates in the . . . State Conventions* 3:641; "Plebeian," *An Address*, in Ford, *Pamphlets on the Constitution*, p. 91; Luther Martin to the Citizens of Maryland, Mar. 25, 1788, in Farrand, *Records* 3:295–96.
36. Edmund Randolph to the Virginia House of Delegates, Richmond, Oct.

10, 1787 [published Dec. 27], in *DHRC* 15:133–34. See also "Plebeian," *An Address*, in Ford, *Pamphlets on the Constitution*, p. 91; remarks of John Tyler, Virginia Convention, June 25, 1788, in Elliot, *Debates in the . . . State Conventions* 3:642.

37. Lutz, "From Covenant to Constitution," pp. 118, 121.
38. John Brown Cutting to William Short, London, Dec. 13, 1787, in *DHRC* 14:480. See also [Webster], *An Examination . . . of the Federal Constitution*, in Ford, *Pamphlets on the Constitution*, pp. 51–52.
39. An excellent contemporary synopsis of this unfolding Federalist argument may be found in "Plain Truth," Philadelphia *Independent Gazetteer*, Nov. 7, 1787, in *DHRC* 14:519–20, and "Reflection II," *Carlisle Gazette*, Mar. 26, 1788, in ibid. 2:2193–94.
40. My survey of the ratification debates revealed a drop-off in Federalists' appeals to the patriotism of the framers after Luther Martin's disclosures in January 1788. The best sign of this change was the appearance in late October 1787 of the "Federalist" series, which increasingly stressed practical and ideological concerns and used patriotism sparingly and with studied effect. On the circulation of the series, see the headnote in *DHRC* 13:490–92.
41. [Webster], *An Examination . . . of the Federal Constitution*, in Ford, *Pamphlets on the Constitution*, p. 54.
42. Washington to John Armstrong, Sr., Mount Vernon, Apr. 25, 1788, and to David Stuart, Oct. 17, 1787, in *Writings of George Washington* 29:465–66, 290. See also his letters to Bushrod Washington, Mount Vernon, Nov. 10, 1787, and to Charles Carter, Jan. 1, 1788, in *DHRC* 14:85, 15:136–37.
43. Federalist nos. 7, 22, *New York Packet*, Nov. 17, Dec. 14, 1787, and no. 26, New York *Independent Journal*, Dec. 22, 1787, all in *DHRC* 13:130–35, 436–44, 15:65, summarized and discussed the weaknesses of the Articles and the potential sources of conflict between the states. Remarks of James Wilson in Farrand, *Records*, 2:10.
44. "Cincinnatus III to James Wilson, Esquire," *New York Journal*, Nov. 15, 1787, in *DHRC* 14:125.
45. Federalist no. 37, New York *Daily Advertiser*, Jan. 11, 1788, and no. 71, *New York Packet*, Mar. 18, 1788, both in ibid. 15:348, 16:412.
46. Federalist no. 37, New York *Daily Advertiser*, Jan. 11, 1788, in ibid. 15:348. See also Howe's discussion of "faculties and factions" in his "Political Psychology of *The Federalist*," pp. 502–5.
47. Federalist no. 50, *New York Packet*, Feb. 5, 1788, in *DHRC* 16:31. See also "A Real Patriot II," *Pennsylvania Mercury*, Feb. 5, 1788, in ibid. 2:1653–56. Furtwangler, *Authority of Publius*, pp. 62–79.
48. Madison's remarks, June 24, 1788, in Elliot, *Debates in the . . . State Conventions* 3:617–18.

49. *An Address to the People of New-York* . . . (New York, [Apr. 17], 1788), in Ford, *Pamphlets on the Constitution*, pp. 77–80.
50. Hamilton's remarks, New York Convention, June 21, 1788, in Elliot, *Debates in the . . . State Conventions* 2:268. See also Thomas Johnson to Washington, Annapolis, Dec. 11, 1787, in *DHRC* 14:404; [Pelatiah Webster], "A Citizen of Philadelphia," *The Weakness of Brutus Exposed*, Nov. 8, 1787, in ibid. 14:64–74; and esp. James Wilson's remarks, Pennsylvania Convention, Nov. 26, 1787, in Elliot, *Debates in the . . . State Conventions* 2:425.
51. "Foreign Spectator," Philadelphia *Independent Gazetteer*, Sept. 21, 1787, in *DHRC* 2:381–82. "A Mechanic," Philadelphia *Independent Gazetteer*, in ibid. 2:513. On the electoral college, see Buel, *Securing the Revolution*, pp. 4–7, and Ketcham, *Presidents above Party*. The more familiar contemporary form of this argument about checks and balances is in Federalist no. 10, New York *Daily Advertiser*, Nov. 22, 1787, in *DHRC* 14:175–81, and no. 51, New York *Independent Journal*, Feb. 6, 1788, in ibid. 16:46. And see [A correspondent], *Pennsylvania Gazette*, Sept. 26, 1787, in ibid. 13:253–54. Panagopoulos, *Checks and Balances*, explores the classical origins of this concept. See also Howe, "Political Psychology of *The Federalist*," pp. 499–502.
52. Bicameralism was supposed to promote concurring majorities whenever possible by forcing the accommodation of minority concerns; see Federalist no. 51, *New York Packet*, Feb. 5, 1788, in *DHRC* 16:29–31. On large assemblies, see comments on Massachusetts's large convention: Nathaniel Freeman to John Quincy Adams, Jan. 5, 1788, in Adams Family Papers, MHS, and Washington to Benjamin Lincoln, Mount Vernon, Feb. 11, 1788, in *Writings of George Washington* 29:412–13. On close divisions, note "Bystander's" remark, Philadelphia *Independent Gazetteer*, Nov. 14, 1787, in *DHRC* 2:1098–1101, that when parties are "nearly equal, the public interest is torn between them like a sheep between two ravenous wolves."
53. Federalist no. 70, New York *Independent Journal*, Mar. 15, 1788, in *DHRC* 16:398–99. Hamilton's remarks, New York Convention, June 25, 1788, in Elliot, *Debates in the . . . State Conventions* 2:316. [Webster], *An Examination . . . of the Federal Constitution*, in Ford, *Pamphlets on the Constitution*, pp. 31, 34–35.
54. Wilson remarks, Pennsylvania Convention, Dec. 1, 1787, in Elliot, *Debates in the . . . State Conventions* 2:447. Federalist no. 75, New York *Independent Journal*, Mar. 26, 1788, in *DHRC* 16:484.
55. Wilson remarks, Pennsylvania Convention, Dec. 3, 4, 1787, in Elliot, *Debates in the . . . State Conventions* 2:452, 499; [Tench Coxe], *An Examination of the Constitution* . . . (Philadelphia, 1788), in Ford, *Pamphlets on the Constitution*, p. 146; C. C. Pinckney remarks, South Carolina House of Representatives, Jan. 1788, in Farrand, *Records* 3:253; Madison remarks, Virginia Convention, June 15, 24, 1788, in Elliot, *Debates in the . . . State Conventions*

3:453, 458, 621–22. Robinson, *Slavery in the Structure of American Politics*, pp. 242–43; Davis, *Slavery in the Age of Revolution*, pp. 130–31.

56. A point well discussed in Robinson, *Slavery in the Structure of American Politics*, pp. 244–45.
57. Federalist nos. 42 and 54, *New York Packet*, Jan. 1, 1788, and Feb. 2, 1788, both in *DHRC* 15:107–10, 429.
58. Federalist no. 37, New York *Daily Advertiser*, Jan. 11, 1788, in ibid. 15:343–48.
59. Federalist no. 62, New York *Independent Journal*, Feb. 27, 1788, in ibid. 16:233. See McDonald, *Novus Ordo Seclorum*, p. 203, about Madison's attachment to principle.
60. Federalist no. 85, in Cooke, *Federalist*, p. 592. Remarks of Hamilton, New York Convention, June 20, 1788, in Elliot, *Debates in the . . . State Conventions* 2:235–37, 251. "Letter from New York," *Connecticut Courant*, Oct. 24, 1787, in *DHRC* 3:383–84. See also "Reply to George Mason's Objections to the Constitution," *New Jersey Journal*, Dec. 26, 1787, in ibid. 3:160–61, and Pierce Butler to Weedon Butler, New York, Oct. 8, 1787, in ibid. 13:352.
61. Certainly the Constitution "touched" slavery at a large number of points simply because the institution, as an economic interest, fell under the instrument's commerce, taxation, militia, and other clauses. Yet the implication that the ratification of the Constitution somehow signified craven capitulation by feckless northerners to southern extortion—a theme pursued in Wiecek, *Sources of Antislavery Constitutionalism*, pp. 61–83, and Finkelman, "Slavery and the Constitutional Convention"—misses the significance of the ratifying conventions' silence on the subject.
62. Madison to Randolph, New York, Jan. 10, 1788, in *DHRC* 15:326–27. Washington to Randolph, Mount Vernon, Jan. 8, 1788, in ibid. 15:288.
63. "Fabius I," in Ford, *Pamphlets on the Constitution*, p. 166; Jay, *An Address*, in ibid., pp. 82, 80–81. See also Federal Committee of the City of Albany, *An Impartial Address*, p. 26. Federalists frequently compared a second convention to the building of the tower of Babel—it would be a confusion of voices. See "Americanus VII," New York *Daily Advertiser*, Jan. 21, 1788, and "G.," *Pittsburgh Gazette*, Nov. 10, 1787, in *DHRC* 2:1078–79.
64. Federalist no. 85, in Cooke, *Federalist*, p. 592. "Conciliator," Philadelphia *Independent Gazetteer*, Jan. 15, 24, 1788, in *DHRC* 2:1494, 1577–78. See also "Socius," *Carlisle Gazette*, Nov. 14, 1787, in ibid. 2:1078–79.
65. "Conciliator," Philadelphia *Independent Gazetteer*, Jan. 15, 1788, in *DHRC* 2:1489; Dickinson, "Fabius VIII," in Ford, *Pamphlets on the Constitution*, pp. 209–10. And see "Americanus VI," New York *Daily Advertiser*, Jan. 12, 1788. Hyneman and Carey pursue this theme in *Second Federalist*.
66. "An Honest American," Philadelphia *Independent Gazetteer*, Jan. 11, 1788, and "Conciliator," ibid., Jan. 15, 1788, both in *DHRC* 2:1468, 1488–89.

"Giles Hickory" [Noah Webster], *American Magazine*, Jan. 1788, pp. 75–80, Feb. 1788, pp. 59–71. Wiecek, *Sources of Antislavery Constitutionalism*, pp. 62–63, mistakenly claims, without qualification, that the slave trade and direct tax clauses "were made unamendable," but Article V permitted amendments after 1808, and the direct tax clause was superseded by the Sixteenth Amendment in 1913. In theory, if not in practice, no part of the Constitution was "unamendable."

67. Hutson, "Creation of the Constitution," pp. 464–66, on the "triple compromise" theme. For questions about defining the Constitution's compromises, see Farrand, "Compromises of the Constitution," [three-fifths]; McDonald, *Formation*, p. 184n [slave trade]; Rakove, "Great Compromise," p. 427; Finkelman, "Slavery and the Constitutional Convention," p. 221.
68. Kendall and Carey, "How to Read 'The Federalist,'" p. 415; McDonald, *Formation*, p. 194.
69. On the fugitive slave clause, see Fehrenbacher, *Dred Scott Case*, p. 25. On the tenuous basis of union in 1788, see Nagel, *One Nation Indivisible*, pp. 14–32, and Pole, *Idea of Union*.
70. Edward Carrington to Madison, New York, Sept. 23, 1787, in *Papers of James Madison* 10:172. These ideas are reminiscent of Edmund Burke, who repudiated the notion of an original social contract in the state of nature while simultaneously arguing that "all government . . . and every virtue and every prudent act, is founded on compromise and barter," for we must trade some liberty in order "to enjoy civil advantages": "Speech on Conciliation with the Colonies," 1775, in *Burke: Selected Writings and Speeches*, p. 181; and see Gough, *Social Contract*, pp. 192–97. On the relationship between compromise and forms of civil association, see the detailed discussion in Freeman, "Process of Covenant," and Kincaid, "Influential Models of Political Association." See also McDonald, *Novus Ordo Seclorum*, pp. 9–55.
71. Gough, *Social Contract*, pp. 2–7, 8, 234–44; Story, *Familiar Exposition*, p. 35. For a discussion of the distinctions between these three terms, see Lutz, *Origins of American Constitutionalism*, pp. 13–22.

CHAPTER 2

1. Story, *Familiar Exposition*, pp. 11, 12, 268–70. Niles epigraph is from "Compromise on the Missouri Question," *NWR* 17 (Feb. 26, 1820): 442.
2. Madison to Henry Lee, Montpelier, June 25, 1824 [my emphasis], in *Writings of James Madison* 9:190–91.
3. Madison to M.L. Hurlbut, Montpelier, May 1830, in ibid.,9:190–91. See also Madison to Thomas Ritchie, Sept. 15, 1821, in ibid. 9:71–73n., and

Madison to C. J. Ingersoll, Montpelier, June 25, 1831, printed in *NWR* 40 (July 16, 1831): 352. On Madison's views of constitutional interpretation, see McCoy's fine analysis, *Last of the Fathers*, pp. 74–82, esp. p. 80, and his discussion of Madison's reasons for accepting a national bank and higher tariff, pp. 94–96. McCulloch, *Concise History*, p. 164.

Madison's advice about interpreting the Constitution has been viewed as an evasion of civic responsibility, coming as it did when southerners were devising seductive constitutional doctrines justifying nullification, secession, and resistance to federal authority. This view, most recently expressed by Kammen in *A Machine That Would Go of Itself*, pp. 56–58, misunderstands Madison's mission as a civic educator. Sensitive to the public's adulation of the framers and their work, Madison well remembered the Constitution's labored entry into the political world, and sought to avoid public statements that, by offering the wisdom of a framer in place of debate and discussion, might derail the deliberative process. That was why he refused Ritchie's request [*supra*] to publish his priceless notes of the Convention's debates "till the Constitution should be well settled by practice & till a knowledge of the controversial part of the proceedings of its framers could be turned to no improper account."

4. Zvesper, *Political Philosophy and Rhetoric*, pp. 181–82, points out that early American political parties did not regard each other as "legitimate" for the purposes of opposition and that by the 1830s they still had not accepted the idea that changing the principles of governance by rotating the parties through office was compatible with a stable constitutional order. Sisson, *American Revolution of 1800*, pp. 23–69, has a similar analysis. On political parties and regime legitimacy, see Huntington, *Political Order in Changing Societies*, pp. 89–91. See Henry Clay's definition of the line between Federalists and Republicans in House Speech on Internal Improvements, Mar. 7, 1818, and House Speech on the Independence of Latin America, Mar. 28, 1818, in *HC* 2:452, 550, 543–44.
5. Sullivan, *Political Class Book*, pp. v–vi, 75. On the pervasive doubts about the early Republic's future, see Somkin, *Unquiet Eagle*; Nagel, *One Nation Indivisible*; Wilson, *Space, Time, and Freedom*.
6. Sullivan, *Political Class Book*, p. 150.
7. *Works of Henry Clay* 9:418.
8. Lienesch, "Constitutional Tradition," pp. 6–7; see also Schechter, "Early History." *Works of Henry Clay* 9:418.
9. Mann quoted in Cremin, *American Education*, p. 107.
10. For other examples of contemporary discussion about compromise in Fourth of July orations, eulogies, and grand-jury charges, see Schechter, "Early History," pp. 726, 732. Formisano, *Transformation of Political Culture*,

explores similar sources for changing attitudes about political parties and their civic context. Smith, *Professors and Public Ethics*, p. 36.

11. *NWR* 34 (June 23, 1828): 281; "Cassius" letter, undated, reprinted in ibid. 38 (July 3, 1830): 341; Niles in ibid. 38 (May 22, 1830): 237.
12. Ibid. 18 (July 29, 1820): 385–86.
13. See May's lucid discussion in *Enlightenment in America*, pp. 307–62. Smith, *Professors and Public Ethics*, p. 36.
14. Thomas Reid, *An Inquiry in the Human Mind, on the Principles of Common Sense* (Edinburgh, 1765), p. 109, quoted in May, *Enlightenment in America*, p. 344.
15. Lieber, *Ancient and Modern Teacher of Politics*, p. 18.
16. May, *Enlightenment in America*, pp. 346–95.
17. Smith, *Professors and Public Ethics*, p. 81, credits Daniel Gros, a German-educated minister in the German Reformed Church and a chaplain in the New York militia during the Revolution, with originating the concept of the respectful citizenry in his work *Natural Principles of Rectitude*, in 1795.

    Howe, *Political Culture of the American Whigs*, pp. 27–32, has a fine summary of Common Sense philosophy and faculty psychology. But Howe's argument on p. 28—that moral philosophy's acceptance of objective moral laws led to moral absolutism in political discourse by calling attention to "value judgments instead of emphasizing . . . questions of means and the technical implementation of policies"—draws too sharp a distinction between moralism and practicality, which many ethicists, including Lieber, believed were inseparable. "Strong conviction of right and wrong and reality early rises to respectful toleration—a generous acknowledgement of the rights, as well as the opinions of others," Lieber argued in his ethics text *On Civil Liberty and Self Government*, pp. 56–57. Nor should Whiggish ethics be confused with the Whig party. Francis Wayland, for instance, considered himself a conservative Democrat; both he and Lieber were ardent free-traders (Smith, *Professors and Public Ethics*, p. 144).
18. Berki, "Distinction between Moderation and Extremism," p. 67. See also Hare, *Freedom and Reason*.
19. See Haddow, *Political Science in American Colleges and Universities*, p. 139. Smith, *Professors and Public Ethics*, p. 100, distills Lieber's moral philosophy from his essays on penal reform.
20. This sketch is based on Freidel, *Francis Lieber*; see also Smith, *Professors and Public Ethics*, pp. 100–127, and Farr, "Francis Lieber."
21. The most common critical reception of Lieber's political works was to admire how "safe" they were; see Freidel, *Francis Lieber*, pp. 163–70. The synthetical approach of Lieber's *On Civil Liberty*, not the originality of its thesis, won the book a favored place in new political science courses, especially in that of Lieber's successor at Columbia, John Burgess, during

the late nineteenth century. Historians tend to regard Lieber as a late bloomer whose closet nationalism could flower only in northern daylight. I think this is overstated; there is little in his pre–Civil War works that smacks of a southern bias. Even a casual reader would notice that his ideas subtly condemned southern lynch law. More important, Lieber was not a statist seeking the melding of all distinct social elements into one homogeneous whole. Instead, he repeatedly stressed that strength lay in diversity so long as institutional cohesion remained intact. See Clark's interesting discussion of Lieber in *Coherent Variety*, pp. 116–19.

22. Lieber, *Ancient and Modern Teacher of Politics*, pp. 20, 24, 25; idem, *Political Ethics* 1:69–70, 81.
23. Lieber, *Political Ethics* 2:16–17, 206–19, 1:337, 2:1–2, 1:158, 2:130, 131, 1:159.
24. Ibid. 2:70–74.
25. Ibid. 1:180–81, 183; Nisbet, *Quest for Community*; idem, *Conservatism*. Lieber grouped American governments within the broader Anglican framework of "institutional self-government": the "mutual guaranteeing of certain rights" defined in the prescriptive English constitution and adapted to American circumstances through its written Constitution; see *Civil Liberty*, pp. 56–57. Institutional self-government was a "mutually moderative contrivance" whose results were "the products of mutual modification and mutual toleration." They were "not originative, but regulative and moderative, or conciliative and adjusting": ibid., pp. 293–94, 253.
26. See Lieber's discussion of the "character of public men," *Political Ethics* 2:452–65.
27. *Civil Liberty*, pp. 346–47.
28. *Political Ethics* 2:55–62; *Civil Liberty*, p. 347.
29. *Political Ethics* 2:184–85.
30. See ibid. 2:412–31 (and esp. pp. 416, 419, 424, 446) for a general discussion; the quotation is on p. 421. See also *Civil Liberty*, pp. 247, 271 n. 1, and Lieber's discussion of party action in *On history and political economy*, pp. 13–14.
31. *Political Ethics* 2:185–86, 424, 134. Lieber made the same argument in *On history and political economy*, p. 14. His stress on language reflected his deep interest in the study of linguistics and the sociology of language, which he explored in his tract *Legal and Political Hermeneutics*.
32. *Political Ethics* 2:212, 213. Lieber defined *patriotism* as "an affection for our country, made up as are all deep-rooted affections, of a thousand associations and influences": ibid. 2:219.
33. *Civil Liberty*, p. 369.
34. Ibid., p. 345; *Political Ethics* 2:511.
35. *Political Ethics* 2:172–76; *Civil Liberty*, p. 373.
36. *Political Ethics* 2:574–75.

37. Ibid. 2:457, 459–61, part of a general discussion on pp. 452–65.
38. Ibid. 2:448n.
39. *Civil Liberty*, p. 196.
40. For a recent discussion of mutuality and of mutual deference as amenability to reason, see Eidelberg, *Discourse on Statesmanship*, chap. 2, esp. p. 87.
41. *Civil Liberty*, p. 329.
42. *Political Ethics* sold briskly at first, but publication ceased with the sale of the first thousand sets by 1855; *Civil Liberty*'s sales were much better, especially after the Civil War: see Freidel, *Francis Lieber*, p. 168n.
43. The literature on political parties as civic educators is remarkably thin for the antebellum period. See Baker, *Affairs of Party*, pp. 71–107, on formal and informal civics education in the common schools.
44. See Raichle, "Image of the Constitution," on Hildreth, Pitkin, Bancroft et al., and Vitzthum, *American Compromise*. On the civics literature in general, see Michael Warner, *Letters of the Republic*; R. E. Kelly, "Writing of Schoolbooks"; Grambs, "Study of Textbooks and Schoolbooks"; Bennett, *Constitution in School and College*.
45. The habit of reprinting fundamental documents of the American founding runs counter to Kammen's claim (in *A Machine That Would Go of Itself*, pp. 77–83) that the Constitution was not widely available in the early Republic. My survey of these texts indicates that the Constitution was *everywhere*—most of the civics manuals reprinted it, along with other founding documents. The real problem was the extent to which students and new citizens read it.
46. McCartney, *Origin and Progress*, p. 403.
47. Story, *Familiar Exposition*, preface; McKinney, *Constitutional Manual*, p. iv. See also Trumbull, *General History*, preface, and Hickey, *Constitution of the United States*, p. xxvii.
48. Burleigh, *American Manual*, preface, p. 229. See also Burleigh's detailed list of objectives, p. 21.
49. See Forgie's discussion of the veneration of the framers in *Patricide*, pp. 13–53.
50. Berrien quoted in Hickey, *Constitution of the United States*, pp. xvii–xviii; Dallas quoted in ibid., p. iii.
51. Lienesch, "Constitutional Tradition," p. 15.
52. See, for example, Young, *First Lessons in Civil Government*, preface.
53. Van Tassel, *Recording America's Past*, p. 73; England, "Democratic Faith in American Schoolbooks"; Lienesch, "Constitutional Tradition," pp. 15, 22; Elson, *Guardians of Tradition*.
54. See, for example, the cases of Andrew Young and Washington McCartney. McCartney (1812–56) was a scholar-dilettante, common-school reformer,

participant in the lyceum movement, state-court justice, county attorney, and educator from Westmoreland County, Pennsylvania. He founded Union Law School in Easton, Pennsylvania, a one-man operation that died with him. McCartney had broad, catholic interests and wrote books, lectures, and unpublished manuscripts on such diverse subjects as "How to Read a Book," *Principles of the Differential and Integral Calculus*, rhetoric, law, optics, and logic, in addition to his civics text, *Origin and Progress of the United States*. He taught mathematics, modern languages, and moral, mental, and natural philosophy at several small colleges in the eastern part of the state. Young (1802–77) was an upstate New York legislator and teacher whose civics manuals, adapted to the state constitutions of his market states, were best-sellers that were still in use in 1900. On McCartney, see Malone and Johnson, *Dictionary of American Biography* 11:571–72. On Young, see Ohles, *Biographical Directory of American Educators* 3: 1451–52.

55. See, for example, Sullivan, *Political Class Book*, pp. 72–73.
56. Young, *Introduction to the Science of government*, preface. See also Samuel Griswold Goodrich, *Young American*, preface, and pp. 244–46; Mansfield, *Political Grammar*, preface; Parker, *The Constitutional Instructor*, pp. 11–12; Young, *First Lessons in Civil Government*, preface.
57. Of course, civics writers were hardly impartial about the Constitution. The civics works smiled proudly on the framers, accentuated their virtues, muted some of their vices, and loudly praised their handiwork. But the authors were not uniform in political affiliation and policy preferences; their opinions ranged from Websterite national unionism to states' rights unionism. They prided themselves on their detachment and brandished expanding sales figures and lavish endorsements from every region, most Christian denominations, and each major party as evidence of the popularity and mildness of their views. See the advertisements and sales figures in Burleigh, *American Manual*, and Hickey, *Constitution of the United States*, pp. v, ix–xxii, and the discussion in Kammen, *Machine That Would Go of Itself*, pp. 77–82.
58. Charles A. Goodrich, *History of the United States* (1833 ed.), pp. 327–28, (1841 ed.), p. 325. This tale of Christian forbearance survived long after the Convention journals and Madison's notes had revealed the delegates' indifference to Franklin's motion. See Lossing, *Primary History of the United States*, p. 169; Taylor, *Universal History of the United States*, p. 238; New York *Herald*, Dec. 5, 1849.
59. Burleigh skillfully used the preamble to illustrate the dangers of disunion and disorder; see his discussion, *American Manual*, pp. 154–56.
60. Story, *Familiar Exposition*, pp. 29–32, 35. See also Duer, *Lectures on the Constitutional Jurisprudence*, p. 35; McCulloch, *Concise History*, pp. 161–64;

Frost, *History of the United States;* Samuel Griswold Goodrich, *Pictorial History of America,* pp. 664–66.

61. Hickey, *Constitution of the United States,* p. 129.
62. Lienesch, "Constitutional Tradition," pp. 10, 14. For a similar view, see Hutson, "Creation of the Constitution."
63. Charles A. Goodrich, *History of the United States,* p. 189; McCartney, *Origin and Progress of the United States,* pp. 237–38, 255; Willard, *Abridged History of the United States,* p. 252.
64. Lord, *New History of the United States of America,* p. 287.
65. Willard, *Abridged History of the United States,* pp. 252–53. See also Brownell, *People's Book of American History* 2:315.
66. Howitt, *Popular History of the United States,* pp. 232–33.
67. Willard, *Abridged History of the United States,* p. 253.
68. Story, *Familiar Exposition,* pp. 68–69; Holmes, *The Statesman,* p. 14.
69. Mansfield, *Political Grammar,* pp. 36–37; Sullivan, *Political Class Book,* p. 76. Civics writers did not shrink from criticizing the Constitution's compromises but couched their complaints in conciliatory language by pointing out what improvements could ameliorate the most objectionable clauses. After criticizing the fugitive slave clause, Andrew Young (*Introduction to the Science of government,* pp. 181–82) urged the use of jury trials to prevent abuses.
70. Story, *Familiar Exposition,* pp. 68–69, 57–58, 142–43. Story also saw the fugitive slave clause as a clear "refutation" of the notion that southerners did not share in the blessings of the Union: ibid., p. 243. See also Young, *Introduction to the Science of government,* p. 64.
71. Duer, *Lectures on the Constitutional Jurisprudence,* p. 41; Mansfield, *Political Grammar* (1855 ed.), preface.
72. McKinney, *Constitutional Manual,* p. 30; the 1859 edition of this manual, *Our Government,* p. 56, adds a footnote to the catechism, quoting George Washington's cover letter to the Confederation Congress.
73. McCartney, *Origin and Progress of the United States,* pp. 237–39.
74. Holmes, *The Statesman,* p. 12. "So long as the line of jurisdiction of the two governments is well defined and distinctly marked, the duties of the citizen can be fulfilled to both. Though the allegiance is *double* it is not *adverse.*" Foreigners would likely fail to appreciate this unique quality of American union, Holmes thought.
75. Young, *Introduction to the Science of government,* p. 59. See also Lossing, *Primary History of the United States,* p. 170.
76. Young, *Introduction to the Science of government,* pp. 302–4; Sullivan, *Political Class Book,* pp. 145, 44, chap. 5, and appendix.
77. Buel, *Securing the Revolution,* p. 5, points out that Americans in the found-

ing period "felt obliged to rationalize what could not be prevented. If they had believed there was any choice, no one would have urged that parties be formed as a positive advantage. Eighteenth-century Americans had no grounds for concluding that such competition would lead to working compromise, or to any functional definition of the public good." See also Zvesper, *Political Philosophy and Rhetoric*, p. 6, and Young, *Introduction to the Science of government*, p. 327.

78. See Formisano, *Transformation of Political Culture*, pp. 10, 95. As Formisano points out, the acceptance of the necessity of parties did not connote an endorsement either of "party spirit" or of the idea of a two-party system.
79. Watson, *History of the United States*, p. 560. See also Samuel Griswold Goodrich, *Pictorial History of America*, p. 667; Lossing, *Pictorial History* 360–61.
80. McCartney, *Origin and Progress of the United States*, p. 255. See also Frost, *History of the United States*, p. 267. For critical commentaries on the effects of party spirit in the early Republic, see Charles A. Goodrich, *History of the United States*, p. 239, (1841 ed.), p. 395; Bradford, *History of the Federal Government*, p. 50; Willard, *Abridged History*, p. 259. For a different view, see Willson, *American History*, pp. 489–500.
81. Young, *Introduction to the Science of government*, 300–301. As Samuel Griswold Goodrich warned in *Young American*, p. 240, "one party always begets another," tempting individuals to slake their ambition for office and creating a "good deal of bitterness between them." See also Formisano, *Transformation of Political Culture*, pp. 84–106.
82. McCartney, *Origin and Progress of the United States*, pp. 298–99, 302.
83. Burleigh, *American Manual*, pp. 237–38, 231, 230.
84. Lossing, *Pictorial History*, pp. 533–34. And see the similar admonition in Samuel Griswold Goodrich, *Young American*, p. 248, that in political discussions, "there should be strict observance of good breeding; there should be no ungentlemanly contradiction; no imputation of bad motives. There should be no heat of words or manner; no display of anger. All should be done in coolness and kindness."
85. The antiparty statement by Young, quoted earlier, was omitted from later editions of his manual. Charles A. Goodrich's histories of the United States became more partisan during the Jacksonian period—a development starkly revealed by Goodrich's layering of new, more partisan chapters on top of unedited old chapters containing antiparty sentiments: Goodrich, *History of the United States* (1841 ed.), pp. 543–45, 588, 625, 633, 640–47.
86. On faction and party, see Willson, *Treatise on Civil Polity*, pp. 41–42.
87. Curtis, *Strength of the Constitution*, p. 13.
88. Cass quoted in Hickey, *Constitution of the United States*, pp. xx–xxi.

CHAPTER 3

1. Epigraphs, Toasts at Jefferson Day Dinner, Apr. 13, 1830, quoted in Niven, *Martin Van Buren*, pp. 256–57. On attendance rates and common schools, see Kaestle, *Pillars of the Republic*, pp. 14–15, 24–25, 60, 109–11, 204, 220, and Kaestle and Vinovskis, *Education and Social Change*.
2. Hollinger, "American Intellectual History." On the peculiar position of the postfounding generation, see Forgie, *Patricide*, pp. 13–53.
3. Peterson, *Olive Branch and Sword*, p. 2.
4. Webster to Dr. William Prescott, Marshfield, Nov. 7, 1850, in *Letters of Daniel Webster*, p. 440. See Nagel's discussion of the "old Union," the spirit of the framers, and compromise, in *One Nation Indivisible*, pp. 124–37.
5. Kelly, Harbison, and Belz, *American Constitution*, p. 258; Fehrenbacher, *Dred Scott Case*, pp. 36–47. A more thorough discussion is in Finkelman, *Imperfect Union*, with a good summary at pp. 338–43. "A citizen of one State would have the same privileges and immunities in another, *as the people of the same class and condition* could enjoy," John Holmes remarked in his 1840 citizen's manual, *The Statesman*, p. 159.
6. Potter, *Impending Crisis*, pp. 44–50, and Potter, "Historian's Use of Nationalism."
7. On colonization, see Dumond, *Antislavery*, pp. 126–32, and Egerton, *Charles Fenton Mercer*, pp. 105–12, 161–73, 237–44. These and other issues are discussed in Robinson, *Slavery in the Structure of American Politics*, pp. 263–306. An obvious exception to this generalization was the Hartford Convention, whose proposals clearly looked to the abandonment of the three-fifths clause and the addition of constitutional restraints against southern power. But the convention did not single out slavery as the mark of distinction between the sections.
8. Fehrenbacher, *Dred Scott Case*, pp. 146–51, 168.
9. The standard narrative of the Missouri crisis is Moore, *Missouri Controversy*, which is a good survey of the debate and of public opinion but which should be supplemented by the more searching discussion of the controversy's implications for the future in Fehrenbacher, *Dred Scott Case*, pp. 101–17, and idem, *Three Sectional Crises*. Peterson, *Great Triumvirate*, pp. 59–66, has an excellent synopsis of the debate and of Clay's role in settling it. A recent addition to the lamentably limited literature on the Compromise of 1820 is Ransom, *Conflict and Compromise*, pp. 33–40, whose insights into the nature and outcome of the Compromise are severely constrained by his overreliance on Moore.

   It has become commonplace to include the twin admissions of Maine and Missouri as part of this Compromise and therefore as a precedent for the paired admissions of slave and free states, an argument championed especially by Fehrenbacher, *Three Sectional Crises*, p. 18. Maine's status as a "sectional hostage" was immediate and temporary; I have seen little contemporary evidence that legislators regarded the separation of the Enabling Act from the Maine bill as a conscious precedent for paired admissions. The historian's search for the "real" compromise in 1820 proves fruitless the more detailed and specific one gets in sifting the evidence, because the compromise—the agreement to restrain sectional passions in the general interest—was abstract and affective, not concrete and specific.

10. *AC* 16:1, Jan. 27, 1820, pp. 951–52. See also remarks of New Hampshire Rep. Clifton Claggett, in ibid. Feb. 1, 1820, p. 1037. For an interesting discussion of the danger to "pure" legislation from making any congressional compromises, see remarks of Sen. Harrison Gray Otis and Rep. Joshua Cushman (Massachusetts), in ibid. Jan. 14, Feb. 14, 1820, pp. 111–12, 1303–4.
11. Ibid. 16:1, Mar. 2, 1820, pp. 1583–86. For similar arguments, see remarks of Rep. William Eustis (Massachusetts), in ibid. 16:2, Dec. 12, 1820, pp. 639–40; Sen. James Barbour (Virginia), in ibid. 16:1, Jan. 31–Feb. 1, 1820, p. 331; Rep. Alexander Smyth (Virginia), in ibid., Jan. 28, 31, 1820, pp. 992–1021; Sen. Benjamin Ruggles (Ohio), in ibid., Jan. 27, 1820, pp. 279–80; Sen. David Morril (New Hampshire), in ibid., Jan. 14, 1820, p. 138.
12. "Mitigation of Slavery, No. 7," *NWR* 16 (Aug. 14, 1819): 402–3.
13. Detweiler, "Congressional Debate on Slavery," pp. 602–4; Moore, *Missouri Controversy*, pp. 44–45.
14. King's speech to the Senate, printed in *NWR* 17 (Dec. 4, 1819): 218–19. Southerners could not call on the treaty power to carry slaves into the territories either, John Taylor believed: *AC* 16:1, Jan. 27, 1820, p. 965.
15. Sergeant speech, *AC* 16:1, Feb. 9, 1820, pp. 1190–92, 1194, 1196; *NWR* 17 (Jan. 8, 1820): 307. These restrictionist arguments were irrefutable, Niles thought; but the more convinced he was of their correctness, the more willing to compromise he became: see ibid. 17 (Dec. 4, 1819): 209. On the three-fifths extension argument, see remarks of Sen. James Burrill, Jr. (Rhode Island), in *AC* 16:1, Jan. 20, 1820, p. 217; resolutions of the New Jersey and Pennsylvania state legislatures, printed respectively in *NWR* 17 (Jan. 22, 1, 1820): 342, 296–97; proceedings of antislavery meeting, in New York *Evening Post*, Nov. 17, 1819; Rufus King, Senate speech, in *NWR* 17 (Dec. 4, 1819): 215–21.
16. *AC* 16:1, Jan. 20, 1820, p. 229.
17. Ibid., Feb. 10, 1820, pp. 1231–32. For supporting views, see Sen. Ninian Edwards (Illinois), in ibid., Jan. 19, 1820, pp. 189–90. Antirestrictionists referred to other slavery "compromises" (such as the fugitive slave clause) as "proof" that the Convention was trying to protect the "peculiar institution." See Mt. Pleasant Baptist Association to Congress, *Missouri Intel-*

ligencer, September 1819, printed in *NWR* 17 (Nov. 27, 1819): 200–201. For other Missouri arguments, see Hodder, "Sidelights on the Missouri Compromises"; Missouri Delegate John Scott to constituents, July 1819, in Cunningham, *Circular Letters* 3:1092–93.

18. *AC* 16:1, Jan. 27–28, 1820, p. 987.
19. Madison to Robert Walsh, Montpelier, Nov. 27, 1819, in *Writings of James Madison* 9:7–10. Resolutions printed in *NWR* 17 (Jan. 22, Feb. 12, 1820): 343, 416.
20. On sectional parties and close divisions, see remarks of Rep. John Holmes, in *AC* 16:1, Jan. 27–28, 1820, p. 988; of Rep. Ben Hardin (Kentucky), in ibid., Feb. 4, 1820, pp. 1090–91; of Rep. Charles Kinsey (New Jersey), in ibid., Mar. 2, 1820, pp. 1579–83, and in Fehrenbacher, *Dred Scott Case*, p. 107.
21. Schmidt, *Hezekiah Niles*, pp. 116, 302; Luxon, "H. Niles"; idem, *Niles' Weekly Register*. On slavery, see Niles's series of editorials "The Mitigation of Slavery," *NWR* 16 (May 8, 15, July 17, Aug. 14, 1819): 177, 193, 342–44, 402–3.
22. *NWR* 17 (Jan. 29, 1820): 362–64; "Compromise on the Missouri Question," ibid. (Feb. 26, 1820): 442.
23. *AC* 16:1, Feb. 24, 1820, p. 1481. When Rep. Daniel Cook of Illinois asked the same question and got the same answer from Lowndes (ibid., Feb. 4, 1820, p. 1111), he cried: "Then away with your compromise. Let Missouri in, and the predominance of a slave influence is settled, and the whole country will be overrun with it." It is easy to forget that slaves did not necessarily accompany proslavery settlers who might enter free territory and try to enact guarantees for their human property.
24. Ibid., Feb. 4, 5, 1820, pp. 1090–91, 1134–35. Other restrictionists also worried about the Compromise's special, irrevocable status. See Lemuel Shaw, "Slavery and the Missouri Question," *North American Review* 10 (1820): 155.
25. *NWR* 18 (Mar. 11, 1820): 26; Holmes to "the People of Maine," Washington, Apr. 10, 1820, in Cunningham, *Circular Letters* 3:1113. Other editors took up Niles's argument about permanence; see the press survey in Moore, *Missouri Controversy*, pp. 206, 208–9, 243, 244–46; Rep. Mark Langdon Hill to "Fellow Citizens of the State of Maine," Mar. 31, 1820, in Cunningham, *Circular Letters* 3:1101–04; Fehrenbacher, *Three Sectional Crises*, p. 29.
26. Section 26, Missouri Constitution, printed in *NWR* 19 (Sept. 23, 1820): 51–52.
27. This compromise on the electoral vote permitted the House to announce two sets of returns: one with and one without Missouri's votes. The outcome was the same in either case. See Moore, *Missouri Controversy*, pp. 152–54, 159, which calls this the second of *three* compromises required to

settle the Missouri dispute. Clay's resolutions and remarks on counting the electoral votes are in *HC* 3:36–40 and *AC* 16:2, Feb. 14, 1821, pp. 1147–66.

28. Moore, *Missouri Controversy*, pp. 129–69, blames antislavery northerners for refusing to accept the compromise of March 1820.
29. See remarks of Rep. John Sergeant (Pennsylvania) and Sen. James Burrill, Jr. (Rhode Island), in *AC* 16:2, Dec. 7, 1820, pp. 517–31, p. 50; Rep. Gideon Tomlinson (Connecticut), in ibid., Feb. 12, 1821, pp. 1101–2; Rep. Joshua Cushman (Maine), in ibid., Feb. 21, 1821, pp. 1017–19, 1022; Moore, *Missouri Controversy*, pp. 148–49.
30. Rep. Charles Pinckney (South Carolina), in *AC* 16:2, Feb. 1, 13, 1821, pp. 1130, 1138, 1140–43; Brown's motion and remarks in ibid., Feb. 12, 21, 1821, pp. 1109–21, 1195–1209.
31. *NWR* 19 (Nov. 4, 1820): 145–46. Rep. William Hendricks (Indiana), an ardent restrictionist, had obviously tired of the "useless debate" as the winter dragged on; see his letter to constituents, Washington, Feb. 28, 1821, in Cunningham, *Circular Letters* 3:1138. A similar evolution of opinion can be traced in the columns of the New York *Evening Post*, which backed Rufus King in the first debate, deplored the paralysis in legislation during the second, and meekly submitted to the result. See issues of Mar. 7, 13, Dec. 1, 1820, Feb. 20, Mar. 1, 2, 1821.
32. Moore, *Missouri Controversy*, pp. 154–56. Clay's resolution, reprinted in ibid., p. 155, was part of a committee report drenched in the rhetoric of conciliation. See his motions, resolutions, and remarks, in *HC* 3:32, and in *AC* 16:2, Feb. 12, 1821, pp. 1093–94, 1116.
33. See Clay's remarks during 1850 debates, in *CG* 31:1, Feb. 6, 1850, Appendix, pp. 122–25.
34. *NWR* 19 (Nov. 4, Dec. 23, 1820): 145–46, 265–66. See Clay's explanation for his actions in Clay to William Woods, Lexington, July 16, 1835, *HC* 8:786–87, and also the rationalizations in Rep. John Rhea (Tennessee) to constituents, Washington, Mar. 5, 1821, in Cunningham, *Circular Letters* 3:1141, 1146–47; remarks of Rep. Robert Clark (New York) and of Rep. Eldred Simkins (South Carolina), in *AC* 16:2, Feb. 13, 1821, pp. 1125–29.
35. *NWR* 19 (Nov. 4, 1820): 145–46.
36. *NWR* 19 (Dec. 23, 1820): 265–66; ibid. 20 (Apr. 7, 1821): 83–84; see also ibid. 19 (Nov. 4, 1820): 145–46, and 18 (July 29, 1820): 385–86; *National Intelligencer*, Feb. 14, 1820, Feb. 28, 1821. See also remarks of Rep. Louis McLane (Delaware), in *AC* 16:2, Dec. 12, 1820, pp. 608–9.
37. Fehrenbacher, *Dred Scott Case*, p. 116. An excellent brief analysis of the Compromise is in Peterson, *Great Triumvirate*, pp. 65–66.
38. Andrew Jackson, for instance, detected incipient disunionism in his opponents' land and internal improvements policies: *MPP* 3:64–65. John C.

Calhoun was a master at uncovering evidence of declension from established constitutional principles in every federal department, from executive appointments to the administration of the territories.

39. On the American System's union-promoting objectives, see Hargreaves, *Presidency of John Quincy Adams*, p. xiii and passim, and the discussion below in chapter 4. Excellent narratives of the nullification crisis and tariff issue have appeared in recent years. See Peterson, *Olive Branch and Sword*; Ellis, *Union at Risk*; Freehling, *Prelude to Civil War*; Wilson, *Space, Time, and Freedom*, pp. 73–93.
40. Johnson, "The Mode of Selecting a New President" (1835), in Johnson, *A Guide to . . . our American union*, p. 94. The question of the Democrats' proslavery origins is still in dispute. See Brown, "Missouri Crisis"; McFaul, "Expediency vs. Morality"; Richards, "Jacksonians and Slavery."
41. See Friedman, *Revolt of the Conservative Democrats*, pp. 17, 101.
42. Richard P. McCormick, *Second American Party System*, pp. 327–56; Shade, "American Political Development"; Kielbowicz, "Party Press Cohesiveness." The last work notes the undeveloped, undisciplined nature of the Jacksonian press in the 1832 campaign.
43. *NWR* 24 (June 28, 1823): 257–59, and Niles's long essay "The Old Landmarks," ibid. (July 5, 12, 1823): 273–80, 291–93; ibid. 42 (June 9, 1832): 266. See also his confusion about parties in ibid. 38 (May 8, 1830): 202–3, and the discussion in Schmidt, *Hezekiah Niles*, pp. 156–63.
44. Ellis, *Union at Risk*, pp. 46–47.
45. "Nullification is not my word," Calhoun told a correspondent in 1831. "I never use it. I always says [*sic*] 'State interposition.'" Calhoun to ?, ca. 1831, in *Papers of John C. Calhoun* 11:533.
46. "South Carolina Exposition and Protest," Dec. 19, 1828, printed both in rough draft and final committee forms in *Papers of John C. Calhoun* 10:444–539; "Fort Hill Address," July 26, 1831, in ibid. 11:413–40; Calhoun, *A Disquisition on Government*.
47. Calhoun to ?, 1831, in *Papers of John C. Calhoun* 11:533.
48. Clyde N. Wilson and William W. Freehling both note the emphasis on compromise in Calhoun's theory, but neither of them places it in the context of mid-nineteenth-century constitutional unionism. Wilson's view is in *Papers of John C. Calhoun* 11:xv; Freehling's is in his "Spoilsmen and Interests." A brief yet broad overview of the context of Calhoun's thinking is in Wiltse, "From Compact to Nation State in American Political Thought."
49. *NWR* 34 (Apr. 12, 1828): 106.
50. Toast at Edisto nullification dinner, printed in *Charleston Courier* and reprinted in *NWR* 43 (Sept. 29, 1832): 77; Message of South Carolina Governor James Hamilton to the state legislature, in *NWR* 43 (Dec. 15, 1832): 260;

Tomlinson Fort to Calhoun, Milledgeville, Ga., July 15, 1831, *Papers of John C. Calhoun* 11:410–11.

51. Ellis, *Union at Risk*, pp. 80–88.
52. Current, *Daniel Webster*, pp. 62, 193–95; Dalzell, *Daniel Webster*, pp. xii–xv, 9–19. Baxter, *One and Inseparable*, pp. 215–18, has an admirable summary of Webster's argument against compact theory; Webster speech reported in *New York American*, Mar. 28, 1831, reprinted in *NWR* 40 (May 9, 1831): 102–3.
53. "Were there no black slaves in the United States, there would be no opposition to a protection of the labor of white freemen," Niles snorted: *NWR* 42 (June 9, 1832): 266. On three-fifths, see ibid. 33 (Nov. 27, 1827): 179; 40 (Apr. 16, 1831): 114–19; 42 (June 30, 1832): 321–22. On the distinction between concession and conciliation, see ibid. 42 (June 16, 1832): 281–82.
54. Freehling, *Prelude to Civil War*, p. 294, and Wilson, *Space, Time, and Freedom*, pp. 73–74, go too far in proclaiming Jackson the "great compromiser" in this controversy. By placing Jackson between the extremes of Clay's protectionism and Calhoun's nullification, these historians exaggerate Clay's commitment to a high tariff and miss the importance of temperament as a measure of the statesman's skill, so crucial an element of contemporary political culture. An excellent corrective may be found in Peterson, *Olive Branch and Sword*, p. 86, from which the quotation is taken.
55. Ellis, *Union at Risk*, pp. 178–98. Ransom argues in *Conflict and Compromise*, pp. 15–16, that the presidency was the pivotal institution in the success of any compromise because the veto could stop legislative compromise. Yet Jackson resisted compromise during the nullification crisis, and in other sectional crises, presidents deliberately refused to take any initiative in compromise, believing that compromise was primarily a legislative matter first and foremost. This pattern of behavior was characteristic of Monroe, Taylor, and Buchanan.
56. Ellis, *Union at Risk*, p. 99.
57. For a detailed discussion of Clay's motives and movements, see Peterson, *Olive Branch and Sword*, pp. 50–55, 64–74.
58. Clay to James B. Harrison, Harrodsburg, Ky., July 24, 1831, in *HC* 8:377; Clay to Edgar Snowden, Lexington, Sept. 25, 1831, in ibid., p. 405; James Barbour to Clay, Barboursville, Va., Mar. 7, 1832, in ibid., p. 470; Clay to Barbour, Washington, Mar. 10, 1832, in ibid., p. 472; Erastus T. Montague to Clay, Waltham, Va., Apr. 4, 1832, in ibid., p. 486; Hezekiah Niles to Clay, [Baltimore?], mid-December 1832, in ibid., pp. 604–5.
59. *MPP* 2:648; Clay to Charles J. Faulkner (confidential), Washington, Jan. 11, 1833, in *HC* 8:611–12; Clay to James Caldwell, Washington, Jan. 6, 1833, in ibid., p. 609; Clay to Francis T. Brooke, Washington, Dec. 12, 1832, in ibid., pp. 602–3.

60. Clay to James Caldwell, Washington, Jan. 6, 1833, in ibid., p. 609; Clay to Francis T. Brooke, Washington, Dec. 12, 1832, in ibid., pp. 602–3. See also the discussion of Clay's constitutionalism and his views of parties in the next chapter.
61. Clay later attributed southern antitariff sentiment to soil exhaustion in the Southeast; see his discussion of this and abolitionism in Clay to William C. Rives, Lexington, Aug. 19, 1844, and to H. M. Brackenridge, Lexington, June 18, 1844, both in PHC. His discussion of the South's interest in maintaining the tariff compromise is in Clay to Waddy Thompson, Jr., Lexington, July 8, 1837, in *HC* 8:57. Harrison Gray Otis of Massachusetts suggested that Clay offer a blunt bargain with the South: colonize the slaves and keep the tariff. "The North would say to the South 'Save our property & we will Save your lives": Otis to Clay, Boston, Mar. 8, 1832, in ibid., p. 471.
62. Some historians argue that the land bill was not part of a compromise package, which actually comprised the Force Bill and the tariff (see Peterson, *Great Triumvirate*, pp. 231–32). But Clay's attempt to salvage the American System did treat the land bill as a compensatory device, if not strictly a prerequisite to compromise itself. Thus, the role of the land bill in the Compromise of 1833 revealed the complex, interlocking nature of the American System, itself an excellent example of Clay's grand vision of union-strengthening policy insulated from the uncertainties of party politics. See the discussion in the next chapter.
63. Peterson, *Olive Branch and Sword*, pp. 78–79.
64. *NWR* 37 (Feb. 13, 1830): 406. Depictions of Clay as a "high tariff partisan" (Ellis, *Union at Risk*, p. 166), are inaccurate. See the discussion in chapter four. Clay was willing to compromise on the tariff in order to save the more important constitutional principle of protection; both, he thought, were in danger from the Verplanck bill, from Jackson (whose stand against the American System had hardened by 1832), and from the protectionists' attempts to postpone the entire issue to the next Congress, which Clay predicted would be filled with free traders. For more detail, see Peterson, *Olive Branch and Sword*; Clay to Henry Clay, Jr., Philadelphia, Dec. 30, 1832, in *HC* 8:606; Clay to Roswell L. Colt, Washington, Jan. 11, 1833, in ibid., p. 610; Peter B. Porter to Clay, Albany, Jan. 21, 1833, in ibid., p. 614; Clay to Porter, Washington, Jan. 29, Feb. 1, 1833, in ibid., pp. 616–17; Clay to Thomas Ellicott, Washington, Feb. 2, 1833, in ibid., pp. 17–18.
65. Clay to James Barbour, Washington, Mar. 2, 1833, in *HC* 8:629. Clay thought he had enough votes to override the veto: Clay to James Brown, Washington, Mar. 3, 1833, in ibid., pp. 629–30.
66. *RD* 22:2, Feb. 12, 1833, pp. 466–69, 481. For a fine narrative of the debate, see Peterson, *Olive Branch and Sword*, pp. 77–83.

67. Ibid. 24:2, Feb. 25, 1837, pp. 971–72.
68. Ibid. 25:1, Oct. 9, 1837, pp. 516–17.
69. See Peterson's remarks about Clay, Calhoun, and compromise, in *Great Triumvirate*, p. 226.
70. The subsequent history of the Compromise of 1833 is a matter of debate among historians. Hodder, "Authorship of the Compromise of 1850," claims that the agreement was "soon thereafter abandoned," but Peterson argues convincingly to the contrary in *Olive Branch and Sword*.
71. Third Annual Message, December 1843, in *MPP* 4:266.
72. *MPP* 3:5, 295–99 (Jackson), 3:315, 319 (Van Buren), 4:15–20 (Harrison), 4:81–82, 180–88, 201, 266, 337 (Tyler). Significantly, Whig presidents emphasized the nonpartisan dimension of the compromise spirit.
73. Charles A. Goodrich, *History of the United States* (1841 ed.), p. 574. Willson, *American History*, pp. 501, 688, similarly relies on statesmanship to avert future crises. More striking, though, is the civics writers' slipshod handling of the basic facts of antebellum compromises, especially of the Missouri Compromise, including wrong dates, inaccurate paraphrasing of legislation, and distorted praise of particular statesmen. For examples, see Mansfield, *Political Grammar*, p. 146; Frost, *History of the United States*, pp. 347–49; Fisher, *Progress of the United States*, p. 175; Sullivan, *Political Class Book*, p. 68; Bradford, *History of the Federal Government*, p. 268; McKinney, *Constitutional Manual*, p. 124; Guernsey, *History of the United States of America*, p. 398. Lossing, *Primary History*, pp. 199–200, says that the Missouri Compromise allowed slaves in Missouri and drew a line "from the southern boundary of Missouri to the Pacific Ocean, and that north of that line there should never be any slaves, in any new State that might be formed there." None of these authors corrected later editions of their histories to account for the acquisition of northwestern territories that were not covered by the Missouri Compromise, implying what Lossing mistakenly declared.
74. The strongest proponent of this view is Silbey, *Partisan Imperative*. See also Agar, *Price of Union*, pp. 328–34.
75. *MPP* 4:376.

CHAPTER 4

1. Clay, House speech on Surveys, Jan. 30, 1824, in *HC* 3:621. Epigraph is from *NWR* 66 (July 1844): 298.
2. Clay to Francis T. Brooke, Washington, Mar. 11, 1833, in *HC* 8:631–32. For an account of their famous duel, see Van Deusen, *Life of Henry Clay*, pp. 219–22. The Compromise of 1850 featured similar bipartisan saluta-

tions among conservatives and old enemies. See chapter six, note 6, for examples.

3. Clay to Henry Clay, Jr., Olympian Springs, Ky., Aug. 24, 1830, in *HC* 8:256. On the irony of Clay's career, see Howe, *Political Culture of the American Whigs*, pp. 125–27.
4. Dangerfield, *Era of Good Feelings*, pp. 10–13. The latest endorsement of this view is Seager, "Clay and the Politics of Compromise."
5. Peterson has reiterated the importance of the Senate as an outpost of opposition to the executive, in *Great Triumvirate*, pp. 234–36.
6. Howe, *Political Culture of the American Whigs*, pp. 123–49; Thomas Brown, *Politics and Statesmanship*, pp. 119, 142, 152–53.
7. For an excellent example of Clay's sensitivity on the "corrupt bargain" charge, see the verbal duel in the Senate between Clay and John C. Calhoun, in *CG* 26:1, Jan. 3, 1840, pp. 96–98.
8. Clay, Senate speech, Jan. 9, 1838, excerpted in *HC* 9:124; Remarks reported by William Henry Sparks, *The Memories of Fifty Years . . .*, 3d ed. (Philadelphia, 1872), p. 232, quoted in *HC* 3:49–50n.
9. Quoted in *Works of Henry Clay* 3:248. See also Peterson, *Great Triumvirate*, p. 6.
10. Clay to Stephen Miller, July 1, 1844, published in *NWR* 66 (Aug. 3, 1844): 372, and in *National Intelligencer*, Aug. 8, 1844. For a discussion of the letter's impact, see Van Deusen, *Life of Henry Clay*, pp. 373–76.
11. "I never studied half enough" for the law, Clay told his son Henry. "I always relied too much upon the resources of my genius." Clay to Henry Clay, Jr., Lexington, Apr. 19, 1829, in *HC* 8:29–30. Schurz, *Henry Clay* 1:23–24, fixes Clay's profession as an "orator," describes him as an "arranger of measures," and notes how his superficial brilliance enabled him "to make little tell for much, and to outshine men of vastly greater learning." See also Van Deusen, *Life of Henry Clay*, pp. 425–26; Eaton, *Henry Clay*, p. 89; Thomas Brown, *Politics and Statesmanship*, pp. 118–19.
12. Most historians call Clay a "nationalist"; for an elaboration on this theme, see Klein, "Henry Clay, Nationalist," which offers many useful insights on Clay's views about parties and statesmanship. On "positive liberalism," see Benson, *Concept of Jacksonian Democracy*, pp. 86–109, esp. p. 103; Van Deusen, "Aspects of Whig Thought"; Howe, *Political Culture of the American Whigs*, p. 20.
13. See esp. Maness, "Henry Clay and the Problem of Slavery," pp. 34, 44, 64. Cf. Schurz, *Henry Clay* 1:301–2, and Clay to Horace Greeley (confidential), Lexington, Nov. 22, 1847, in PHC.
14. Seager, "Clay and the Politics of Compromise," p. 6.
15. Resolution of Thanks to Speaker of the House, Mar. 3, 1821; Speech at Public Dinner, Lewisburg, Va., Aug. 30, 1826; Clay to General Robert

Swartwout, Lexington, Oct. 5, 1838; all in *HC* 3:57, 5:655, 8:237. Several historians have challenged the supposed opposition of states' rights to nationalist unionism; see Ellis, *Union at Risk*, and the fine essay by Belz, "The South and the American Constitutional Tradition."

16. Clay, House speech on Cumberland Road, Jan. 17, 1825, in *HC* 4:24–25.
17. Clay, House Speech on Internal Improvements, Mar. 7, 1818, in ibid. 2:451–52, 449; Clay to Edward Everett, Lexington, Apr. 22, July 3, 1824, in ibid. 3:738, 791–92.
18. Antinullification speech at Cincinnati, Aug. 3, 1830, in ibid. 8:242–44. Most historians describe Clay as an organic Unionist, contrary to the view expressed here. See Nagel, *One Nation Indivisible*, p. 256; Thomas Brown, *Politics and Statesmanship*, pp. 137–53; Howe, *Political Culture of the American Whigs*, p. 148.
19. Clay to Francis T. Brooke, Lexington, May 1, 1831, in *HC* 8:343; Clay, Senate speech on abolition, Feb. 7, 1839, in *Works of Henry Clay* 1:227, 8:157 (unfortunately only parts of this important speech are excerpted in *HC* 9:277–83); Clay, antinullification speech in Cincinnati, in *HC* 8:243. See also Clay's toast at a public dinner in Yellow Springs, Ohio, July 27, 1830, in ibid., p. 241. For striking examples of the depth of Clay's fears about the stability of the Union, see Clay to George Corbin Washington, Lexington, May 17, 1830; Clay to Charles Hammond, Lexington, Nov. 17, 1832; Clay to Henry Clay, Jr., Washington, Jan. 3, 18[33]; Clay to Francis T. Brooke, Lexington, Aug. 2, 1833; Clay to David F. Caldwell, Lexington, June 25, 1835; Clay to Francis T. Brooke, Lexington, June 27, 1835; all in ibid., pp. 208, 599, 607–8, 660–62, 774–76. See also Clay to Peter Cromwell (private), Lexington, Feb. 17, 1845, and to John R. Thompson, Lexington, Apr. 23, 1845, both in PHC.
20. Van Deusen, *Life of Henry Clay*, p. 69. For an excellent example of Clay's use of Madison's words, see Madison to Clay, Apr. 2, 1833, and then Clay to Richard Henry Wilde (confidential), Lexington, Apr. 27, 1833, both in *HC* 8:639–41.
21. Madison to Reynolds Chapman, Montpelier, Jan. 6, 1831, in *Writings of James Madison* 9:434; Clay, House Speech on Internal Improvements, Feb. 4, 1818, and Clay, Remarks on Resolution Concerning Internal Improvements, Mar. 6, 1818, both in *HC* 2:308–11, 446–47. See also Peterson, *Great Triumvirate*, p. 48, and McCoy's discussion of the evolution of Madison's opinions about protection, in *Last of the Fathers*, p. 186.
22. George Tucker to Clay, Charlottesville, Va., ca. June 30, 1836, in *HC* 8:859. Madison's "Advice" was first published by the *National Intelligencer*, Feb. 6, 22, 1851, as "The Dying Injunction of Mr. Madison"; see Brant, *James Madison*, pp. 530–31. On Madison's unionism, see McCoy, *Last of the Fathers*, pp. 190–92, 274.

23. Clay, Campaign speech at Hanover County, Va., June 27, 1840, in *Works of Henry Clay* 8:200. See also Clay, House Speech on Internal Improvements, Mar. 7, 1818, in *HC* 2:449, and Clay's discussion of legislative precedent, executive powers, and the importance of established policy, in Clay to Francis Lieber, Washington, Feb. 12, 1838, in ibid. 9:142–43. On Madison's views of constitutional interpretation, see McCoy's fine analysis, *Last of the Fathers*, pp. 74–82, esp. p. 80, and his discussion of Madison's reasons for accepting a national bank and higher tariff, pp. 94–96.
24. See Clay, House Speeches on Internal Improvements, Mar. 7, 13, 1818, Jan. 14, 1824; Clay to Edward Everett, Apr. 22, 1824; Clay to Francis T. Brooke, Lexington, May 1, 1831; Clay, Speech at Clay Festival, Lexington, June 9, 1842; all in *HC* 2:448, 449, 468, 3:581, 738, 8:343, 9:709. See also Clay, Senate Speech on Omnibus Bill, in *CG* 31:1, July 22, 1850, Appendix, p. 1411.

    Clay's intellectual debt to Jefferson was more apparent than real. He praised Jefferson's statesmanship but always referred to *Madison*'s, not Jefferson's, Resolves. And Madison's views on the perpetuity of the Union were more moderate than Jefferson's. See Malone, *Jefferson and the Ordeal of Liberty*, pp. 395–424 and sources cited therein, and Peterson, *Jefferson Image in the American Mind*, pp. 57–58.
25. Kelly, Harbison, and Belz, *American Constitution*, pp. 136–41. On Madison and the moderate Republicans, see Ellis, *Jeffersonian Crisis*, pp. 21–24, 236–37, and McCoy, *Last of the Fathers*, pp. 139–42.
26. Clay, House Speeches on Internal Improvements, Mar. 13, 7, 1818, Jan. 14, 1824, in *HC* 2:468, 448, 451, 3:581.
27. Clay, House Speech on Internal Improvements, Mar. 13, 1818, in ibid. 2:470–71.
28. Clay to Francis T. Brooke, Lexington, Aug. 28, 1823, in ibid. 3:478. See also Clay to Littleton W. Tazewell, Washington, Feb. 1, Apr. 5, 1834, and Clay, Senate Speech and Resolutions on the Executive, Mar. 7, 1834, both in *HC* 8:693, 710–11, 703; Clay, Response to House Resolution of Thanks, May 15, 1820, in ibid. 2:862.

    Clay's belief in legislative supremacy stemmed from both his Madisonian heritage and his experience as Speaker and opposition leader. His denunciation of "King Andrew" Jackson was an almost point-for-point rehashing of the style and substance of Madison's "Address to the People" of Virginia, which accompanied the Virginia Resolves. See the discussion of this theme below; Clay's speech at Fowler's Garden, Lexington, May 16, 1829, in ibid. 8:41–54, which outlined the essentials of the antiexecutive argument; Banning, *Jeffersonian Persuasion*, pp. 264–66, 301–30.
29. *RD* 22:2, Feb. 12, 1833, pp. 466–69; Clay, House Speech on Internal Improvements, Mar. 7, 1818, in *HC* 2:451.
30. See McCoy, *Last of the Fathers*, pp. 79–83, 96–105, 115, which does not

reconcile Madison's support for legislative precedent as a source of constitutionality with his vehement opposition to congressional declarations of constitutionality.

31. Clay, House Speeches on Internal Improvements, Mar. 7, 13, 1818, Jan. 14, 1824, in *HC* 2:456–57, 463, 473–74, 3:580, 587.
32. Clay, House Speech on Internal Improvements, Mar. 7, 1818, in ibid. 2:449, 448; Thomas Brown, *Politics and Statesmanship*, pp. 123–24; on Madison's postwar views, see McCoy, *Last of the Fathers*, pp. 94–95, 177–92.
33. Clay, House Speech on Bill to Raise an Additional Military Force, Jan. 8, 9, 1813, in *HC* 1:762.
34. Clay, Speech Adjourning the House of Representatives, Mar. 3, 1817, in ibid. 2:321; Schurz, *Henry Clay* 2:413.
35. On Madison's political economy, see McCoy, *Elusive Republic*, esp. pp. 209–59.
36. Clay, Speech at Hopkinsville, Ky., Sept. 21, 1829, and Clay to Charles Wilkins et al., Lexington, June 3, 1820, both in *HC* 8:104–5, 2:867–68. On the American System's primary goal of preserving and strengthening the Union, see Clay, House Speech on Cumberland Road, Jan. 17, 1825, in ibid. 4:24–25; Clay, House Speeches on Internal Improvements, Mar. 7, 1818, Jan. 14, 1824, in ibid. 2:449, 450–51, 458–59, 462–63, 3:586–87; Clay, Senate Speech on Land Bill, in *RD* 24:1, Apr. 26, 1836, pp. 1296–98; Clay, Senate Speech on the Bank of the United States, in ibid. 25:1, Sept. 27, 1837, p. 298.

    Clay's favoritism for eastern manufacturers (Van Deusen, *Life of Henry Clay*, pp. 254–55, 307, 308, 425–26) has been exaggerated; he never repudiated his assertion to E. I. Du Pont in 1824 that agriculture was "the first and greatest of all our interests": *HC* 3:640.
37. Clay, House Speech on the Tariff, Mar. 30, 31, 1824, and Clay, Speech at Natchez, Miss., Mar. 13, 1830, both in *HC* 3:724, 8:180–81; Schurz, *Henry Clay* 1:52. Clay later told a biographer that this 1824 tariff speech was "the most elaborate" he had "ever delivered": Clay to Epes Sargent, Lexington, Aug. 20, 1842, in *HC* 9:758.
38. Clay, House Speeches on the Tariff, Apr. 26, 1820, Mar. 30, 31, 1824, in *HC* 2:833, 3:723–26. See also Clay to Francis T. Brooke, Lexington, Aug. 28, 1823; Clay, Remarks on Tariff Bill, Feb. 17, 1824; Clay to Edward Everett, Washington, Apr. 22, 1824; all in *HC* 3:479–80, 647, 737–38.
39. Clay, House Speech on Internal Improvements, Feb. 14, 1817, in *HC* 2:309. See also his Speech on the Bank of the United States, June 3, 1816, in ibid. 2:202–4.
40. Toasts and speech at public dinner, June 17, 1824, in ibid. 3:779. On the distribution of benefits to strengthen the Union, the best summary is in Clay's House Speech on Establishing Additional Military Academies, Jan.

2, 1816, in ibid. 2:119–21. Clay's support for moderate tariff rates was stronger and more consistent than some historians allow. Extremely high or low rates only make protection a party issue, which Clay hoped to avoid. For the evolution of his ideas on this, see Clay's statements in the following: Motion to Amend Tariff Bill, Mar. 25, 1816; House Speech on the Tariff, Apr. 26, 1820; to Peter B. Porter, Washington, Apr. 2, 12, 1828; to George Featherstonhaugh, Washington, Feb. 18, 1828; to Hezekiah Niles (confidential), Lexington, Oct. 4, 1829; to Dr. F. S. Bronson, Lexington, Sept. 13, 1843; all in ibid. 2:182–83, 3:479–80, 7:212, 225, 102, 8:108–9, 9:856. And see Clay, Campaign Speech at Hanover County, Va., June 27, 1840, in *Works of Henry Clay* 8:206; Clay to *Tennessee State Agriculturist*, Lexington, Aug. 1843, in *HC* 9:842–43; Clay to E. Roussel, Lexington, May 18, 1846, in PHC.

41. Clay, Senate Speech on Abolition, Feb. 7, 1839, in *Works of Henry Clay* 8:149; Clay, notes for oral arguments in Groves *v.* Slaughter (40 Peters 449–517), in *HC* 9:476. See also Clay, House Speech on Internal Improvements, Jan. 14, 1824, in *HC* 3:586–87.
42. Clay, Speech on the Tariff, Apr. 26, 1820, in *HC* 2:836. In 1843, Clay remarked that the Lowell system was "in respect to Manufactures, what the U. States" were "in respect to self-government." Both were experiments, one in the compatibility of industrialism with "the social virtues" and the other in the ability of men to govern themselves wisely. "Both have shown that they are not perfect, and therefore not always free from error." Clay to William Schouler, Lexington, Nov. 10, 1843, in ibid. 9:888. Hargreaves, *Presidency of John Quincy Adams*, pp. xiii, 165–87, stresses the antisectional thrust of the American System's design.
43. See McCoy, *Last of the Fathers*, pp. 63–64.
44. Peterson, *Great Triumvirate*, pp. 380–81; Clay to Henry Clay, Jr., Washington, Mar. 2, 1838, in *HC* 9:152. See also the latter's observations of Clay's winning ways in Henry Clay, Jr. MS Diary, Dec. 29, 18[31], Special Collections, Margaret King Library, University of Kentucky, Lexington.
45. The three standard biographies of Clay—by Schurz, Van Deusen, and Eaton—narrate Clay's party activities with little attention to the problem of party conflict as I am discussing it here. Poage, *Henry Clay and the Whig Party*, is the only monograph about Clay's party career after 1833, and it assumes that he fully endorsed the new democratic politics.
46. The literature on party development is massive, rich, and full of controversy. See McCormick, *Second American Party System*, and idem, "Party Period and Public Policy." Hofstadter, *Idea of a Party System*, has become a classic, but the section on the rise of mass parties relies mainly on the New York experience analyzed in Wallace, "Concepts of Party in the United States." Silbey's argument is in his *Partisan Imperative*, pp. 50–68, at p. 55.

47. On this point, see Formisano, *Transformation of Political Culture*, pp. 84–106, 313.
48. Clay to William Ellery Channing, Washington, Dec. 13, 1837, in *HC* 9:104. Wilson, *Space, Time, and Freedom*, p. 55, notes that the advocates of the American System offered a consensus view of politics, one that "ruled out the idea of a permanent two-party system."
49. See Clay, House Speech on Internal Improvements, Mar. 7, 1818, and Clay, Speech to Whig Senate Caucus, Sept. 13, 1841, both in *HC* 2:452, 9:608; Van Deusen, *Life of Henry Clay*, p. 211.
50. See Clay to William Woods, Lexington, July 16, 1835, in *HC* 8:786–87.
51. Clay, House Speech on Internal Improvements, Mar. 7, 1818, and Clay, House Speech on the Independence of Latin America, Mar. 28, 1818, both in *HC* 2:452, 550, 543–44. See also Clay to Henry Rutgers (private and confidential), Lexington, June 4, 1827, in ibid. 6:644–45.
52. Clay to Peter B. Porter (confidential), Lexington, Oct. 22, 1822; Clay to Josephus B. Stuart, Washington, Dec. 19, 1823; Clay to Charles Hammond (confidential), Frankfort, Oct. 25, 1824; all in ibid. 3:300–301, 545, 870.
53. Clay to Benjamin W. Crowninshield, Washington, Mar. 18, 1827, and Clay to Peter B. Porter, Washington, Apr. 28, 1828, both in ibid. 6:320, 7:211–12. Clay's sluggish reaction to the early evidence of Jackson's coalition is evident in Clay to Francis T. Brooke (confidential), Washington, Feb. 18, 1825, in ibid. 4:74.
54. Clay to Allen Trimble, Washington, Dec. 24, 1827; Clay to Francis T. Brooke (confidential), Washington, Nov. 24, 1827; Henry Shaw to Clay, Lanesboro, Mass., Nov. 17, 1828; Clay to Peter B. Porter (private and confidential), Washington, Jan. 14, 1828; all in ibid. 6:1377, 1312, 1279–80, 7:36. See also Clay to Richard Peters, Jr. (private and confidential), Washington, Oct. 16, 1826, in ibid. 5:798–99.
55. Clay to Denison Wattles, Washington, Nov. 10, 1828, in ibid. 7:534.
56. David Lee Childs to Clay, Boston, Apr. 11, 1829, and Clay to Denison Wattles, Jr., Washington, Dec. 6, 1828, in ibid. 8:25–26, 7:559.
57. Clay to John Sloane, Washington, May 20, 1827, in ibid. 6:572–73.
58. The speech, whose audience Clay expected would include "many Jacksonians," is in ibid. 8:41–54, which is the source of the quotations in the next two paragraphs. For similar themes, see Clay, Speech at Bardstown, Ky., July 30, 1829, in *HC* 8:81. Clay sensed the potency of this issue from his network of Washington informants, who reported throughout 1829 and 1830 the administration's patronage turnover and the conflicts within the cabinet. See Thomas Patterson (former clerk of the House of Representatives) to Clay, Hagerstown, Md., June 8, 1829, in ibid., pp. 67–68, and the reports from Sen. Josiah Johnston, esp. his letter to Clay from Maysville, Ky., July 8, 1829, in ibid., p. 73.

59. Clay to George Featherstonhaugh, Washington, Feb. 18, 1828, and Clay to Marquis de Lafayette, Washington, Jan. 1, 1828, both in *HC* 7:101, 2. Clay here echoed Madison's alarms over the intensity of party competition for the presidency. See McCoy, *Last of the Fathers*, pp. 125–26.
60. See Peterson, *Great Triumvirate*, p. 235.
61. Clay to John Quincy Adams, Lexington, Apr. 12, 1829, and Adams to Clay, Apr. 21, 1829, both in *HC* 8:26, 33. See also James Brown to Clay, Paris, Dec. 12, 1828; Lewis P. W. Balch to Clay, Frederick, Md., Jan. 27, 1829; John L. Lawrence to Clay, New York City, Oct. 6, 1831; all in ibid. 7:565, 607, 8:416.
62. See White, *The Jacksonians*, pp. 27–49, 564–65. Madison believed that Whig attempts to restrict the executive went too far; see McCoy, *Last of the Fathers*, pp. 104–5.
63. Clay to Brantz Mayer, Washington, Jan. 21, 1832, *HC* 8:447.
64. Clay's confidence in the weakness of his foes and the strength of the American System runs throughout his correspondence in the early 1830s; see, for example, Clay to Jesse B. Harrison, Lexington, Jan. 3, 1830, and Clay to George Corbin Washington, Lexington, May 17, 1830, both in ibid., pp. 167, 209.

    Clay urged his followers to organize but gave them little more than advice. His plan for party organization—laid out in Clay to John F. Henry (confidential), Washington, Sept. 27, 1827, in *HC* 6:1074–76—amounted to a national literature distribution system along the lines of Jeffersonian party organizations in the early 1810s. See also Clay to William Greene (confidential), Nov. 11, 1830, in ibid. 8:295–96.
65. Although Clay said this many times, a good summary is in Clay to [John M. Bailhache], Lexington, July 14, 1835, in ibid., pp. 784–85. Eaton, *Henry Clay*, pp. 81, 84.
66. Clay's financial and family circumstances intruded on his political life more than historians have recognized. The deaths of children, business failures, and low prices for the hemp produced at his magnificent plantation in Lexington made his long absences from home even harder to bear. The death of his favorite daughter, Anne—the sixth of Clay's daughters to die—might have led him away from seeking a Whig nomination in 1836. See Clay to Francis T. Brooke, Washington, Jan. 1, 1836 in *HC* 8:820–21; ibid., p. 809n; Van Deusen, *Life of Henry Clay*, pp. 149–52, 231–33, 272–75, 379–80, on family and business matters.
67. Van Deusen, *Life of Henry Clay*, pp. 245–63.
68. Clay to Nathaniel P. Tallmadge, Lexington, Apr. 12, 1839, in *HC* 9:304.
69. Clay to Francis T. Brooke, Washington, Jan. 17, 1833, in ibid. 8:613–14; see also Clay to Brooke, Lexington, Aug. 2, 1833, in ibid., pp. 660–62.
70. Clay to Francis T. Brooke, Washington, Mar. 23, 1834; Clay to David F.

Caldwell, Lexington, June 25, 1835; Clay to Francis T. Brooke, Lexington, June 27, 1835; all in ibid., pp. 706–7, 775–76.

71. Clay to S. L. Southard, Lexington, June 27, 1835; Clay to James Heaton, Lexington, June 12, 1835; Clay to Christopher Hughes, Lexington, Aug. 25, 1835; all in ibid., pp. 776–77, 788–89, 773, 798–99. On 1836, see Peterson, *Great Triumvirate*, pp. 244, 247–49, and Clay to Matthew L. Davis (confidential), Lexington, July 3, 1837, in *HC* 9:54–55.

72. On the Calhoun resolutions, see Clay to Peter B. Porter (confidential), Washington, Jan. 10, 1838; Clay to Francis T. Brooke, Washington, Jan. 13, 1838; Clay to Harrison Gray Otis, Washington, June 26, 1838; all in *HC* 9:127, 129, 208. Calhoun would "die a traitor or a madman," Clay predicted to Otis.

73. Clay to Thomas Speed, Lexington, June 19, 1833, and Clay, Speech to Kentucky chapter of American Colonization Society, Dec. 17, 1829, both in ibid. 8:652–53, 156–59. There is an extensive literature on Clay's views about race and slavery. See Maness, "Clay and the Problem of Slavery," and Van Deusen, *Life of Henry Clay*, pp. 136–38. The evolution of his ideas can be traced in Clay's statements in the following: House Speech on Fugitive Slave Bill, Jan. 28, 1818; House Speech on the Tariff, Mar. 30–31, 1824; Speech at Public Dinner, Lewisburg, Va., Aug. 30, 1828; to Alexander W. Stow, Lexington, Apr. 26, 1837; to Jacob Gibson, Lexington, July 26, 1842; all in *HC* 2:432–33, 3:702, 5:660, 9:43, 745–47.

74. Clay, Speech to American Colonization Society, Jan. 20, 1827; Clay to John W. White, Washington, Dec. 15, 1838; Henry Clay, Jr., diary entry, 1831; all in *HC* 6:84–85, 9:257, 8:85.

75. Clay, Senate Speech on Abolition, Feb. 7, 1839, in *Works of Henry Clay* 8:150; Clay to Thomas Speed, Lexington, June 19, 1833, and Clay to Charles Hammond, Washington, Apr. 19, 1826, both in *HC* 8:652–53, 5:253; Clay to Mrs. Martha K. Buckingham (private), Lexington, Mar. 31, 1845, in PHC. The government could act "*after* emancipation," which Clay regarded as a state matter; see Clay to Joseph Berry, Lexington, June 15, 1833, in *HC* 8:649–50.

76. Clay to Charles Hammond, Washington, Apr. 19, 1825, in ibid. 5:253.

77. Clay to James Brown, Lexington, July 7, 1833, in ibid. 8:656.

78. Clay to Birney, Lexington, Sept. 16, 1834; Birney to Clay, New York City, Dec. 22, 1837; Clay to Tappan, Washington, July 6, 1838; Clay to Birney, Nov. 3, 1838; all in ibid. 8:748, 9:111–13, 212, 244–45. See also Clay to John Greenleaf Whittier (private), Lexington, July 22, 1837, and Clay to John Pendleton Kennedy, Lexington, May 16, 1839, both in ibid. 9:64, 314–15; and Clay to Joshua Giddings (confidential), Lexington, Oct. 6, 1847, in PHC.

79. See Clay to John C. Crump et al., Lexington, May 25, 1839, in *HC* 9:318–19.
80. Clay to John Pendleton Kennedy, Lexington, May 16, 1839, in ibid., pp. 314–15. See his analysis of the party situation in Clay, Senate Speech on Abolition, Feb. 7, 1839, in *Works of Henry Clay* 1:224, 8:145, and in Clay to C. C. Baldwin, Lexington, Aug. 28, 1838, and Clay to Willie Mangum, Washington, May 31, 1838, both in *HC* 9:222–23, 194. On third parties, see Clay to Brantz Mayer and Morrison Harris (confidential), Lexington, Feb. 1, 1845; Clay to Dudley Selden, Lexington, Apr. 23, 1845; Clay to John L. Littell, Lexington, Nov. 17, 1846; all in PHC.
81. Clay letters: to John C. Crump et al., Lexington, May 25, 1839; to James D. Allen, Washington, June 22, 1840; to John Pendleton Kennedy, Lexington, Apr. 17, 1839; to Committee of Henry County, Tennessee Whigs, Lexington, Oct. 1, 1838; all in *HC* 9:318–19, 425, 306, 234–36.
82. Clay letters: to Peter B. Porter, Washington, June 3, 1838; to Harrison Gray Otis, Washington, Dec. 13, 1838; to Alexander Hamilton, Washington, Feb. 24, 1839; to John Leeds Kerr, Washington, May 22, 1838; all in ibid., pp. 197–98, 252, 291, 188. See Van Deusen, *Life of Henry Clay*, pp. 326–29, on the tour.
83. Clay to Jones Green, Washington, May 12, 1840, in *HC* 9:411–12. Harrison's nomination was "a measure of relief to" Clay, he wrote Harrison Gray Otis. "I feel, once more, a free man, at liberty to pursue my own inclinations, and unembarrassed by ten or twelve months of turmoil": Clay to Otis, Washington, Dec. 19, 1839, in ibid., p. 368. Van Deusen, *Life of Henry Clay*, p. 334, says that in the "log cabin" campaign, "Clay worked zealously for the Whig ticket," but Van Deusen does not say how. Clay did endorse some campaign literature, but as Van Deusen admits, he found the entire campaign's antics a regrettable appeal to the passions of the people, the only excuse for which was the Jacksonians' adoption of such tactics: Clay to John J. Crittenden, July 31, 1840, in PHC, and Van Deusen, *Life of Henry Clay*, p. 335. This important letter, strangely, is not printed in *HC*, vol. 9.
84. See Clay letters: to Daniel Webster, Washington, Nov. 10, 1828; to Hezekiah Niles, Washington, Nov. 25, 1828; to ?, Lexington, May 23, 1829; to Waddy Thompson, Jr., Lexington, July 8, 1837; especially that to Nathaniel P. Tallmadge, Lexington, Oct. 30, 1841; to John Sloane, Lexington, Oct. 23, 1841; all in *HC* 7:552–53, 548–49, 8:56–57, 57–58, 9:619, 615–16.
85. Clay to John M. Clayton (confidential), Wilmington, Del., May 29, 1840, in ibid. 9:416; Clay's program outlined in a speech at Taylorsville, in Hanover County, Va., June 27, 1840, in *Works of Henry Clay* 6:195–214; Van Deusen, *Life of Henry Clay*, p. 335. On the rift with Harrison, see Clay to Harrison (confidential), and Harrison to Clay, Washington, Mar. 13, 1841, both in *HC* 9:514–15.

86. See Clay to Pierce M. Butler, Lexington, Aug. 8, 1842, and Clay, Speech to Senate Whig Caucus, Sept. 13, 1841, both in *HC* 9:752, 608–9.
87. Cunningham, *Process of Government under Jefferson*; Young, *Washington Community*, pp. 157–212. Clay letters: to Robert Swartwout, Washington, Jan. 14, 1842; to Samuel C. Morton, Washington, Apr. 18, 1842; to Francis L. Smith et al., Washington, Apr. 1, 1842; all in *HC* 9:631, 701, 696.
88. Letters and other items from Clay's tour in the spring of 1844 in the files of PHC offer some revealing insights into presidential campaigning. The itinerary, from New Orleans across the South and then up to Washington, is in Clay to William C. Preston, New Orleans, Jan. 19, 1844, in PHC; on the trip, see esp. Clay to Lucretia Clay, Mobile, Ala., Mar. 2, 1844, and Clay to William A. Graham, New Orleans, Feb. 6, 1844, both in PHC. The campaigning remark is from Charles Hammond to Clay, Cincinnati, Jan. 21, 1840, in *HC* 9:382.
89. Clay quoted in Peterson, *Great Triumvirate*, p. 364, which also has a spirited narrative of the campaign.
90. Clay to Crittenden, New Orleans, Feb. 15, 1844, and from Savannah, Mar. 24, 1844, and Clay to Willie P. Mangum, Raleigh, Apr. 17, 1844, and from Petersburg, Va., Apr. 19, 1844, all in PHC.
91. Clay to Thomas Ewing, Lexington, June 19, 1844, and Ewing to Clay, Laurentia, [Ohio?], June 23, 1844, both in PHC.
92. Clay to Peter Cromwell (private), Lexington, Feb. 17, 1845, in PHC. Phillip Hone could not understand why Clay ever wanted to be president. After Harrison's nomination, Hone remarked that Clay should have been relieved, for he had "reached a higher eminence." Hone noted, "He has sacrificed personal interest to the public good." In 1847, after a pleasant visit with Clay at Ashland, Hone wondered, "Why should such a man, so situated, desire to succeed in public office a man like James K. Polk?" *Diary of Phillip Hone*, Dec. 20, 1839, and June 24, 1847, pp. 444, 806–7.
93. The speech is printed in *NWR* 78 (Nov. 27, 1847): 197–200. Clay to Horace Greeley, Lexington, June 23, 1846; Clay to Mrs. Octavia LeVert, New Orleans, Nov. 6, 1846; Clay to John Pendleton Kennedy, New Orleans, Nov. 27, 1847; John Davis to Clay, Worcester, Nov. 13, 1846; all in PHC.
94. Clay letters: to John M. Clayton (confidential), Lexington, Apr. 16, 1847; to Adam Beatty, Lexington, Apr. 29, 1847; to Daniel Ullmann (confidential), Lexington, May 12, 1847; to Lucretia Clay, Cape May, May 18, 1847; to John Sloane, Washington, Feb. 12, 1848; to James E. Harvey (confidential), Lexington, May 8, 1848; all in PHC. See also Van Deusen, *Life of Henry Clay*, pp. 379–93. For fears about Clay's renomination as a sign of Whig declension, see G. B. Kinkead to John J. Crittenden, Frankfort, Jan. 2, 1847, in *Life of John J. Crittenden* 1:265.

95. Thomas B. Stevenson to Clay, Frankfort, Ky., Aug. 10, 1848, and Clay to Morton McMichael (private), Lexington, Sept. 16, 1848, both in PHC.
96. On conservatism as a "philosophy" of limits, see O'Sullivan, *Revolutionary Theory and Political Reality*, introduction.
97. Peter B. Porter to Clay, Black Rock, N.Y., Apr. 22, 1838, in PHC.

CHAPTER 5

1. Farrand, "Compromises of the Constitution," p. 479; "X," Baltimore *Sun*, Feb. 25, Sept. 9, 1850. Epigraph from *CG* 31:1, Apr. 5, 1850, p. 647.
2. The party's emergence capped a long period of internal adjustments, tactical disputes, and philosophical debate within the broader antislavery community that had long existed in the country. See Stewart, *Holy Warriors*, pp. 21–26, and Sewell, *Ballots for Freedom*, pp. 3–6.
3. On Weld and Chase, see Wiecek, *Sources of Antislavery Constitutionalism*, pp. 189–93. See also Lynd, "Abolitionist Critique of the United States Constitution."
4. Kelly, Harbison, and Belz, *American Constitution*, pp. 254–57; Finkelman, *Imperfect Union*, esp. pp. 234–39.
5. Resolutions, Dec. 27, 1837, in *Papers of John C. Calhoun* 14:31–32; February 1847 resolutions in *Works of John C. Calhoun* 3:141; Calhoun, remarks in Senate, Jan. 10, 1838, in *Papers of John C. Calhoun* 14:85.
6. Calhoun, remarks in Senate, Dec. 18, 1837, Jan. 5, 1838, in *Papers of John C. Calhoun* 14:12, 58, 61, 73. See also Cooper, *The South and the Politics of Slavery*, pp. 64, 96–97, 234–35, 243–44.
7. Calhoun, remarks in Senate, Jan. 11, 1828, in *Papers of John C. Calhoun* 14:92; see also *Works of John C. Calhoun* 4:347. On Garrison's rejection of compromise, see Dumond, *Antislavery*, pp. 169, 173; on abolitionists in general and political compromise, see Davis, *Slavery and Human Progress*, pp. 129–53, esp. pp. 150–53. In *Professors and Public Ethics*, pp. 186–200, Wilson Smith traces the replacement of moderate, whiggish ethics in the 1840s with an uncompromising politics of conscience.
8. Parties seized control of the election process in the states and were instrumental in seeking ballot reforms and uniform registration practices. In 1845 Congress began to regularize elections by requiring all states to have presidential ballots cast on the Tuesday after the first Monday in November. See Barney, *Battleground for the Union*, p. 56.
9. Stewart, *Holy Warriors*, pp. 47, 53, 64.
10. See Dillon's discussion of the abolitionists' problems with their disunionist image in his *Abolitionists*, pp. 142, 151–56.
11. For typical expressions of faith in the compromises of the Constitution, see

report of Detroit Whig meeting, in *National Intelligencer*, Sept. 18, 1848; Reverdy Johnson speech reported in ibid., Sept. 20, 1848; presidential addresses in *MPP* 3:175, 243 (Jackson), 314, 319 (Van Buren), 4:376, 607–8, 639 (Polk), 5:92–93 (Fillmore). Kohl, *Politics of Individualism*, pp. 84–86, discusses the Whig proclivity to compromise.

12. See Belz, "The South and the American Constitutional Tradition," pp. 29–31.
13. See Fehrenbacher, *Three Sectional Crises*, p. 29.
14. Fehrenbacher, *Dred Scott Case*, p. 630 n. 46, and in *CG* 29:2, Feb. 1, 1847, p. 303.
15. Sheldon Leake (Virginia), quoted in Fehrenbacher, *Dred Scott Case*, p. 134.
16. Morrison, *Democratic Politics and Sectionalism*, pp. 77–78.
17. James Buchanan to Charles Kessler et al., Washington, Aug. 25, 1847, in *Works of James Buchanan* 7:386.
18. Fehrenbacher, *Dred Scott Case*, pp. 142–47. On Cass, see Klunder, "Lewis Cass and Slavery Expansion."
19. On popular sovereignty as a compromise, see Henry L. Benning to Howell Cobb, Columbus, Ga., Feb. 23, 1848, in Phillips, *Robert Toombs, Alexander H. Stephens, and Howell Cobb*, p. 103. Fehrenbacher, *Dred Scott Case*, p. 146, argues that because popular sovereignty was not an "ultimate disposition of the problem" it therefore "was not a substantive compromise." Certainly it was clear that *no* "ultimate disposition" of the crisis could be a substantive compromise, but this did not rule out a temporary compromise settlement. As Nevins, *Ordeal of the Union* 1:33, points out: "A mere compromise of the Territorial question would not be enough, for it would leave the deeper issues untouched. It would simply afford a foundation on which constructive statesmanship, if the nation had it, might operate to deal with slavery itself, the root of the sectional quarrel."
20. *National Intelligencer*, July 20, 1848; Fehrenbacher, *Dred Scott Case*, pp. 148–50.
21. *National Intelligencer*, July 20, 1848, and also issues of July 31, Sept. 20, 1848.
22. The Georgia Whig Alexander Stephens opposed Clayton's bill and led the move to table it in the House. A strong supporter of the Missouri line, Stephens opposed the transfer of the issue to the Supreme Court while Oregon was left free. He reasoned that if Congress had the power to prohibit slavery in Oregon, then it had the power to reaffirm noninterference elsewhere. See his letter to the Milledgeville *Federal Union*, Aug. 30, 1848, in Phillips, *Robert Toombs, Alexander H. Stephens, and Howell Cobb*, pp. 117–24.
23. See Alexander Stephens to James Thomas, Washington, May 17, 1844, in Phillips, *Robert Toombs, Alexander H. Stephens and Howell Cobb*, pp. 57–58;

Robert Toombs to Stephens, Washington, Ga., Feb. 6, 1845, in ibid., p. 64; *National Intelligencer*, July 7, 1848; Thomas Corwin speech, reprinted in ibid., Sept. 6, 1848.

24. "Remarks on the Resolutions and Manifesto of the Southern Caucus," *American Whig Review* 9, no. 15 (March 1849): 221–34; "Opinions of the Council of Three: The Nature of This Government," ibid. 6, no. 4 (October 1847): 370–75; "Dangers and Safeguards of the Union," ibid. 9, no. 14 (February 1849): 111–20. See also Willie Mangum speech, reported in *National Intelligencer*, July 18, 1848; Graebner, "Thomas Corwin and the Election of 1848"; Fowler, "The Anti-Expansionistic Argument in the United States."
25. "Freedom of Opinion," *American Whig Review* 9, no. 18 (June 1849): 551–60; H. W. Warner, "The Republic," and "The Republic II," ibid. 9, nos. 16, 17 (April, May 1849): 399–406, 476–87. See also Daniel D. Barnard, "The Constitution Written and Unwritten," ibid. 6, no. 1 (July 1847): 1–17; Ames, *History of the National Intelligencer*, p. 300.
26. *New York Tribune*, reprinted in *National Intelligencer*, July 27, 1848. Robert Toombs called for "a patriot not a partisan in the Presidential chair," in ibid., July 19, 1848. See also ibid., July 6, 1848. On the revival of Whig fortunes by 1848, see Holt, "Winding Roads to Recovery."
27. On Free-Soil influence, see Sewell, *Ballots for Freedom*, pp. 168–69. See also Caleb Cushing to constituents, in *National Intelligencer*, July 20, 1848. On southern Democrats' charges of Whig disunionism, see Howell Cobb to Committee of Citizens of Charleston, S.C., Athens, Ga., Nov. 4[?], 1848, in Phillips, *Robert Toombs, Alexander H. Stephens, and Howell Cobb*, pp. 133–35.
28. See Georgia Whig resolutions, in *National Intelligencer*, Sept. 17, 1848; letter of John Pendleton Kennedy, in ibid., Sept. 19, 1848; Speech of John Bell at Murfreesboro, Tenn., in ibid., Oct. 12, 1848; *Cincinnati Chronicle* editorial, reprinted in ibid., Nov. 21, 1848; Auburn Birdsall to Howell Cobb, Binghampton, N.Y., Sept. 8, 1848, in Phillips, *Robert Toombs, Alexander H. Stephens, and Howell Cobb*, p. 125; Fillmore letter to Buffalo *Commercial Advertiser*, in *National Intelligencer*, Nov. 20, 1848.
29. For southern Whigs' criticism of the Southern Address as a typical Democratic disunionist trick, see Robert Toombs to John J. Crittenden, Washington, Jan. 3, 1849, in Phillips, *Robert Toombs, Alexander H. Stephens, and Howell Cobb*, pp. 139–40; "Remarks on the Resolutions and Manifesto of the Southern Caucus," pp. 221–22. On fears of geographical parties, see, for instance, Hopkins Holsey to Howell Cobb, Athens, Ga., Jan. 29, 1849, in ibid., pp. 143–44. On state resolutions for and against the Wilmot Proviso, the abolition of the District's slavery, and other sectional questions, see Nevins, *Ordeal of the Union* 1:219–20.
30. New York *Herald*, Dec. 4, 1849.

31. See Whig Congressman David F. Outlaw's daily chronicle of the decay and personal bitterness within his North Carolina delegation during this session, in David F. Outlaw Papers, SHC.
32. Hamilton, *Prologue to Conflict*, p. 40, notes that over half of the representatives were novices; 44 percent of them would not return in the next Congress. For more on this, see Bogue, *Congressman's Civil War*, pp. 10–12.
33. New York *Herald*, Dec. 5, 1849, Jan. 15, 19, 1850; New York *Mirror*, quoted in Baltimore *Sun*, Dec. 17, 1849; "Ion's" Washington correspondence in ibid. On the disintegration of the old parties into sectional alignments, see ibid., Dec. 31, 1849, Apr. 2, 1850. Religious periodicals routinely denounced parties for their "counter excitements, the stir and vehemence of party issues, the absorption of the attention, the neglect of private prayer," that threatened anyone dragged into "the maelstrom *suck* of party politics." *Southern Christian Advocate* (Richmond), July 14, 1848, in Norton, "Religious Press and the Compromise of 1850," pp. 161–62, and also pp. 165, 34–35, 38–39, 146.
34. Cole, *Whig Party in the South*, pp. 147, 152; Poage, *Henry Clay and the Whig Party*, pp. 192–96; Potter, *Impending Crisis*, pp. 88–89.
35. The messages are in *MPP* 5:19, 26–30. Nevins, *Ordeal of the Union* 1:235, 239, 244–47, 256–57, is highly critical of Taylor. Hamilton, *Zachary Taylor*, pp. 257–58, firmly backs Taylor; Potter, *Impending Crisis*, pp. 91–96, has a measured analysis of the plan.
36. New York *Herald*, Dec. 5, 1849, Jan. 21, 1850; Charles S. Morehead to Crittenden, Washington, Mar. 30, 1850, *Life of John J. Crittenden* 1:361–64.
37. See Webster to Franklin Haven, Washington, Jan. 13, 1850, Webster to Peter Harvey, Washington, Feb. 14, 1850, and headnote in *Papers of Daniel Webster* 7:5, 10, 14–16.
38. For apprehensions about Clay's return, see John M. Clayton to John J. Crittenden, Washington, Feb. 5, 1850, in Special Collections, Margaret King Library, University of Kentucky, Lexington; David F. Outlaw to his wife, Washington, Mar. 1, 1850, in Outlaw Papers, SHC; Jefferson Davis and Alexander Stephens, remarks reported in Schurz, *Henry Clay* 2:322–23; Robert Toombs to John J. Crittenden, Washington, Jan. 3, 1849, in Phillips, *Robert Toombs, Alexander H. Stephens, and Howell Cobb*, p. 140.
39. On Clay's motives, see Clay letters: to Thomas B. Stevenson (private), Lexington, Dec. 19, 1848; to A. Peirse, New Orleans, Feb. 16, 1849; to James Harlan, New Orleans, Mar. 13, 1849; to Jesse M. Christopher, Lexington, Apr. 19, 1849; to Dr. Boyd McNairy (private), Washington, Mar. 7, 1850; to Stevenson, Washington, Apr. 3, 25, 1850; all in PHC. And see Van Deusen, *Life of Henry Clay*, p. 399 n. 13. On his role in the Compromise, see ibid., pp. 394–413; Poage, *Henry Clay and the Whig Party*, pp. 197–264; Peterson's excellent narrative, *Great Triumvirate*, pp. 449–76.

40. Report of Baltimore remarks in New York *Herald*, Dec. 1, 2, 1849. Accounts of Clay's first compromise speeches are in Nevins, *Ordeal of the Union* 1:266, 269–71; Poage, *Henry Clay and the Whig Party*, pp. 200–201, 202–4; Potter, *Impending Crisis*, pp. 99–100; Van Deusen, *Life of Henry Clay*, pp. 399–402.
41. Proposals and initial speech are in *CG* 31:1, Jan. 29, 1850, pp. 244–47. See also Nevins, *Ordeal of the Union* 1:265–67.
42. Quotations in this and the next three paragraphs are from defense of first and second resolutions in *CG* 31:1, Feb. 5, 1850, Appendix, pp. 116–19, 125–26.
43. On the Wilmot Proviso, see ibid., May 21, 1850, p. 613. On the price of labor and conditions in California, see Clay's remarks in ibid., May 15, 1850, pp. 1003–5, and Clay to R. H. Walworth, Washington, Mar. 11, 1850, in PHC.
44. Defense of third and fourth resolutions in *CG* 31:1, Feb. 5, 1850, Appendix, p. 119; Webster's remark in ibid., June 7, 1850, p. 1164.
45. Defense of fifth and sixth resolutions in ibid., Feb. 6, 1850, Appendix, pp. 120–21.
46. Quotations in this and the following paragraph are from defense of seventh and eighth resolutions in ibid., pp. 122–25. Clay's personal servant, Levi, had disappeared briefly during Clay's visit to New York the previous summer.
47. In late February, southern Whigs in the House had stopped a California statehood bill, demanding a settlement of other slavery issues as the price of passage. For details, see Poage, *Henry Clay and the Whig Party*, pp. 206–8.
48. *CG* 31:1, Feb. 5, 1850, Appendix, pp. 115–16.
49. Ibid., Feb. 6, May 21, 1850, Appendix, pp. 126–27, 616. See also Sen. James Shields's remarks on sectional equilibrium, in ibid., Apr. 5, 1850, p. 648.
50. But it is worth noting that Webster did not outline a historical argument for compromise, as Clay had. The Compromises of 1820 and 1833, which he opposed, did not in his mind constitute a moderate tradition of mutual concessions. And he accepted the antislavery view that the compromises of the Constitution were restricted to the original thirteen states and anticipated no further additions of slave territory. The speech is in ibid., Mar. 7, 1850, pp. 467–83, and in *Webster: Speeches and Formal Writings* 2:515–53. On Webster's earlier views about the West, see his speeches "The Admission of Texas," Dec. 22, 1845, "The Mexican War," Mar. 1, 1847, and "Exclusion of Slavery from the Territories," Aug. 12, 1848, all in ibid. 2:357, 358, 440, 441–43, 465, 468, 480–82.
51. Calhoun's speech is in *Works of John C. Calhoun* 4:542–73. On Davis's speech, see *CG* 31:1, Feb. 13, 1850, Appendix, pp. 149–57, 202–11; Nevins, *Ordeal of the Union* 1:266, 276–78; Eaton, *Jefferson Davis*, pp. 74–75. Note also Davis's defense of the policy of static equilibrium, in *CG* 31:1, June 7,

1850, p. 1162. The other criticisms of Clay are in ibid., Feb. 20, 1850, p. 396, and May 8, pp. 950–51 (Clemens), Feb. 12, 1850, Appendix, p. 209 (Berrien), May 8, 1850, p. 953 (Yulee), May 8, 1850, pp. 953–54 (Borland). For further discussion of southern reaction to Clay's proposals, see Hamilton, *Prologue to Conflict*, pp. 54–55, 60–62.

52. On Seward, see Nevins, *Ordeal of the Union* 1:299–301; *CG* 31:1, July 25, 1850, Appendix, p. 1442. See also Hale's anticompromise argument, in ibid., Apr. 8, May 8, 1850, pp. 663, 954–55.

53. Donald, *Liberty and Union*, pp. 47–48. See also Forgie's excellent discussion of Clay, Douglas, and the Compromise of 1850 in *Patricide*, pp. 12, 123–58.

54. *CG* 31:1, Jan. 24, 1850, pp. 226–28; Clay to Leslie Combs, Washington, Dec. 22, 1849, Jan. 22, 1850, in PHC; Schurz, *Henry Clay* 2:328; Clay, remarks in Annapolis reported in Baltimore *Sun*, June 6, 1850; rebuke of Clemens in *CG* 31:1, Dec. 20, 1849, pp. 51, 56–57; clash with Henry S. Foote discussed in Poage, *Henry Clay and the Whig Party*, p. 203; attack on Robert Barnwell Rhett in *CG* 31:1, July 22, 1850, Appendix, p. 1414. On Clay's attempts to force militants to offer moderate counterproposals, see his running battle with Pierre Soulé, in ibid., May 21, 1850, Appendix, pp. 612–14. On the rhetoric of compromise in 1850, see Armold, "Compromise of 1850."

55. See procompromise editorials and letters in New York *Herald*, Jan. 31, Feb. 2, 1850; "X," Baltimore *Sun*, Feb. 16, Feb. 25, 27, and esp. June 21, 1850. Many of the procompromise letters that Webster and Clay received at this time were from former opponents as well as friends. See, for example, Isaac Hill to Webster, Concord, N.H., Apr. 17, 1850, and Webster's appreciative response, in *Papers of Daniel Webster* 7:69–70, 72–73; as for Clay, see letters from James F. Bayard, Wilmington, Del., July 1, 1850 (which Clay read to the Senate two days later—see *CG* 31:1, July 3, 1850, pp. 1332–33); John Pendleton Kennedy, Baltimore, Feb. 9, 1850; John Smith and twenty-eight others, Clinton, Mich., Mar. 8, 1850; A. D. Choloner et al., Philadelphia, Feb. 22, 1850; all in PHC.

56. New York *Herald*, Feb. 26, 1850. See also Baltimore *Sun*, Feb. 26, 1850; on St. Louis, see report in ibid., Mar. 22, 1850.

57. New York *Herald*, Mar. 3, 1850; proceedings of Baltimore Union meeting, reported in Baltimore *Sun*, Mar. 5, 1850.

58. See Clay's discussion of his strategy, in *CG* 31:1, Feb. 14, 1850, pp. 365–69, and "Ion" and "X," Baltimore *Sun*, Mar. 18, Apr. 26, 1850.

59. See Henry S. Foote's comments on the committee, in *CG* 31:1, Apr. 11, 1850, pp. 713–14, and "Ion," Baltimore *Sun*, Mar. 9, 1850. On select committees, see Galloway, *History of the House of Representatives*, p. 78.

60. The committee report is in *CG* 31:1, May 8, 1850, pp. 944–48.

61. Ibid., p. 945. See also Baltimore *Sun*, May 3, 5, 1850.

62. For similar sentiments, see "Ion," Baltimore *Sun*, Apr. 17, 1850; letter of David Stewart to Washington *Union*, May 16, reported in ibid., May 20, 1850.
63. *CG* 31:1, May 13, 1850, Appendix, pp. 567–73. The opponents of the omnibus, Bennett pointed out, forgot "that the Constitution itself was a compromise, an 'omnibus' measure of the same kind": New York *Herald*, May 21, 1850.
64. *CG* 31:1, May 21, 1850, Appendix, p. 613.
65. Ibid., pp. 614, 616.
66. "X," Baltimore *Sun*, Mar. 11, 1850.
67. Schurz, *Henry Clay* 2:365–66; *CG* 31:1, May 21, 1850, Appendix, pp. 614, 616.
68. *CG* 31:1, May 24, 1850, Appendix, p. 783. For similar northern attacks on the ambiguity of the omnibus, see ibid., May 28 (Hale) and June 6 (Baldwin), 1850, pp. 1084–85, 1146–47.
69. Clay's remark in ibid., June 15, July 19, 1850, Appendix, pp. 903, 1399; Soulé's remark in ibid., June 15, 1850, Appendix, pp. 903, 904, 907.
70. Ibid., July 5, 1850, Appendix, p. 1095. The Baltimore *Sun* called noninterference the "*mezzo termine* of the two extremes," a "permanent principle in accordance with reason and the Constitution": March 20, June 17, 1850.
71. Fehrenbacher, *Dred Scott Case*, p. 178.
72. David Outlaw to Mrs. Outlaw, Washington, June 21[?], 1850, in Outlaw Papers, SHC.
73. On Fillmore, see esp. Potter, *Impending Crisis*, pp. 110–11.
74. *CG* 31:1, July 22, 1850, Appendix, pp. 1405–14, from which the quotations in the next two paragraphs are drawn. Curiously, historians tend to focus more on Clay's attack on the administration's plan in this speech than on his more elaborate defense of compromise. Clay thought that Taylor had forced a confrontation; see Clay to James B. Clay, Washington, May 27, 1850, and Clay to Lucretia Clay, Washington, July 6, 1850, both in PHC.
75. "X," Baltimore *Sun*, Feb. 6, 1850. For reactions to the speech, see David Outlaw to Mrs. Outlaw, July 22, 23, 1850, in Outlaw Papers, SHC.
76. The best treatment of Douglas's motives and movements is Johannsen, *Douglas*, pp. 262–303. But see also Harmon, "Douglas and the Compromise of 1850."
77. *CG* 31:1, June 3, 1850, p. 1114.
78. Roll-call analyses may be found in Hamilton, *Prologue to Conflict*, pp. 141–50, 191–200; Alexander, *Sectional Stress and Party Strength*, p. 211; Poage, *Henry Clay and the Whig Party*, p. 213; Fehrenbacher, *Dred Scott Case*, pp. 162–63, 169.
79. Note the differing assessments of the Compromise in Fehrenbacher, *Dred Scott Case*, pp. 174–77, and Russell, "What Was the Compromise of 1850?"

80. The "truce" argument is best articulated in Potter, *Impending Crisis*, pp. 116–20, and Fehrenbacher, *Dred Scott Case*, p. 163; see also Thomas Brown, *Politics and Statesmanship*, p. 152; Seager, "Clay and the Politics of Compromise," p. 4; Freehling, *Road to Disunion*, pp. 487–510, esp. 509.
81. See, for example, the repeated urgings that statesmen at least talk to each other, avoid rigidity, and pass any measure that would pacify the country, in Baltimore *Sun*, Feb. 25, 27, Mar. 1, 11, Apr. 17, May 6, 20, June 4, 21, Aug. 5, 1850.
82. On Foote, Clemens, King, Downs, and Toombs, see John Cooper Warner, "Winning the Lower South to the Compromise of 1850," pp. 65, 115–16, 174–76, 180, 183–84, 253–54, 260–61, 278, 283. On Bell, see Parks, *John Bell of Tennessee*, pp. 260, 262, 267–68.
83. David Outlaw to Mrs. Outlaw, Sept. 18, 1850, in Outlaw Papers, SHC.
84. Clay joined in efforts to choke off negotiation on the fugitive slave law. See Clay to Hamilton Fish, Washington, Feb. 23, 1851, in PHC, and Van Deusen, *Life of Henry Clay*, pp. 416–18. But the Democrats excelled at declaring the act an extension of "the solemn compact" on fugitive slaves in 1787. See "The Fugitive Slave Law: Shall It Be Enforced?" *United States Magazine* 28, no. 154 (April 1851): 355.
85. Three works—Hodder, "Authorship of the Compromise of 1850"; Harmon, "Douglas and the Compromise of 1850"; and Seager, "Clay and the Politics of Compromise"—all declare Douglas "responsible" for or the "author" of the Compromise. But he was no more responsible for it than was James Murray Mason, the author of the fugitive slave act. There was no single author of the Compromise of 1850. Clay devised the plan's comprehensive pattern and scope; the bills were written in several different committees and were amended on the floor. See Poage, *Henry Clay and the Whig Party*, p. 259 n. 20.
86. Federalist no. 50, *New York Packet*, Feb. 5, 1788, in *DHRC* 16:31.

CHAPTER 6

1. For a discussion of this literature on compromise, see Knupfer, " 'Union As It Was,' " pp. 32–40. Epigraph, Lincoln Speech at Peoria, Oct. 16, 1854, in *Works of Abraham Lincoln* 2:272.
2. Holt, *Political Crisis of the 1850s*, and Barney, *Battleground for the Union*, offer good summaries of this argument.
3. See esp. Summers, *Plundering Generation*, pp. 183–200, 290–92.
4. "Appeal of the Independent Democrats," in Commager, *Documents of American History* 1:329–31.
5. Douglas quoted in Dixon, *True History*, p. 445.

6. Van Deusen, *Life of Henry Clay*, p. 414; Klunder, "Lewis Cass and Slavery Expansion," p. 423. Major compromises did evince a pattern of bipartisan reconciliation. Clay and Thomas Ritchie patched up their old quarrel; Webster, Clay, and a host of conservative Democrats, including Dickinson, Foote, Shields, Cass, and others, exchanged rare public and private greetings, apologies, and expressions of warmth and sympathy. See Clay to James O. Harrison, Oct. 1850; Clay to Benjamin Gratz et al., Lexington, Oct. 10, 1850; Clay, Speech at Barbeque, Lexington, Oct. 17, 1850; Clay to A.H.H. Stuart, Lexington, Nov. 18, 1850; all in PHC. See also Nevins, *Ordeal of the Union* 1:273; Webster to Daniel S. Dickinson, Washington, Sept. 27, 1850, and Dickinson to Webster, Binghamton, N.Y., in *Correspondence of Daniel Webster* 2:392–93; John Davis to Dickinson, Norwich, Conn., July 25, 1850, and Invitation and Responses to Public Dinner in honor of Dickinson, May 20, 1850, in *Correspondence, etc., of . . . Dickinson* 2:446, 431. On the brief conservative coalition of the early 1850s, see Potter, *Impending Crisis*, pp. 124–30; Nevins, *Ordeal of the Union* 1:346–79.
7. Johnson, "Philosophy of Our Union," (January 1, 1850), in his *Guide to the right understanding of our American union*, p. 23; "Constitutional Compromises," *United States Magazine* 28, no. 155 (May 1851): 389–91.
8. Johnson, "Philosophy of Our Union," (January 1, 1850), in his *Guide to the right understanding of our American union*, p. 23, and also p. 36. "Compromises," *United States Magazine* 3, no. 1 (July 1854): 5, 11.
9. Quoted in Johannsen, *Douglas*, p. 298.
10. On Douglas and the Kansas-Nebraska Act, see ibid., pp. 401–34; his Missouri Compromise extension argument is on page 421. Other quotations from Johnson, "The Kansas-Nebraska Question," in his *Guide to the right understanding of our American union*, p. 27; C.S.H. Binghampton, "The Missouri Prohibition," *United States Magazine* 3, no. 2 (August 1854): 129; *MPP* 5:401–2 (Pierce quotation), 346, 348–49. And see Capen's attack on the Missouri Compromise in *Plain Facts and Considerations*, p. 26, and Johnson, "Reserved Rights of American Citizens," in his *Guide to the right understanding of our American union*, p. 23. See also Russell, "Kansas-Nebraska Bill," and Nichols, "Kansas-Nebraska Act."
11. Johannsen, *Douglas*, pp. 431, 432, 434. See also Nichols, *Disruption of American Democracy*, pp. 56, 60–61, 66–67.
12. See Binghampton, "The Missouri Prohibition," p. 141.
13. Capen, *Plain Facts and Considerations*, pp. 31–32; see also Johnson, "Principles of American Liberty" and "Our Political Disorders and Their Remedy," both in his *Guide to the right understanding of our American union*, pp. 60–64, 58.
14. See, for example, Douglas's attempts, during his debates with Abraham Lincoln in 1858, to attract old Whigs and Democrats by stressing the

bipartisan nature of the Compromise of 1850: Johannsen, *Lincoln-Douglas Debates*, pp. 37–38.

15. Crittenden to Archibald Dixon, Frankfort, Mar. 7, 1854, in *Life of John J. Crittenden* 2:102–3; see also Crittenden to Presley Ewing, Frankfort, Mar. 6, 1854, in ibid., 2:103–4, in which Crittenden stated his belief that only a "numerical concurrence of Northern representatives as would fairly indicate the assent of the North to such substitution" of "the rule *fixed* by the *Missouri Compromise*" would be acceptable to him. Crittenden's crucial position in a key border state, as well as his identification with centrist politics and his tremendous longevity in national office, made him a natural communications center for compromisers and conservatives throughout the crisis of the 1850s. For his views on the Kansas question, from the Kansas-Nebraska Act through the Lecompton controversy, see Kirwan, *Crittenden*, pp. 289–335.
16. Forgie, *Patricide*, pp. 159–99, esp. p. 186.
17. On the Madisonian roots of the Constitutional Unionists, see McCoy's discussion, *Last of the Fathers*, pp. 338–45. On the Constitutional Unionists, see Stabler, "History of the Constitutional Union Party."
18. Crittenden to W. M. Smallwood and Jonathan P. Bowman, [Frankfort?], [Sept.] 1860, in *Life of John J. Crittenden* 2:216.
19. See esp. excerpts from Crittenden's speech in Senate, Jan. 3, 1861, and his Farewell Speech to Senate, Mar. 3, 1861, both in ibid. 2:252, 270–90.
20. Kirwan, *Crittenden*, pp. 319, 374–76, 290, 349.
21. For a discussion of these proposals, see esp. Crofts, *Reluctant Confederates*, pp. 195–214.
22. See Crofts's discussion, ibid., pp. 262–73.
23. Stampp, *And the War Came*, p. 158, and pp. 123, 126, 131, 132, 158–78; Hyman, "Narrow Escape from a 'Compromise of 1860,'" pp. 158–59.
24. Summers, *Plundering Generation*, pp. 289–92. On the language of compromise in the secession crisis, see Auer, *Antislavery and Disunion*, and Fisher, "The Failure of Compromise in 1860–1861."
25. This is one theme of Silbey, *Respectable Minority*, esp. pp. 32–39, 51.

Bibliography

PRIVATE CORRESPONDENCE

Unpublished

Massachusetts Historical Society, Boston.
  Adams Family Papers.
  William Heath Diary.
Boston Public Library.
  Thatcher Papers, Chamberlain Collection.
Southern Historical Collection, University of North Carolina, Chapel Hill.
  David F. Outlaw Papers.
Library of Congress, Washington, D.C.
  John Jordan Crittenden Papers.
  Letterbook, George Washington Papers.
Margaret King Library, University of Kentucky, Lexington.
  Papers of Henry Clay.
  Henry Clay, Jr., MS Diary, Special Collections.
  Miscellaneous Letters, Special Collections.

Published

Buchanan, James. *The Works of James Buchanan: Comprising His Speeches, State Papers, and Private Correspondence*. Edited by John Bassett Moore. 16 vols. 1908–11. Reprint. New York, 1960.

Burke, Edmund. *Edmund Burke: Selected Writings and Speeches*. Edited by Peter J. Stanlis. Gloucester, Mass., 1968.

Calhoun, John C. *The Papers of John C. Calhoun*. Edited by Robert L. Meriwether, W. Edwin Hemphill, et al. 16 vols. to date. Columbia, Mo., 1959–.

———. *The Works of John C. Calhoun*. Edited by Richard K. Cralle. 6 vols. 1853–57. Reprint. New York, 1968.

Clay, Henry. *The Papers of Henry Clay*. Edited by James F. Hopkins et al. 9 vols. to date. Lexington, Ky., 1959–88.

———. *The Works of Henry Clay: Comprising His Life, Correspondence, and Speeches*. Edited by Calvin Colton. 10 vols. New York, 1904.

Crittenden, John J. *The Life of John J. Crittenden, with Selections from his*

Correspondence and Speeches. Edited by Mrs. Chapman Coleman. 2 vols. Philadelphia, 1871.

Dickinson, Daniel S. *Speeches, Correspondence, etc., of the Late Daniel S. Dickinson, of New York. . . .* Edited by John R. Dickinson. 2 vols. New York, 1867.

Hone, Phillip. *The Diary of Phillip Hone, 1828–1851*. Edited by Allan Nevins. 2 vols. in 1. New York, 1927.

King, Rufus. *Life and Correspondence of Rufus King*. Edited by Charles R. King. 6 vols. New York, 1894.

Lincoln, Abraham. *The Collected Works of Abraham Lincoln*. Edited by Roy P. Basler. 8 vols. New Brunswick, 1953–55.

Madison, James, Jr. *The Papers of James Madison*. Edited by Robert A. Rutland et al. Mult. vols. Chicago, 1975.

———. *The Writings of James Madison: Comprising His Public Papers and His Private Correspondence. . . .* Edited by Gaillard Hunt. 9 vols. New York, 1901.

Mason, George. *The Papers of George Mason*. Edited by Robert Rutland. 3 vols. Chapel Hill, 1970.

Phillips, Ulrich B., ed. *The Correspondence of Robert Toombs, Alexander H. Stephens, and Howell Cobb*. Vol. 2 of *Annual Report of the American Historical Association for the Year 1911*. Washington, D.C., 1913.

Washington, George. *The Writings of George Washington from the Original Manuscript Sources, 1745–1799*. Edited by John C. Fitzpatrick. 39 vols. Washington, D.C., 1939.

Webb, Samuel Blacheley. *Correspondence and Journal of Samuel Blacheley Webb*. Edited by Worthington C. Ford. 3 vols. New York, 1894.

Webster, Daniel. *The Letters of Daniel Webster: From Documents Owned Principally by the New Hampshire Historical Society*. Edited by C. H. Van Tyne. 1902. Reprint. New York, 1968.

———. *The Papers of Daniel Webster*. Edited by Charles M. Wiltse and Michael J. Birkner. 8 vols. to date. Hanover, N.H., 1974.

———. *The Papers of Daniel Webster: Speeches and Formal Writings*. Edited by Charles M. Wiltse and Alan R. Berolzheimer. 2 vols. Hanover, N.H., 1986–87.

———. *The Private Correspondence of Daniel Webster*. Edited by Fletcher Webster. 2 vols. Boston, 1875.

PUBLISHED DOCUMENTS, COMMENTARIES, AND HISTORIES

Constitutional Documents, Pamphlets, and Government Papers

Calhoun, John C. "A Disquisition on Government." In *A Disquisition on Government and Selections from the Discourse*, edited by C. Gordon Post, pp. 3–81. Indianapolis, 1953.

Cunningham, Noble, ed. *Circular Letters of Congressmen to Their Constituents, 1789–1829*. 3 vols. Chapel Hill, 1978.

Elliot, Jonathan, ed. *The Debates in the Several State Conventions on the Adoption of the Federal Constitution. . . .* 4 vols. 1836–45. Reprint. New York, 1888.

Farrand, Max, ed. *The Records of the Federal Convention of 1787*. 4 vols. 1911. Reprint. New Haven, 1937.

Federal Committee of the City of Albany. *An Impartial Address to the Citizens of . . . Albany. . . .* Albany, 1788.

A Flatbush Farmer. *To the Inhabitants of King's County*. New York, [April 21, 1788]. Broadside Collection, Massachusetts Historical Society, Boston.

Ford, Paul L., ed. *Pamphlets on the Constitution of the United States Published during its Discussion by the People*. Brooklyn, 1888.

Jensen, Merrill, et al., eds. *Documentary History of the Ratification of the Constitution*. 9 vols. to date. Madison, 1976–90.

Madison, James, Alexander Hamilton, and John Jay. *The Federalist*. Edited by Jacob Cooke. Middletown, Conn., 1961.

Richardson, James D., comp. *A Compilation of the Messages and Papers of the Presidents, 1789–1897*. 10 vols. Washington, D.C., 1898.

Civics Literature and Contemporary Histories

Bradford, Alden. *History of the Federal Government, for Fifty Years from March 1789 to March 1839*. Boston, 1840.

Brownell, Henry Howard. *The People's Book of American History, Comprising the New World*. 2 vols. Hartford, Conn., 1854.

Burleigh, Joseph. *The American Manual, Containing a Brief Outline of the Origin and Purpose of Political Power, and the Laws of Nations; a Commentary on the Constitution of the United States of North America, and a Lucid Exposition of the Duties and Responsibilities of Voters, Jurors, and Civil Magistrates, . . . Adapted to the Use of Schools, Academies, and the Public*. Philadelphia, 1848.

[Capen, Nahum.] *Plain Facts and Considerations: Addressed to the People of the United States, Without Distinction of Party, in Favor of James Buchanan, of Pennsylvania, for President, and John C. Breckinridge, of Kentucky, for Vice President. By an American Citizen*. Boston, 1856.

Curtis, George Ticknor. *The Strength of the Constitution. A Discourse delivered at the Lowell Institute, in Boston, 7 February 1850, at the Conclusion of a course of Twelve Lectures on the history of the Constitution of the United States*. Boston, 1850.

Duer, William. *A Course of Lectures on the Constitutional Jurisprudence of the United States; designed as a text book for lectures, as a class book for academies and common schools, and as a manual for popular use*. 1833. Reprint. New York, 1843.

Fisher, Richard S. *The Progress of the United States of America From the Earliest Periods, Geographical, Statistical, Historical*. New York, 1854.

Frost, John. *The History of the United States of North America*. London, 1838.

Goodrich, Charles A. *A History of the United States of America . . . to the Present Time. . . .* Bellows Falls, Vt., 1824.

Goodrich, Samuel Griswold. *A Pictorial History of America; Embracing the Northern and Southern Portions*. Hartford, Conn., 1850.

———. *The Young American; or, Book of Government and Law; Showing Their History, Nature and Necessity. For the Use of Schools*. 5th ed. New York, [1844].

Guernsey, Egbert. *History of the United States of America. . . .* 7th ed. New York, 1850.

Hickey, William. *The Constitution of the United States of America, with an Alphabetical Analysis. . . .* Washington, D.C., 1854.

Holmes, John. *The Statesman; or, Principles of Legislation and Law*. Augusta, Maine, 1840.

Howitt, Mary. *A Popular History of the United States of America from the Discovery of the American Continent to the Present Time*. New York, 1860.

Johnson, Alexander Bryan. *A Guide to the right understanding of our American union; or, Political, economical, and literary miscellanies. . . .* New York, 1857.

Lieber, Francis. *The Ancient and Modern Teacher of Politics. An introductory discourse of lectures on the state. Delivered on the 10th of October, 1859 in the law school of Columbia College*. New York, 1860.

———. *Legal and Political Hermeneutics. . . .* Enl. ed. Boston, 1839.

———. *Manual of Political Ethics Designed Chiefly for the Use of Colleges and Students at Law*. 2 vols. Boston, 1838.

———. *On Civil Liberty and Self Government*. Philadelphia, 1859.

———. *On history and political economy, as necessary branches of superior education in free states. An inaugural address delivered in South Carolina College, before his excellency the governor and the legislature of the State, on Commencement day the 7th of December, 1835*. Columbia, S.C., 1836.

Lord, John. *A New History of the United States of America, For the Use of Schools*. Philadelphia, 1854.

Lossing, Benson J. *A Pictorial History of the United States, For Families and Libraries*. New York, 1857.

———. *A Primary History of the United States, For Schools and Families*. New York, 1857.

McCartney, Washington. *The Origin and Progress of the United States*. Philadelphia, 1847.

McCulloch, John. *A Concise History of the United States, From the Discovery of America, Till 1813*. 4th ed. Philadelphia, 1813.

McKinney, Mordecai. *Our Government: An Explanatory Statement of the System of Government of the Country. . . . A Manual for schools, Academies, and popular use*. Philadelphia, 1859.

———. *The United States Constitutional Manual; being a Comprehensive Compendium of the System of Government of the Country . . . in the form of Questions and Answers; designed for Academies, schools, and readers in general*. Harrisburg, 1845.

Mansfield, Edward D. *The Political Grammar of the United States, or a Complete View of the Theory and Practice of the General and State Governments, with the Relations Between Them. Dedicated and Adapted to the Young Men of the United States*. New York, 1834.

Parker, Rev. Daniel. *The Constitutional Instructor, for the Use of Schools*. Boston, 1848.

Story, Joseph. *A Familiar Exposition of the Constitution of the United States: containing a brief commentary on Every Clause. . . .* N. p., 1840.

Sullivan, William. *The Political Class Book: intended to instruct the Higher Classes in Schools in the Origin, Nature, and Use of Political Power*. Boston, 1831.

Taylor, C. B. *A Universal History of the United States to the Present Time*. New York, 1831.

Trumbull, Benjamin. *A General History of the United States of America; From the Discovery [in] 1492; or, Sketches of the Divine Agency, In their Settlement, Growth, and Protection; and especially in the late Memorable Revolution . . . to 1765*. Boston, 1810.

Watson, Henry C. *History of the United States of America, From the Discovery to the Present Time*. Philadelphia, 1853.

Willard, Emma. *Abridged History of the United States or Republic of America*. New York, 1857.

Willson, Marcius. *American History*. New York, 1847.

———. *A Treatise on Civil Polity and Political Economy: With an Appendix, Containing a Brief Account of the Powers, Duties, and Salaries of National, State, County, and Town Officers, For the Use of Schools and Academies*. 3d stereotyped ed. New York, 1845.

Young, Andrew W. *First Lessons in Civil Government; including a Comprehensive View of the Government of the State of New-York, and an Abstract of the Laws, Showing the Rights, Duties, and Responsibilities of Citizens in the Civil and Domestic Relations; with An Outline of the Government of the United States: Adapted to the Capacities of Children and Youth, and Designed for the Use of Schools*. 8th ed. Auburn, N.Y., 1845.

———. *Introduction to the Science of government and Compend of the Constitution and Civil Jurisprudence of the United States. With a Brief Treatise on Political Economy. Designed for the Use of Families and Schools*. Warsaw, N.Y., 1836.

NEWSPAPERS AND PERIODICALS

American Magazine
American Whig Review
Baltimore *Sun*
Maryland Gazette (Baltimore)
National Intelligencer (Washington, D.C.)
New Hampshire Recorder (Keene)
Newport Herald
New York *Daily Advertiser*
New York *Evening Post*
New York *Herald*
New York Journal
Niles' Weekly Register
North American Review
United States Magazine

REFERENCE WORKS

Commager, Henry Steele, ed. *Documents of American History*. 9th ed. 2 vols. Englewood Cliffs, N.J., 1973.
McCarthy, Eugene. *A Current Dictionary of American Politics*. New York, 1962.
Malone, Dumas, and Allen Johnson, eds. *Dictionary of American Biography*. 11 vols. and supplements. New York, 1958–64.
Ohles, John F., ed. *Biographical Directory of American Educators*. 3 vols. Westport, Conn., 1978.
Plano, Jack, and Milton Greenberg. *The American Political Dictionary*. 5th ed. New York, 1978.
Smith, Edward C., and Arnold J. Zurcher. *New Dictionary of American Politics*. New York, 1949.
Webster, Noah. *A Compendious Dictionary of the English Language*. 1806. Reprint. Fac. ed. New York, 1970.

SECONDARY SOURCES (BOOKS, ARTICLES, AND DISSERTATIONS)

Agar, Herbert. *The Price of Union*. Boston, 1950.
Alexander, Thomas B. *Sectional Stress and Party Strength: A Study of Roll-call Voting Patterns in the United States House of Representatives, 1836–1860*. Nashville, 1967.
Ames, William E. *A History of the National Intelligencer*. Chapel Hill, 1972.

Armold, Jack David. "The Compromise of 1850: A Burkean Analysis." Ph.D. dissertation, University of Illinois-Urbana, 1959.

Arnston, Paul, and Craig R. Smith. "The Seventh of March Address: A Mediating Influence." *Southern Speech Communications Journal* 40 (Spring 1975): 288–301.

Auer, J. Jeffrey, ed. *Antislavery and Disunion, 1858–1861: Studies in the Rhetoric of Compromise and Conflict*. New York, 1963.

Baker, Jean H. *Affairs of Party: The Political Culture of the Northern Democrats in the Mid-Nineteenth Century*. Ithaca, 1983.

Ball, Terence, James Farr, and Russell Hanson, eds. *Political Innovation and Conceptual Change*. Cambridge, Eng., 1989.

Ball, Terence, and J.G.A. Pocock, eds. *Conceptual Change and the Constitution*. Lawrence, 1988.

Banning, Lance. "James Madison and the Dynamics of the Constitutional Convention." *Political Science Reviewer* 17 (Fall 1987): 5–48.

———. *The Jeffersonian Persuasion: Evolution of a Party Ideology*. Ithaca, 1978.

———. "The Practicable Sphere of a Republic: James Madison, the Constitutional Convention, and the Emergence of Revolutionary Federalism." In *Beyond Confederation*, edited by Richard Beeman et al., pp. 162–87.

Barnes, Gilbert Hobbes. *The Antislavery Impulse, 1830–1844*. New York, 1964.

Barney, William J. *Battleground for the Union: The Era of Civil War and Reconstruction, 1848–1877*. Englewood Cliffs, N.J., 1990.

Baxter, Maurice. *One and Inseparable: Daniel Webster and the Union*. Cambridge, Mass., 1984.

Beeman, Richard, et al., eds. *Beyond Confederation: Origins of the Constitution and American National Identity*. Chapel Hill, 1987.

Belz, Herman. "The South and the American Constitutional Tradition at the Bicentennial." In *An Uncertain Tradition*, edited by Kermit Hall and James W. Ely, Jr., pp. 17–59.

Benditt, Theodore M. "Compromising Interests and Principles." In *Compromise*, edited by J. Roland Pennock and John W. Chapman, pp. 26–37.

Bennett, Henry Arnold. *The Constitution in School and College*. New York, 1936.

Benson, Lee. *The Concept of Jacksonian Democracy: New York As a Test Case*. Princeton, 1961.

Berki, R. N. "The Distinction between Moderation and Extremism." In *The Morality of Politics*, edited by R. N. Berki and Bhirkhu Parekh, pp. 66–80. London, 1972.

Bogue, Allan G. *The Congressman's Civil War*. Cambridge, Eng., 1989.

Bourke, Paul. "The Pluralist Reading of James Madison's Tenth *Federalist*." *Perspectives in American History* 9 (1975): 271–95.

Bouwsma, William J. "From History of Ideas to History of Meaning." *Journal of Interdisciplinary History* 12 (Autumn 1981): 279–91.

Boyd, Stephen R. *The Politics of Opposition: Antifederalists and the Acceptance of the Constitution*. Millwood, N.Y., 1979.

Brant, Irving. *James Madison: Commander in Chief, 1812–1836*. Indianapolis, 1961.

Brown, Richard H. "The Missouri Crisis, Slavery, and the Politics of Jacksonianism." *South Atlantic Quarterly* 65 (Winter 1966): 55–72.

Brown, Thomas. "Henry Clay and the Politics of Consensus." *Politics and Statesmanship: Essays on the American Whig Party*. New York, 1983.

Buel, Richard, Jr. *Securing the Revolution: Ideology in American Politics, 1789–1815*. Ithaca, 1972.

Carens, Joseph H. "Compromises in Politics." In *Compromise*, edited by J. Roland Pennock and John W. Chapman, pp. 123–40.

Carr, Lois Green. "The Foundations of Social Order: Local Government in Colonial Maryland." In *Town and County*, edited by Bruce Daniels, pp. 72–110.

Clark, Michael D. *Coherent Variety: The Idea of Diversity in British and American Conservative Thought*. Westport, Conn., 1983.

Colbourn, Trevor, ed. *Fame and the Founding Fathers: Essays by Douglass Adair*. New York, 1974.

Cole, Arthur C. *The Whig Party in the South*. 1914. Reprint. Gloucester, Mass., 1962.

Cooper, William E. *The South and the Politics of Slavery, 1828–1856*. Baton Rouge, 1978.

Cremin, Lawrence. *American Education: The National Experience, 1783–1876*. New York, 1980.

Crofts, Daniel W. *Reluctant Confederates: Upper South Unionists in the Secession Crisis*. Chapel Hill, 1989.

Cunningham, Noble E. *The Process of Government under Jefferson*. Princeton, 1978.

Current, Richard N. *Daniel Webster and the Rise of National Conservatism*. Boston, 1955.

Curti, Merle. *The Growth of American Thought*. 3d ed. New York, 1964.

Dahl, Robert. *Pluralist Democracy in the United States: Conflict and Consent*. Chicago, 1967.

Dalzell, Robert F. *Daniel Webster and the Trial of American Nationalism, 1843–1852*. Boston, 1973.

Dangerfield, George. *The Era of Good Feelings*. New York, 1952.

Daniels, Bruce, ed. *Town and County: Essays on the Structure of Local Government in the American Colonies*. Middletown, Conn., 1978.

Davis, David Brion. "The Emergence of Immediatism in British and

American Antislavery Thought." *Mississippi Valley Historical Review* 49 (September 1962): 209–30.
———. *The Problem of Slavery in the Age of Revolution, 1770–1823*. Ithaca, 1975.
———. *Slavery and Human Progress*. New York, 1984.
De Jouvenel, Bertrand. *The Pure Theory of Politics*. New Haven, 1963.
Detweiler, Philip F. "Congressional Debate on Slavery and the Declaration of Independence, 1819–1821." *American Historical Review* 63 (April 1958): 598–616.
Dillon, Merton L. *The Abolitionists: The Growth of a Dissenting Minority*. De Kalb, Ill., 1974.
Dixon, Mrs. Archibald. *The True History of the Missouri Compromise and Its Repeal*. Cincinnati, 1898.
Donald, David Herbert. *Liberty and Union*. New York, 1978.
Doty, Franklin A. "Florida, Iowa, and the National Balance of Power, 1845." *Florida Historical Quarterly* 35 (July 1956): 30–59.
Dumond, Dwight L. *Antislavery: The Crusade for Freedom in America*. New York, 1961.
Eaton, Clement. *Henry Clay and the Art of American Politics*. Boston, 1957.
———. *Jefferson Davis*. New York, 1977.
Egerton, Douglas R. *Charles Fenton Mercer and the Trial of National Conservatism*. Jackson, Miss., 1989.
Eidelberg, Paul. *A Discourse on Statesmanship: The Design and Transformation of the American Polity*. Urbana, Ill., 1974.
Ellis, Richard E. *The Jeffersonian Crisis: Courts and Politics in the Young Republic*. New York, 1971.
———. *The Union at Risk: Jacksonian Democracy, States' Rights, and the Nullification Crisis*. New York, 1987.
Elson, Ruth Miller. *Guardians of Tradition: American Schoolbooks of the Nineteenth Century*. Lincoln, Nebr., 1964.
England, J. Merton. "The Democratic Faith in American Schoolbooks, 1783–1860." *American Quarterly* 15 (1963): 191–99.
Ernst, Robert. *Rufus King: American Federalist*. Chapel Hill, 1968.
Farr, James. "Conceptual Change and Constitutional Innovation." In *Conceptual Change*, edited by Terence Ball and J.G.A. Pocock, pp. 13–34.
———. "Francis Lieber and the Interpretation of American Political Science." *Journal of Politics* 52, no. 4 (November 1990): 1027–49.
———. "The History of Political Science." *American Journal of Political Science* 32 (November 1988): 1075–95.
Farrand, Max. "Compromises of the Constitution." *American Historical Review* 9 (April 1904): 479–80.
———. *The Framing of the Constitution of the United States*. New Haven, 1914.

Fehrenbacher, Don E. *The Dred Scott Case: Its Significance in American Law and Politics*. Oxford, Eng., 1978.

———. *The South and Three Sectional Crises*. Baton Rouge, 1980.

Finkelman, Paul. *An Imperfect Union: Slavery, Federalism, and Comity*. Chapel Hill, 1984.

———. "Slavery and the Constitutional Convention: A Covenant With Death." In *Beyond Confederation*, edited by Richard Beeman et al., pp. 188–225.

Fisher, Walter R. "The Failure of Compromise in 1860–1861: A Rhetorical View." *Speech Monographs* 33 (August 1966): 364–71.

Follett, Mary Parker. "Constructive Conflict" and "The Psychology of Conciliation and Arbitration." In *Dynamic Administration: The Collected Papers of Mary Parker Follett*, edited by Henry C. Metcalf and L. Urwick, pp. 30–49, 230–46. New York, [1940].

Forgie, George. *Patricide in the House Divided: A Psychological Portrait of Lincoln and His Age*. Chapel Hill, 1979.

Formisano, Ronald P. *The Transformation of Political Culture: Massachusetts Parties, 1790s–1840s*. Oxford, Eng., 1983.

Fowler, Nolan. "The Anti-Expansionistic Argument in the United States prior to the Civil War." Ph.D. dissertation, University of Kentucky, 1955.

Fowler, Robert Booth. *Believing Skeptics: American Political Intellectuals, 1945–1964*. Westport, Conn., 1978.

Freehling, William W. *Prelude to Civil War: The Nullification Crisis in South Carolina, 1816–1836*. New York, 1966.

———. *The Road to Disunion: Secessionists at Bay, 1776–1854*. New York, 1990.

———. "Spoilsmen and Interests in the Thought and Career of John C. Calhoun." *Journal of American History* 52 (June 1965): 25–42.

Freeman, Gordon M. "The Process of Covenant." *Publius* 10 (Fall 1980): 71–81.

Freidel, Frank. *Francis Lieber: Nineteenth Century Liberal*. Baton Rouge, 1947.

Friedman, Jean E. *The Revolt of the Conservative Democrats: An Essay in American Political Culture and Political Development, 1837–1844*. Ann Arbor, 1979.

Furtwangler, Albert. *The Authority of Publius: A Reading of the Federalist Papers*. Ithaca, 1984.

Galloway, George B. *History of the House of Representatives*. 2d ed., rev. Sidney Wise. New York, 1976.

Golding, Martin P. "The Nature of Compromise: A Preliminary Inquiry." In *Compromise*, edited by J. Roland Pennock and John W. Chapman, pp. 3–25.

Gough, J. W. *The Social Contract: A Critical Study of Its Development*. 2d ed. Oxford, Eng., 1957.

Graebner, Norman A. "Thomas Corwin and the Election of 1848: A Study in Conservative Politics." *Journal of Southern History* 17 (May 1951): 162–79.
Grambs, Jean Dresden. "The Study of Textbooks and Schoolbooks: A Selected Bibliography." In *Improving the Use of Social Studies Textbooks*, edited by William E. Patton, pp. 61–76. National Council for the Social Studies Bulletin no. 63. Washington, D.C., 1980.
Greene, Jack P. "From the Perspective of Law: Context and Legitimacy in the Origins of the American Revolution: A Review Essay." *South Atlantic Quarterly* 85 (Winter 1986): 56–77.
———. "The Growth of Political Stability: An Interpretation of Political Development in the Anglo-American Colonies, 1660–1760." In *American Revolution*, edited by John Parker and Carol Urness, pp. 26–52.
———. *Peripheries and Center: Constitutional Development in the Extended Polities of the British Empire and the United States, 1607–1788*. Athens, Ga., 1986.
Haddow, Anna. *Political Science in American Colleges and Universities, 1636–1900*. New York, 1939.
Hall, Kermit, and James W. Ely, Jr., eds. *An Uncertain Tradition: Constitutionalism and the History of the South*. Athens, Ga., 1989.
Hallowell, John H. "Compromise As a Political Ideal." *Ethics* 54 (April 1944): 157–73.
Hamilton, Holman. *Prologue to Conflict: The Compromise of 1850*. Lexington, Ky., 1960.
———. *Zachary Taylor: Soldier in the White House*. Indianapolis, 1951.
Hare, R. M. *Freedom and Reason*. London, 1963.
Hargreaves, Mary H. M. *The Presidency of John Quincy Adams*. Lawrence, 1985.
Harmon, George. "Douglas and the Compromise of 1850." *Journal of the Illinois State Historical Society* 21 (1929): 453–99.
Hartog, Hendrik, ed. *Law in the American Revolution and the Revolution in the Law: A Collection of Review Essays in American Legal History*. New York, 1981.
Hodder, Frank. "The Authorship of the Compromise of 1850." *Mississippi Valley Historical Review* 22 (June 1935): 525–36.
———. "Sidelights on the Missouri Compromises." *Annual Report of the American Historical Association for the Year 1909*, pp. 151–61. Washington, D.C., 1911.
Hofstadter, Richard. *The Idea of a Party System: The Rise of Legitimate Opposition in the United States, 1780–1840*. Berkeley, 1969.
Hollinger, David. "American Intellectual History: Issues for the 1980s." *Reviews in American History* 10 (December 1982): 306–27.
Holt, Michael F. *The Political Crisis of the 1850s*. New York, 1978.

———. "Winding Roads to Recovery: The Whig Party from 1844 to 1848." In *Essays on Antebellum American Politics*, edited by Stephen Maizlish and John J. Kushma, pp. 122–65.

Howe, Daniel W. *The Political Culture of the American Whigs*. Chicago, 1979.

———. "The Political Psychology of *The Federalist*." *William and Mary Quarterly* 44 (July 1987): 485–509.

Huntington, Samuel P. *Political Order in Changing Societies*. New Haven, 1968.

Hutson, James. "Country, Court, and Constitution: Antifederalism and the Historians." *William and Mary Quarterly* 38 (July 1981): 337–68.

———. "The Creation of the Constitution: Scholarship at a Standstill." *Reviews in American History* 12 (December 1984): 463–77.

Hyman, Harold M. "The Narrow Escape from a " 'Compromise of 1860': Secession and the Constitution." In *Freedom and Reform: Essays in Honor of Henry Steele Commager*, edited by Harold M. Hyman and Leonard W. Levy, pp. 149–66. New York, 1967.

Hyneman, Charles S., and George W. Carey. *A Second Federalist: Congress Creates a Government*. Columbia, S.C., 1967.

Jillson, Calvin. "Constitution-Making: Alignment and Realignment in the Federal Convention of 1787." *American Political Science Review* 75 (1981): 598–612.

Jillson, Calvin, and Thornton Anderson. "Realignments in the Convention of 1787: The Slave Trade Compromise." *Journal of Politics* 39 (1977): 712–29.

Johannsen, Robert W. *Stephen A. Douglas*. New York, 1973.

———, ed. *The Lincoln-Douglas Debates of 1858*. New York, 1965.

Kaestle, Carl F. *Pillars of the Republic: Common Schools and American Society, 1780–1860*. New York, 1983.

Kaestle, Carl F., and Maris Vinovskis. *Education and Social Change in Nineteenth-Century Massachusetts*. New York, 1980.

Kammen, Michael. *A Machine That Would Go of Itself: The Constitution and American Culture*. New York, 1986.

Kelly, Alfred H., Winfred Harbison, and Herman Belz. *The American Constitution: Its Origins and Development*. 6th ed. New York, 1983.

Kelly, George Armstrong. "Mediation versus Compromise in Hegel." In *Compromise*, edited by J. Roland Pennock and John W. Chapman, pp. 87–103.

Kelly, R. E. "Writing of Schoolbooks in the Late Eighteenth and Early Nineteenth Centuries." *History of Education Quarterly* 15 (Summer 1975): 207–11.

Kendall, Willmoore, and George W. Carey. "How to Read 'The Federalist.' " In *Willmoore Kendall: Contra Mundum*, edited by Nellie D. Kendall, pp. 387–420. New Rochelle, N.Y., 1971.

Ketcham, Ralph. *Presidents Above Party: The First American Presidency, 1789–1829*. Chapel Hill, 1984.

Kielbowicz, Richard B. "Party Press Cohesiveness: Jacksonian Newspapers, 1832." *Journalism Quarterly* 60 (1983): 518–21.

Kincaid, John. "Influential Models of Political Association in the Western Tradition." *Publius* 10 (Fall 1980): 31–58.

Kirwan, Albert D. *John J. Crittenden: The Struggle for Union*. Lexington, Ky., 1962.

Klein, Larry. "Henry Clay, Nationalist." Ph.D. dissertation, University of Kentucky, 1977.

Kloppenberg, James T. "The Virtues of Liberalism: Christianity, Republicanism, and Ethics in Early American Political Discourse." *Journal of American History* 74 (June 1987): 9–33.

Klunder, Willard Carl. "Lewis Cass and Slavery Expansion: The Father of Popular Sovereignty and Ideological Infanticide." *Civil War History* 32 (December 1986): 293–317.

———. "Lewis Cass, 1782–1866: A Political Biography." Ph.D. dissertation, University of Illinois-Urbana, 1981.

Knupfer, Peter B. "'The Union As It Was': The Civic Tradition of Compromise before the Civil War." Ph.D. dissertation, University of Wisconsin, 1988.

Kohl, Lawrence Frederick. *The Politics of Individualism: Parties and the American Character in the Jacksonian Era*. New York, 1989.

Konig, David Thomas. "English Legal Change and the Origins of Local Government in Northern Massachusetts." In *Town and County*, edited by Bruce Daniels, pp. 12–43.

Konvitz, Milton J. "John Morley on Liberty and Compromise." In *Essays in Political Theory*, edited by Milton J. Konvitz and Arthur E. Murphy, pp. 194–205.

Konvitz, Milton J., and Arthur E. Murphy, eds. *Essays in Political Theory Presented to George H. Sabine*. Ithaca, 1948.

Kuflick, Arthur. "Morality and Compromise." In *Compromise*, edited by J. Roland Pennock and John W. Chapman, pp. 38–65.

Kukla, Jon. "Order and Chaos in Early America: Political and Social Stability in Pre-Restoration Virginia." *American Historical Review* 90 (April 1985): 275–98.

Lienesch, Michael. "The Constitutional Tradition: History, Political Action, and Progress in American Political Thought." *Journal of Politics* 42 (February 1980): 1–30, 47–48.

Lutz, Donald S. "From Covenant to Constitution in American Political Thought." *Publius* 10 (Fall 1980): 101–33.

———. *The Origins of American Constitutionalism*. Baton Rouge, 1988.

Luxon, Norval Neil. "H. Niles: The Man and the Editor." *Mississippi Valley Historical Review* 28 (June 1941): 27–40.

———. *Niles' Weekly Register*. Baton Rouge, 1947.

Lynd, Staughton. "The Abolitionist Critique of the United States Constitution." In *The Antislavery Vanguard: New Essays on the Abolitionists*, edited by Martin Duberman, pp. 209–39. Princeton, 1965.

———. "The Compromise of 1787." *Political Science Quarterly* 81 (June 1966): 225–260.

McCarthy, Eugene. "Compromise and Politics." In *Integrity and Compromise*, edited by R. M. McIver, pp. 19–28. New York, 1957.

McCormick, Richard L. "The Party Period and Public Policy: An Exploratory Hypothesis." *Journal of American History* 66 (September 1979): 279–98.

McCormick, Richard P. *The Second American Party System: Party Formation in the Jacksonian Era*. Chapel Hill, 1966.

McCoy, Drew R. *The Elusive Republic: Political Economy in Jeffersonian America*. Chapel Hill, 1980.

———. *The Last of the Fathers: James Madison and the Republican Legacy*. Cambridge, N.Y., 1989.

McDonald, Forrest. *The Formation of the American Republic, 1776–1790*. 1965. Penguin ed. Boston, 1970.

———. *Novus Ordo Seclorum: The Intellectual Origins of the Constitution*. Lawrence, 1985.

McFaul, John M. "Expediency vs. Morality: Jacksonian Politics and Slavery." *Journal of American History* 62 (June 1975): 24–39.

Main, Jackson Turner. *The Antifederalists: Critics of the Constitution, 1781–1788*. 1961. Norton ed. Chapel Hill, 1974.

Maizlish, Stephen, and John J. Kushma, eds. *Essays on Antebellum American Politics*. College Station, Tex., 1982.

Malone, Dumas. *Jefferson and the Ordeal of Liberty*. Boston, 1962.

Maness, Lonnie. "Henry Clay and the Problem of Slavery." Ph.D. dissertation, Memphis State University, 1980.

Marshall, Lynn L. "Opposing Democratic and Whig Concepts of Party Organization." In *New Perspectives on Jacksonian Parties and Politics*, edited by Edward S. Pessen, pp. 38–68.

May, Henry F. *The Enlightenment in America*. Oxford, Eng., 1976.

Moore, Glover. *The Missouri Controversy, 1819–1821*. Lexington, Ky., 1953.

Morley, John Viscount. *On Compromise*. 1874. Reprint. London, 1923.

Morrison, Chaplain. *Democratic Politics and Sectionalism: The Wilmot Proviso Controversy*. Chapel Hill, 1967.

Nagel, Paul C. *One Nation Indivisible: The Union in American Thought, 1776–1860*. New York, 1964.

Nelson, William E. "Reason and Compromise in the Establishment of the Federal Constitution." *William and Mary Quarterly* 44 (July 1987): 458–84.

Nevins, Allan. *Ordeal of the Union*. 2 vols. New York, 1947.
Nichols, Roy Franklin. *The Disruption of American Democracy*. New York, 1948.
———. "The Kansas-Nebraska Act: A Century of Historiography." *Mississippi Valley Historical Review* 43 (1956): 187–212.
Nisbet, Robert. *Conservatism: Dream and Reality*. Minneapolis, 1986.
———. *The Quest for Community: A Study in the Ethics of Order and Freedom*. New York, 1953.
Niven, John. *Martin Van Buren: The Romantic Age of American Politics*. New York, 1983.
Norton, L. Wesley. "The Religious Press and the Compromise of 1850: A Study of the Relationship of the Methodist, Baptist, and Presbyterian Press to the Slavery Controversy, 1846–1851." Ph.D. dissertation, University of Illinois, 1959.
O'Connor, John E. *William Paterson: Lawyer and Statesman, 1745–1806*. New Brunswick, 1979.
Ohline, Howard A. "Republicanism and Slavery: Origins of the Three-Fifths Clause in the United States Constitution." *William and Mary Quarterly* 28 (October 1971): 563–84.
Onuf, Peter S. *The Origins of the Federal Republic: Jurisdictional Controversies in the United States, 1775–1787*. Philadelphia, 1983.
O'Sullivan, Noel, ed. *Revolutionary Theory and Political Reality*. New York, 1983.
Panagopoulos, E. P. *Essays on the History and Meaning of Checks and Balances*. Lanham, Md., 1985.
Parker, John, and Carol Urness, eds. *The American Revolution: A Heritage of Change*. Minneapolis, 1975.
Parks, Joseph. *John Bell of Tennessee*. Baton Rouge, 1950.
Pennock, J. Roland, and John W. Chapman, eds. *Compromise in Ethics, Law, and Politics*. NOMOS XXI. New York, 1979.
Pessen, Edward S. *New Perspectives on Jacksonian Parties and Politics*. Boston, 1969.
Peterson, Merrill D. *The Great Triumvirate: Webster, Clay, and Calhoun*. New York, 1987.
———. *The Jefferson Image in the American Mind*. New York, 1960.
———. *Olive Branch and Sword: The Compromise of 1833*. Baton Rouge, 1982.
Poage, George R. *Henry Clay and the Whig Party*. Chapel Hill, 1936.
Pole, J. R. *The Idea of Union*. Alexandria, Va., 1977.
Potter, David M. "The Historian's Use of Nationalism and Vice Versa." *The South and the Sectional Conflict*. Baton Rouge, 1968.
———. *The Impending Crisis, 1848–1861*. Edited by Don E. Fehrenbacher. New York, 1976.

Raichle, Donald Roderick. "The Image of the Constitution in American History: A Study in Historical Writing from David Ramsay to John Fiske, 1789–1888." Ph.D. dissertation, Columbia University, 1956.

Rakove, Jack. "The Great Compromise: Ideas, Interests, and the Politics of Constitution Making." *William and Mary Quarterly* 44 (July 1987): 424–57.

Ransom, Roger L. *Conflict and Compromise: The Political Economy of Slavery, Emancipation, and the American Civil War*. Cambridge, Eng., 1989.

Reid, John Phillip. "In Our Contracted Sphere: The Constitutional Contract, the Stamp Act Crisis, and the Coming of the American Revolution." *Columbia Law Review* 76 (1976): 21–47.

———. "The Irrelevance of the Declaration." In *Law in the American Revolution*, edited by Hendrik Hartog, pp. 46–89.

Remini, Robert. *Andrew Jackson and the Course of American Democracy, 1833–1845*. New York, 1984.

Resnick, David. "Justice, Compromise, and Constitutional Rules in Aristotle's *Politics*." In *Compromise*, edited by J. Roland Pennock and John W. Chapman, pp. 69–86.

Richards, Leonard L. "The Jacksonians and Slavery." In *Antislavery Reconsidered: New Perspectives on the Abolitionists*, edited by Lewis Perry and Michael Fellman, pp. 99–118. Baton Rouge, 1979.

Riker, William H. "The Heresthetics of Constitution-Making, with Comments on Determinism and Rational Choice." *American Political Science Review* 78 (March 1984): 1–16.

———. "Political Theory and the Art of Heresthetics." In *Political Science: The State of the Discipline*, edited by Ada Finifter, pp. 47–67. Washington, D.C., 1983.

Robinson, Donald L. *Slavery in the Structure of American Politics, 1765–1820*. New York, 1971.

Roche, John P. "The Founding Fathers: A Reform Caucus in Action." *American Political Science Review* 55 (1962): 799–806.

Rossiter, Clinton. *1787: The Grand Convention*. New York, 1966.

Russell, Robert R. "The Issues in the Congressional Struggle over the Kansas-Nebraska Bill, 1854." *Journal of Southern History* 29 (May 1963): 187–200.

———. "What Was the Compromise of 1850?" *Journal of Southern History* 22 (February 1956): 292–309.

Rutland, Robert. *The Ordeal of the Constitution: The Antifederalists and the Ratification Struggle of 1787–1788*. Norman, 1966.

Schechter, Frank I. "The Early History of the Tradition of the Constitution." *American Political Science Review* 9 (November 1915): 707–34.

Schmidt, Philip R. *Hezekiah Niles and American Economic Nationalism: A Political Biography*. New York, 1982.

Schurz, Carl. *Henry Clay*. 2 vols. New York, 1888.
Seager, Robert F., II. "Henry Clay and the Politics of Compromise and Non-compromise." *Register of the Kentucky Historical Society* 85 (Winter 1987): 1–28.
Seltser, Barry Jay. *The Principles and Practice of Political Compromise: A Case Study of the United States Senate*. Studies in American Religion, vol. 12. New York, 1984.
Sewell, Richard H. *Ballots for Freedom: Antislavery Politics in the United States, 1837–1860*. New York, 1976.
Shade, William. "American Political Development, 1789–1840." *Current History* 67 (July 1974): 6–8, 40.
Silbey, Joel. *The Partisan Imperative: The Dynamics of American Politics before the Civil War*. New York, 1985.
———. *A Respectable Minority: The Democratic Party in the Civil War Era, 1860–1868*. New York, 1977.
Simpson, Albert F. "The Political Significance of Slave Representation, 1787–1821." *Journal of Southern History* 7 (August 1941): 315–42.
Sisson, Daniel. *The American Revolution of 1800*. New York, 1974.
Slonin, Shlomo. "The Electoral College at Philadelphia: The Evolution of an Ad Hoc Congress for the Selection of a President." *Journal of American History* 73 (June 1986): 35–58.
Smith, Craig R. "Daniel Webster's July 17th Address: A Mediating Influence in the 1850 Compromise." *Quarterly Journal of Speech* 71 (1985): 349–61.
Smith, Thomas V. *The Ethics of Compromise and the Art of Containment*. Boston, 1956.
Smith, Wilson. *Professors and Public Ethics: Studies of Northern Moral Philosophers before the Civil War*. Ithaca, 1956.
Somkin, Fred. *Unquiet Eagle: Memory and Desire in the Idea of American Freedom, 1815–1860*. Ithaca, 1967.
Stabler, John B. "A History of the Constitutional Union Party: A Tragic Failure." Ph.D. dissertation, Columbia University, 1954.
Stampp, Kenneth M. *And the War Came . . . : The North and the Secession Crisis, 1860–61*. Chicago, 1950.
Stewart, James Brewer. *Holy Warriors: The Abolitionists and American Slavery*. New York, 1976.
Stroh, Guy W. *American Ethical Thought*. Chicago, 1979.
Summers, Mark W. *The Plundering Generation, Corruption, and the Crisis of the Union, 1849–1861*. New York, 1987.
Tate, Thad W. "The Social Contract in America, 1747–1787: Revolutionary Theory As a Conservative Instrument." *William and Mary Quarterly* 22 (July 1965): 375–91.
Thompson, Martyn P. "The History of Fundamental Law in Political

Thought from the French Wars of Religion to the American Revolution." *American Historical Review* 91 (December 1986): 1103–28.

Van Deusen, Glyndon G. *The Life of Henry Clay*. Boston, 1937.

———. "Some Aspects of Whig Thought and Theory in the Jacksonian Period." *American Historical Review* 63 (January 1958): 305–22.

Van Tassel, David D. *Recording America's Past: An Interpretation of Historical Studies in America, 1607–1884*. Chicago, 1960.

Vitzthum, Richard C. *The American Compromise: Theme and Method in the Histories of Bancroft, Parkman, and Adams*. Norman, 1974.

Wallace, Michael. "The Concepts of Party in the United States: New York, 1815–1828." *American Historical Review* 74 (December 1968): 453–91.

Warner, John Cooper. "Winning the Lower South to the Compromise of 1850." Ph.D. dissertation, Louisiana State University, 1974.

Warner, Michael. *The Letters of the Republic: Publication and the Public Sphere in Eighteenth-Century America*. Cambridge, Mass., 1990.

Weber, Max. "Politics As a Vocation." In *From Max Weber: Essays in Sociology*, translated and edited by H. H. Gerth and C. Wright Mills, pp. 77–128. New York, 1946.

Welter, Rush. *The Mind of America, 1820–1860*. New York, 1975.

Wharton, Leslie. *Polity and the Public Good: Conflicting Theories of Republican Government in the New Nation*. Ann Arbor, 1980.

White, Leonard D. *The Jacksonians: A Study in Administrative History, 1829–1861*. New York, 1954.

Wiecek, William M. *The Sources of Antislavery Constitutionalism in America, 1760–1848*. Ithaca, 1977.

Wilson, Major L. *Space, Time, and Freedom: The Quest for Nationality and the Irrepressible Conflict, 1815–1860*. Westport, Conn., 1974.

Wiltse, Charles M. "From Compact to Nation State in American Political Thought." In *Essays in Political Theory*, edited by Milton J. Konvitz and Arthur E. Murphy, pp. 153–78.

Wood, Gordon. *The Creation of the American Republic, 1776–1789*. Chapel Hill, 1969.

Young, Alfred F. "Conservatives, the Constitution, and the 'Spirit of Accommodation.'" In *How Democratic Is the Constitution?* edited by Robert A. Goldwin and William A. Schambra, pp. 117–47. Washington, D.C., 1980.

Young, James Sterling. *The Washington Community, 1800–1828*. New York, 1966.

Zemsky, Robert. *Merchants, Farmers, and River Gods: An Essay on Eighteenth Century American Politics*. Boston, 1971.

Zvesper, John. *Political Philosophy and Rhetoric: A Study of the Origins of American Party Politics*. Cambridge, N.Y., 1977.

Index